BREAKING CHARACTER

A Memoir

By David Christopher and David Umbach

Edited by Dustin Ballard

"I once planned a book which was to consist entirely of dedications, but abandoned the idea because I could not think of a dedication for it."

~ P. G. Wodehouse on Dedications

In a brief tome about a vast life, it is impossible to touch upon every incident or include every person who has touch one's life.

But I dedicate this to them all.

~ David Umbach

Photographer credits:
David Umbach
Jonathan Umbach
Lake Forest College Yearbook
Roselle Park High School Yearbook
Len Chandros
David Munro
Gary P. Cohen
Warren Westura
Rich Kowalski
Howard Fischer

Table of Contents

Prologue	OH THOSE EYES	7
1	ALWAYS THE NEW KID	13
2	HAPPY HIGH SCHOOL	29
3	HI HO, THE COLLEGE LIFE	43
4	ON THE TOWN	64
5	OF SHIPS AND PLANES AND EURAIL PASS	78
6	THE TRAVELING TROUBADOUR	87
7	EUROPE, *SANS* REYNOLDS	102
8	LOOK, MA, I'M A PROFESSIONAL ACTOR	115
9	THE DRAMA CLUB	123
10	THE SWINGIN' SIXTIES	136
11	FIRST HIPPIE ON LBI	153
12	MAKE A CELEBRATION	160
13	INSIDE THE ACTING STUDIO	183
14	THE MUNRO DOCTRINE	197
15	TRAVELOSITY	214
16	RELATIVE-ITY	238
17	THE END OF BOBBY	265
18	PLAYING IN THE PARK	274
19	ARBAD-A-CARBA	288
20	COMING OUT TO MOTHER, IN EUROPE, YET	295
21	EQUITY AND INEQUITY	300
22	MERCK WORK	319
23	SPIN YOUR PARTNER, DO-SI-SO	326
Epilogue	GOOD NIGHT, SWEET PRINCE	334

6

Prologue

Oh, Those Eyes!

It was an age of moral innocence and sexual ignorance. The Fifties. Doris Day and Rock Hudson were the perfect pair of chaste lovers. No one even dreamed that she was a battered wife or that his homosexual affairs would eventually kill him.

If all the families were trying to emulate "Ozzie and Harriet", college life at the small mid-western college that I went to was more like "Mickey and Judy Putting on a Play". It was a far cry from the campuses of the Sixties or today. We were completely insulated in a cocoon of academia and spiffy social life. The outside world and reality made very little impression on us, especially those of us in the Drama Department. Even Sex wasn't talked about, much. I'm sure it was done, but not by me – there was no shame in being a virgin in those days. My education was strictly out of books and lectures – but that changed during Spring Break my Junior year.

Several of my friends were discussing a trip to New York City during our break to see some Broadway shows. I was ecstatic! I had only been there once before with my parents and I had fallen in love with the city. In the beginning of our planning, there were three or four people who wanted to drive and I had to choose whose car I would ride in. But as we neared zero hour, every one of my once adventurous friends copped out, and I was the only one who still wanted to make the journey.

Although I had no transportation, I was still determined to get to New York, even if I had to hitchhike. Then, in a Chicago paper, I happened to see a personal ad, reading *"Going to New York City, need passenger to share expenses and driving. Car is a new convertible. Call Kurt at ...."* I ran to the phone and dialed the number, convinced that this was my ticket to Broadway. Kurt turned out to be an advertising man, who sounded nice over the phone, but he said that he'd already accepted someone else as a passenger. Close to begging, I asked if he could possibly take two riders and he agreed to meet with me during his lunch break. I rushed into Chicago, rode up to the 24th floor of the Prudential Building and met the man who was to change my life.

His appearance didn't impress me particularly, besides seeming to be clean cut and pleasant. He was in his thirties, with a crew cut, and he reminded me of George Gobbel, a popular comedian of the day. After a short but friendly interview, we made a deal that if I didn't bring too much luggage, he could fit me in and we'd share the expenses three ways. It happened that he was leaving one day after my spring vacation started, so it worked out perfectly. Fate was definitely smiling at me.

So off to "Theatrical Mecca" I went. My life centered around the theater, and Broadway was where it was all happening. In those days Chicago was a barren desert, as far as theater was concerned, only hosting road shows from Broadway. And now I was going to be able to see the Original! I couldn't have been more excited.

When the car arrived to pick me up, I was delighted to see that it was a shiny green Pontiac convertible. The top was up because it was a cool spring morning, but I knew that the trip was going to be very comfortable, as well as exhilarating. My fellow passenger was a scruffy youth, older than me, but still with a collegiate appearance. His name was Buster and that fit his personality. He wasn't very friendly, even from the start, very self-absorbed. He had no interests in New York City, except that he had family there and was summoned back because of a wedding that he didn't want to go to. He complained about it the whole trip.

Kurt, however, was very congenial and seemed as excited about going to the Big Apple as I was. During our long trip, Kurt and I gabbed away, while Buster sat in the back seat and smoked. Not much happened during the ride to New York, except that Kurt and I formed a bond, mostly because of our dislike of Buster and our anticipation of The City. We didn't stop over for a night, but drove 20 hours straight through, sharing the driving three ways.

When we arrived in New York, we dropped Buster off at a subway station and Kurt deposited me at the Sloan House YMCA on 34th Street. He gave me a phone number of where he was staying and invited me to make the return trip with him, *sans* Buster. I was delighted, because I hadn't really thought about how I was going to get back to Chicago. He said to contact him before the end of the week to make arrangements.

Sloan House was very different from what I expected. It had more the feel of a huge dormitory than a hotel, even though everyone had their own room. There were lots of rules, like having to sign in at the desk to get your key and forbidding guests in the rooms. But it wasn't like college, because the men were all types and ages, from Skid Row bums, to squeaky-clean Bible thumpers. My room was the size of a closet, with just a single bed and a dresser. It was on the 10th floor, with a window over-looking a grimy airshaft, but I didn't care; I was just using it to sleep. The rest of the time I was going to explore New York and see as much theater as I could fit in.

And theater I saw! Although there were no performances on Sundays then, I attended eight plays in seven days, by seeing Wednesday and Saturday matinees. My first Broadway play was Noel Coward's *Fallen Angels,* with Nancy Walker. The best drama I saw was Julie Harris playing Joan of Arc in *The Lark.* And the best musical by far was *My Fair Lady*, with Rex Harrison and Julie Andrews. It was opening week, so I had to wait in line from 5:00 AM to get a standing room ticket, and it was well worth it.

But the play that led to my Life Lesson was *A Most Happy Fella*. In that musical, a handsome leading man stands center stage and sings the haunting ballad, "Joey! Joey, Joey!". I remember being moved by the song, but enjoying more the peppier numbers, like "Big D, Little A, Double L. A. S". It wasn't until that night after the show that the song "Joey!" entered my personal life.

I wanted to explore Greenwich Village, so after the play I took a subway down to Christopher Street and wandered around looking for "beatniks". I ended up at a rustic bar called *The Ninth Circle,* which had sawdust on the floors and a long bar with a brass rail. I sat on a bench along the wall at one of the tables and ordered a beer and a hamburger.

Suddenly, sitting next to me, on the same bench but at the adjoining table, was a good looking young man in a tee shirt and jeans. This was not the current style of dress in my circle, so it looked quaintly Bohemian to me. He was very friendly and introduced himself as "Joey". I commented that I had just seen a play that had a song in it with his name in the title. As our conversation continued he moved closer to me and put his hand on my leg – I couldn't have been more startled. As he cheerfully chatted on, he kept his hand there and rubbed my leg, getting closer and closer to my crotch. I totally panicked! My emotional reaction was so powerful that I knocked over my beer. I apologized, hastily called for the check, and stumbled out the door.

I couldn't fathom what I was feeling. I wasn't appalled by what had happened, I was more shocked – and yes, thrilled! But I couldn't understand why? Remember this was in the Fifties and in those "I-

Like-Ike" years, the subject of homosexuality just wasn't discussed or written about like it is today. There were no Gay Pride Parades; no After-School Specials where Scott Baio falls in love with his high school chum, no tales about the happy homosexuals in San Francisco, no hilarious and sensitive plays by Harvey Fierstein, and certainly no "Queer As Folk". Oh, there were a few depressing novels in which the guilt-ridden queers always committed suicide in the end, but I hadn't read any of them. I was completely ignorant of this aspect of life, and yet the touch of Joey's hand on my leg had sent chills up my spine that blew my head apart.

Somehow I got back to the "Y", went to my cubicle and spent a sleepless night reliving the event. I couldn't get the incident out of my mind. Little did I know that Sloan House was a hot bed of homosexual activity, and that liaisons of that nature were going on all around me.

During the remaining three days of my New York holiday, I must have seen lots of the city and I certainly went to whatever plays I had tickets for, but all I remember was wandering around singing to myself, "Joey, Joey, Joey!". I went back to *The Ninth Circle* every evening, hoping, yet dreading, to meet up with Joey again. I never did.

On the day I was to leave New York, I went to an apartment on the Upper West Side, to meet with my driver, Kurt. I had never been in a Manhattan apartment and I was excited about seeing one. If I expected it to look like Margo Channing's apartment in "All About Eve", I certainly wasn't ready to have the man who answered the door talk like Bette Davis. He was extremely flamboyant, a type which today I would classify as "an old Queen". He introduced himself as Oliver and welcomed me to his "humble dwelling". I was agog at the grandiose décor. There was lots of gilt furniture, a plush purple carpet, large paintings and marble statues – I'd never seen anything like it in the Midwest, or even in my imagination. He ushered me in and began interrogating me about my New York experiences. I was intrigued by him and his place, thinking it was very "theatrical", but I made no other connections. Kurt entered with a friendly greeting and said that he was in the bedroom packing and wouldn't be long.

Then, coming out of the bedroom behind him, I saw a vision that made me go numb. A blond boy, about my age, in a pair of shorts and a turquoise shirt, stood there with his hand on his hip and a smirk that said, "I'm aware how good looking I am, so enjoy!". And his eyes – oh, those eyes – were huge and deep blue. I felt that I would fall right into them. I couldn't imagine why I was so entranced with him, but he seemed like the most perfect thing I had ever seen and I couldn't stop staring at him.

Kurt turned to go back into the bedroom, saying "Come on Eric, we have more to do in here". He touched the shoulder of the boy, who immediately followed him with a grin on his face. Oliver then continued our conversation about the plays I had gone to, most of which he had seen, too. I was torn between talking about my favorite topic and thinking about those blue eyes. As we were discussing "Get Me To The Church On Time", I kept hearing echoes of "Joey, Joey, Joey!".

Finally, Kurt came out of the bedroom with his arm around the boy. Oliver suggested we all go out for lunch before Kurt and I started our long journey back to Chicago. As we were leaving, Kurt came up to me and said quietly, "I hope you don't mind that we're gay." Now this may seem incredible, but I had no idea what he was talking about. The word "gay" only meant happy, to me, so I couldn't figure out why I should mind that they were happy. I thought, perhaps, that they were taking drugs to make them "gay", but I also knew very little about drugs.

During our meal, conversation was awkward, with Oliver valiantly trying to keep it going with witty chatter. The boy seemed sad and sullen and Kurt embarrassed, with little to say. Although I made no inferences about what was going on between these men, I was painfully aware of the effect that Eric's blue eyes were having on me.

After lunch we packed up the convertible, and I sneaked my last looks at Eric. Then just before we drove away, I happened to notice Eric behind me, in the side-view mirror. He didn't know I was looking at him and he pointed at me, giving a thumbs-up sign to Kurt. I couldn't imagine what he meant. Then the car pulled out into the New York traffic, leaving the beautiful Eric waving on the curb.

After we had gotten through the Holland Tunnel and onto the New Jersey Turnpike, Kurt began what would become my most important college course. He started simply with, "So, you liked Eric, huh?" I didn't know what to say. I think I said something stupid, like, "He seemed very nice." But Kurt wouldn't let me get away with that. He pressed and pushed until I confessed to him that I found Eric magnificent but that I couldn't understand why.

"You're gay, too", he said nonchalantly, "Don't you know that?" This was followed by my admitting ignorance of the word and his explaining it. And on and on it went. His making revelations to me, about me and about the vast underground world of the homosexual.

I told him about "Joey" and about all the feelings I'd had when I was growing up that had confused me. He told me that I was a member of a very large, exclusive club that had members in every city in the world. That I could go anywhere and always find friends who would accept me into their group, just because I was one of them. He said that those not "in the club" were called "straight" and were ignorant of how many gays there were in every walk of life. He told me that a high percentage of the great Artists in the world were gay, citing people like Tennessee Williams, Michaelangelo, Walt Whitman and Noel Coward.

I asked him how he had met Eric. He told me that he had picked him up at a "gay beach" and that they had spent most of the week together. *The Ninth Circle,* he said, was a gay restaurant, and that there were hundreds of gay bars and restaurants in New York City. He explained that Joey would have been my friend, too, if I had let him. That his touching my leg was his way of letting me know that he was "in the club". This sent a chill of regret through me that I still feel today.

This conversation went on through Pennsylvania, Ohio and Indiana. I was utterly fascinated. I can't say that I felt any guilt or regret about being gay, because Kurt presented it in such a rational and guilt-free manner. I will always thank him for this.

I'm sure you would like to hear that Kurt also introduced me to the wondrous world of sex, but no. As we took separate motel rooms over night, he confessed to being exhausted from his week with the blond "godling". That part of my education came later and is a different tale. But I can easily say that that trip changed my life for the better, and formed in me a "gay pride" that was way before its time. I never saw Kurt again after he dropped me off, but he will always remain my favorite college professor.

One

Always The New Kid

I was always the new kid. I was constantly being torn from one school and put into another school. I was pudgy and non-athletic, so I was never a popular new kid. Although my family lived in three states while I grew up (Illinois, Tennessee and Massachusetts), I consider Highland Park, Illinois to be my home town, because we kept moving back there.

For a time we had our own house, but primarily we would retreat to the house on Glenview Avenue that my mother grew up in, and where my Grandmother Guyot lived. My father suffered emotional difficulties, so any attempts to free ourselves from my Grandmother always ultimately failed. I was never aware of what my father was dealing with all his life, because he never showed it to us kids – my mother dealt with it in her own way. So I didn't know why we kept moving all the time, I just went along and coped.

When I was in preschool we lived with my Grandmother, then an apartment in Chicago, then in another suburb, Deerfield, then Paris, Tennessee with my father's family. During grammar school, we lived in an apartment upstairs from my Grandmother, then we got our own house in Highland Park, then we moved to Massachusetts, then we moved back upstairs from my Grandmother. In high school, we were still in Grandmother's house, then we moved to Onarga – a small town in Central Illinois – then we moved back to my Grandmother's, but she had the apartment upstairs.

We weren't exactly gypsies, but we did moved around a lot.

Me and my "Denton".
When my mother asked, "Why don't you say 'elephant'?"
I distinctly told her,
"I cannot say Elephant, I have to say Denton."

Highland Park, a large, Chicago suburb on the North Shore of Lake Michigan, is populated by a majority of mostly wealthy, Jewish families, as well as great many wealthy WASPs (White, Anglo-Saxon Protestants). Along the lake front were huge mansions and other grand houses that fill the "fashionable side of town", including many homes designed by Frank Lloyd Wright. The downtown area boasted classy and pricy department stores that we certainly didn't custom. There was also an old fashioned drug store with a soda fountain, where we'd get cherry cokes. But my favorite landmark was the Highland Park Movie theater.

When I was three years old, my father, Robert, took me to my first movie, "Pinocchio". To prepare me, he made a scrapbook of pictures from the Disney movie and told me the story many times, so that I would be familiar with it. I was utterly enchanted. My second movie was with my mother, Mary, who was a Jane Austen fan. It was "Pride and Prejudice" with Laurence Olivier. I didn't understand much of the plot, but I think I fell in love with Olivier. From these exposures, the movies became an integral part of my life ever after.

The Northwestern Railroad runs right through the middle of the town, with all the wealthier homes on the side of Lake Michigan. "The other side of the tracks", where my Grandmother had lived since her marriage, was much humbler. In our neighborhood there were Italian and Polish families and the houses were smaller and closer together. Gramma's house on Glenview Avenue was covered in dirty grey stucco and was squeezed into a skinny lot, with a tiny garden in the back. The driveway to a garage in back completely filled the one side of the lot, while a small path on the other side, led to the back yard.

At one end of the street was the Highland Park Hospital, which was much smaller than it is today. On the other end was the house where the Manony's lived, with an Italian grocery store, which was run by the Manony family. Their house had a larger, fenced-in lawn that contained a horse, Manony's Pony, the delight of all us neighborhood kids.

Gramma Guyot

Our house on Glenview Ave. with my mother as a little girl

My first grammar school was fairly close to Glenview Avenue, on our side of town. I'm told that in first grade I was asked what I wanted to be when I grew up, and I answered, "An actor, a teacher or a preacher." I guess 2 out of 3 isn't bad.

The actor side of me got its first chance in second grade. The class was doing a staging of "The Nutcracker Suite" (from Disney's "Fantasia") and I was one of the group of dancing mushrooms. I enjoyed being part of the mushroom band, which circled together, doing basically all the same movements. But the best role was of the Rebel Mushroom, who doesn't dance with the rest of the group, but dances on the outside of the circle doing his own movements.

On the day of the show, that boy got sick and Miss Whelock made me his understudy. I took my new responsibilities to heart, and on the day of the show, I took off improvising all my movements that the other mushrooms didn't do, twirling, leaping, cavorting around with abandon – and I was a HIT. As we did our curtain call the audience of mothers applauded, and I felt that it was just for me - and I loved it. You have to start somewhere.

Second Grade, standing right in front of Miss Whelock

After third grade I had to go across town to Elm Place School, which was larger and a very different affair, because we were mixed in with the kids from the other side of the tracks. Passing all those elegant homes, with vast tree-covered lawns, multiple cars in long driveways, tall wrought iron fences surrounding them, was awe inspiring. I always had a favorite stick, which I clicked along the iron fences as I walked to school each morning, and parked behind some bush so I could pick it up on my way home. To this day, I like to have a stick to hold whenever I take a walk.

Elm Place School extolled nature and art, but maybe not individualism. In one art class when we were asked to draw an underwater scene. I created a fanciful, Disneyesque drawing with the anthropomorphic fish wearing hats and canes and moustaches. The teacher was not pleased and told me this was not the assignment. My eight year old self was crushed. This was the same art teacher who told me that blue and green shouldn't be used together. Clearly her artistic pursuits had never led her to drawing any scenes from nature. Anytime I see a painting depicting a scene of sky and trees, I am reminded of her and how dumb she was. However, I still shirk at putting on a green shirt with blue pants.

Though we were from the "other side of the tracks", we were not ignorant of the lake side of Highland Park, since we ventured over there in the summer to go to the beach. Lake Michigan's beaches on the north shore were far down a bluff. So the view from the top of the bluff was quite magnificent with blue water, stretching as far as eye could see. But the paths down to the beach could be treacherous and it was an arduous climb back up. There was a road to drive down, but it was hard to walk on because it was curvy and teenagers in cars tended to barrel up and down it. But the climb down and up again never hampered my cousins and me, who spent many happy hours splashing in the waves and building castles on the bright yellow sand. I grew up swimming in this clean, fresh-water lake, so saltwater and the ocean were quite a surprise when I encountered them years later.

Me and my cousins, Billy, Charles and Marianne.
(do you think my pose was telling)

At some point in these grammar school days, we moved out of Glenview Avenue to a house on Sunset Road, a newer sub-division next to Sunset Park. I'm sure my parents were very relieved to have a home of their own, but still close to my Grandmother. The house was one of those 1920s, A-roof houses, on a small hill with a sloping lawn around it. The yard was certainly bigger than Glenview, but better yet, across the street was this huge park with wooded areas, picnic areas, a club house with skating rink, baseball, hockey and football fields. It was a perfect location for a sports-loving kid to live.

The house on Sunset as it is today.
The tree in the front yard was very small when I lived there.

I, on the other hand, was more into putting on plays in our basement. I would drag the neighborhood kids, who I'm sure would have preferred to be in the park, to perform these "plays" for our parents. The director even then, I created these swash-buckling dramas with fervor and enough enthusiasm to con my casts into believing we were making great theater. My mother told me later how hard it was for the parents to sit through them, so they must have been pretty bad.

For one play I used a Decca album of "Alice in Wonderland", on three 78 RPM records, that starred Ginger Rogers as Alice. I had the kids act out all the parts, lip-syncing to the record. I forced a shy, little sister of one of my friends to be Alice, because Alice had to be a girl. I played multiple roles, but my favorite was the snooty caterpillar, who said "Who are You?"

I could also sing all the songs from an album by Danny Kaye, who was my hero. "Anatole of Paris" was a favorite, which I learned word for word, but didn't understand most of the jokes until I was an adult. The song was so gay, no wonder I loved it.

"I'm the Anatole of Paris, I reek with chic, my hat of the week:
Called, Six Divorces, three run-away horses"

Another Kaye song that I still use as a warm-up before any performance I give, was his Americanized version of Gilbert and Sullivan's "The Nightmare Song".

The Nightmare Song
by W.S. Gilbert, from *Iolanthe*
(Americanized dream by Danny Kaye)

When you're lying awake with a dismal headache, and repose is
    taboo'd by anxiety,
I conceive you may use any language you choose to indulge in,
    without impropriety;
For your brain is on fire; the bedclothes conspire of usual
    slumber to plunder you:
First your counterpane goes and uncovers your toes,
    and your sheet slips demurely from under you.
Then your blanketing tickles, you feel like mixed pickles
    so terribly sharp is the pricking,
And you're hot and your cross, and you tumble and toss
    till there's nothing 'twixt you and the ticking.
Then the bedclothes all creep to the ground in a heap,
    so you pick them all up in a tangle;
Next our pillow resigns and politely declines to remain at its
    usual angle.

Well, you get some repose, in the form of a doze, with eye-balls
    and head ever aching,
But your slumbering teams with such horrible dreams, that
    you'd very much better be waking.
For you dream you are ill, having swallowed a pill that was made
    out of ossified onyx.
And the doctor you've found has been traveling around
    on a subway that's bound for the "Bron-ix".
Oh, you must find him fast, as the hours go past,
    you're convinced that you're headed for tragedy,
For you saw him on Sunday, felt much worse on Monday,
    and here it's the following "Sagedy".
You're full of suspicion, this traveling physician, he fed you some
    stuff with a barb in it.
So you rush down the street as you frantically eat
    a souffle made of sodium bi-carbonate.
To a druggist you rush, but he gives you the brush, saying
    "Who let this asthmatic gasper in?"
You plead with the villain, you need penicillin,

> he won't even give you an aspirin.
> Then a pill on the shelf leaps down by itself
> > and it lands on your head like a lead post.
> You suddenly awake, and no wonder you ache,
> > you've been hitting yourself with the bed-post.

You're a regular wreck, with a crick in your neck, and no wonder you snore, for your head's on the floor, and you've needles and pins from your soles to your shins, and your flesh is a-creep, for your left leg's asleep, and you've cramps in your toes, and a fly on your nose, and some fluff in your lung, and a feverish tongue, and a thirst that's intense, and a general sense, that you haven't been sleeping in clover.

But the darkness is past and it's daylight at last,
and the night has been long
Ditto ditto my song
And thank goodness they're both of them over.

    One summer I staged an elaborate "Western" play on our lawn, full of heroes (me I'm sure), villains and maidens in distress, and I decided to open it up to the public and sell tickets. So I covered the town of posters which described the play, in colorful crayon, and at the bottom it read: "**At David's House – Tickets 10 Cents**". Oh, I expected the Highland Park people, young and old, to flock to my house resulting in a packed lawn and a booming return. Then when absolutely no one came, because no one knew "David" or where "his house" was, my play was a flop. I was shattered, but I was forced to learn the hard way that show business ain't easy.

    Being in our own house there was a sense of freedom and exuberance for life on Sunset Road for our family. My mother was always, even to the end of her life, a fanatic lover of Christmas. For most of my childhood, my parents would stay up very late the night before Christmas, putting up the tree, wrapping presents, stuffing stockings and generally creating a miraculous surprise for me (and later my brother) on Christmas morning. It was her favorite time of year and she always tried to make the most of it. So even though I was way past the Santa age, Christmas on Sunset Road was a spectacle.

    That year my mother's cousin Mary Schrey came to visit us for a short stay. She loved Christmas too and she was very artistic so the two of them tried to out-do each other in their gift wrappings. And my creative father joined in as well. Each present was a work of art, like one with cotton puffs covering the package, and a mirror in the middle like an ice pond in the snow, with tiny skaters on top. These gifts were *almost* too beautiful to open. The present that year that I remember most was a hand-illustrated booklet, made by Mary, of the song "Swinging on a Star", which Bing Crosby had made popular that year. We all sang it all the time and she had drawn an adorable comic book to lyrics like:

> "A mule is an animal with long funny ears
> Kicks up at anything he hears
> His back is brawny but his brain is weak
> He's just plain stupid with a stubborn streak
> And by the way, if you hate to go to school
> You may grow up to be a mule."

    My imagination ruled my life in those days on Sunset Road. I acquired a large plaster statue of a Swami, wearing a turban with an enormous red glass gem, which I was convinced was a ruby, a prized possession. Each week I sat on my bed the nights my parents went to choir practice, listening to the forbidden "Inner Sanctum" on the radio, holding two croquet mallets across my chest for protection. In a pedestrian tunnel under the train station, which was clammy and dark, I claimed that a square mound on the floor was "Queen Elizabeth's Tomb", which I brought people to see.

    My parents were Depression-raised and it affected them like it did so many of that generation. We lived frugally. Though my mother was a fine cook, we ate simple food in our house. "Plain Cheap Food", my mother proudly called it. When I was a baby, the only job my college-graduate father could get was stirring apples for Mrs. Wagner's Pie Factory. He finally got a job for Lewis Melind Ink Co., a company that he hated, but he kept working there off and on for most of his life, afraid to be out of work.

    For all his troubles, my father was a terrific dad. During the war, new bicycles were impossible to get, but like all young boys, I too wanted a bike. So one day he bought a second hand bike from somewhere near his work in Chicago. The only way to get it home was to ride it. We lived in the suburbs, about 25 miles from his job, but he proceeded to ride the bike all the way to our house on Sunset Road. He was laid up for a couple of days from the exertion and strained muscles. When he recovered, he tried to teach me to ride it. I took one shaky ride, fell off, and would never touch the bike again.

Because he hated Lewis Melind, my father wanted to change professions and he was quite skilled at making up games. He invented a game he called "Murder". It involved cards with suspects, weapons and rooms on them; the object being to find out who murdered the victim, in what room, and with what weapon. He showed "Murder" to the powers-that-be at Parker Brothers, Inc., who told him that the public didn't want games about crime. Not long after that rejection, Parker Brothers released "Clue", which is my father's game with a board added. Unfortunately he was too naïve to take out a patent beforehand.

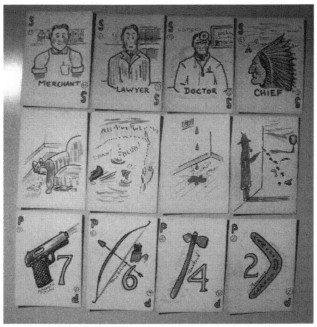

Some of the cards my father made for the prototype of his game "Murder" (which was stolen by Parker Bros. for "Clue")

Encouraged by Parker Brothers' interest, he applied for other jobs in the game business and he first got a job with Milton Bradley Co. in Springfield, Massachusetts. But after a year in this huge company, a year of fiddling with silly toys, he quit that job. It wasn't long before he got a much better job with Electric Game Co., which was a smaller company, where he was given truly creative projects. Among several games that he developed there, he made the first Electric Football which was very successful.

I was in 5th or 6th grade at the time and once my father was securely in a job, his family naturally had to follow. So off to the East Coast we moved, to Longmeadow, Massachusetts, which is a suburb of Springfield. It is quite a beautiful town, long and thin, with some lovely homes along the main road that went through it from Springfield to the Connecticut border. The centerpiece of the town was a tall, white, Congregational church that was certainly unlike our squat, old fashioned Bethany church in Highland Park. My parents joined it, my father sang in the choir, and I went regularly to Sunday School.

Our house was on Barrington Road, backed by a ravine, which the locals called a "dingle". We kids named it "Jo-Jo Jungle" and it was a perfect place for my movie-loving imagination to act out Tarzan movies, swinging on the vines, sliding down the steep hill, and crashing through the stick weeds. It was during one of these enactments that I broke my arm, the one and only time in my life I broke a bone. We also had an abandoned old chicken coop in our back yard, which had a trap door in the roof and a climbable pine tree next to it, which made a perfect pirate ship for Long John Silver – "Treasure Island" being my then favorite movie at the time. From the top of the mast I would growl in my best Robert Newton accent, "Arrrr, Matey, Fire that musket and I cuts 'is throat".

Although my spare time was fun because of my imagination, school was not a happy time for me. I was chubby and my friends were limited. I was hounded by a school bully whose last name, hilariously enough, was O'Golly. He waited for me to walk home from school to terrorize me every day. Junior high school proved to be just as disappointing, though O'Golly didn't pass sixth grade, so I was free of him at least.

Acting for an audience wasn't in my life in those days, but I was in a choral group that was going to sing in a variety show. We rehearsed the beautiful song "Deep Purple" and I was so excited to do this, because I would be on the stage in front of a real audience. But as luck would have it, I got sick the day of the performance and couldn't make it. I was heart sick about missing this show, and hearing that song, even today, makes me sad.

My primary joy in those days was the movies. Since my parents took me to my first movie, "Pinocchio", I was hooked. Realizing that I was unhappy at school, they gave me a 16 mm movie projector. I would rent short movies, with sub-titles instead of sound, because I didn't have a sound projector. Laurel and Hardy and WC Fields were top on my list and I rented every one of their films I could. So now I had my own movie theater in the basement, and it was a way to get kids to come over to my house to watch them.

I also went to the movies as much as I could. I would take the bus into Springfield every Saturday to go to one of the many movie palaces. I can remember every movie theater in Springfield and many of the films that I saw in them. One hot Saturday I watched a Johnny Weissmuller "Tarzan" through laced fingers, because I had a migraine headache and the light hurt my eyes. It didn't stop me from watching the whole thing, though, as well as devouring a box of cinnamon candies, causing me to vomit in the men's room after the movie finished.

One year my grades in eighth grade were not so good and my father said that if they didn't improve, I'd be banned from movies until they improved. Unfortunately, my grades went down, and I went movie-less for a marking period. I vividly recall the last movie before the ban, Disney's "Song of the South", and the first one when my grades went up, "Joan of Arc" with Ingrid Bergman.

My excursions to Springfield were usually by myself and besides the movie I'd see, I often played solitary, movie-based games. I would see how long I could pretend to be blind by closing my eyes and feeling my way down the street, hoping some kind stranger would assist me. Or pick some person to "follow", pretending to be a Private Eye – sometimes going so far as to follow them on a bus to their home. I prided myself on never being spotted by my subject, but I imagine I looked just silly, this little kid skulking around corners, dashing up to hide behind lampposts, probably with an imaginary gun in his jacket? Today, I'd get picked up for stalking, I suppose. After the movie and my play-acting adventures, I'd ride the bouncy bus back to Longmeadow, usually getting an embarrassing pre-adolescent erection.

My parents, realizing that I was a lonely kid, thought it would be good for me to have a sibling. Mother was unable to have another child, so they decided to adopt, which altered my life completely. I wasn't aware of the process they went through, but finally they brought home a 5 year old boy with club feet, who they called Jonathan Kurt. He'd had a very hard first year of his life and it was quite courageous and warm hearted of my parents to choose him, over an infant. I suppose they wanted a more mature child that I could be brothers with, right off the bat. He was a sweet kid, but I don't think I was particularly nice to him at the time – kid brother syndrome – I remember whacking him often on the head.

Before Jonathan came to us, he had, for some reason, been passed to five different foster homes in his first five years, making a very unstable beginning for a child. When my parents adopted him, they constantly reassured him that we were his final, permanent family – that he would never have to leave us, ever. My father took him to the school where he would start kindergarten in the fall, and I'm sure he tried to believe that this was his future.

But a couple weeks before kindergarten began, my parents received a letter from the Shriner's Hospital for Children stating that Jonathan's name had finally come up on the list and that he should check in immediately for surgery on his club feet. The stay in the hospital would be months. So instead of going to the promised school, he was packed off to the hospital. My parents and I visited him constantly and tried to convince him that he would be coming home to his family, but I don't imagine that this traumatized, five year old boy had much faith in their assurances after yet another disappointment.

Jonathan did return home, although he had to sleep with a ghastly metal brace, spreading his legs with his feet in bulky boots. But he went to kindergarten and we did become a family. Jonathan and I played together a lot in those days, reenacting movies in Jo-Jo Jungle and in the deep snow that fell during those frigid New England winters. One Sunday, we were supposed to go to Sunday School, but instead I took him across the Connecticut border to a movie theater that had triple features. "You better not tell Mom", I threatened him, which he honored. That's my kind of playing hooky. I think it was three Westerns, including one starring Roy Rogers, the blond, singing cowboy. He was my favorite cowboy and I probably had a crush on him, but didn't realize it at that age.

With Jonathan posing for an early portrait and in the New England snow.

Since my father was employed in these game companies, our family was constantly being subjected to his new ideas. Besides the ones for his job, he invented two games independently, Lawn Billiards and Lawn Quoits. The first was too elaborate to manufacture, so it was never commercial. It required six aluminum scoop "pockets", which were set around the lawn in a rectangle like a pool table, with a string connecting them to define the "table". The balls were struck with croquet mallets and when hit correctly, scooped in and out of the pockets, which constituted getting in "in the pocket". It was actually lots of fun and we played in on our lawn for years with his homemade set.

But more successful was Lawn Quoits, which incorporated the new toy, Flying Saucers (later called Frisbies). Five of the Flying Saucers were used for the game, one yellow, two red and two blue ones. One team was chosen to throw the yellow one out first and where it landed constituted the point to reach. Then, like bocce ball, the red and blue team would try to see how close they could get to the yellow one.

Because these Flying Saucers could be purchased wholesale, my father bought a bunch of them and put together a kit for his game. He then travelled around New England on weekends to tourist cabins selling them. One summer I accompanied him several times, which was great fun for me, bonding alone with my father, away from the rest of the family. I have always cherished those trips with him.

During one of these excursions, I encountered the ocean for the first time, on the coast of Connecticut. Having been brought up on fresh water lakes, I was excited and scared, not knowing what to expect in the vast, salty ocean. After my father and I changed in a locker room, he encouraged me to enter the salt water, warning me not to swallow it. It felt very different from Lake Michigan and I was imagining all kinds of sea monsters and sharks. Suddenly, after I had immersed myself in the brine, I felt this "thing" grasping at my neck. I screamed and frantically tried to pull it off, to no avail. Hysterical, I fled from the water, frantically pulling on this "sea monster". Crying with fear, I ran to my father, who pointed out that it was just the locker key on an elastic rope around my neck.

Much to my surprise, in the middle of the first semester of 9th grade, which in Longmeadow was the last year of junior high school, we had to return to Highland Park. My father evidently had another crisis (again I was unaware), and back to Grandmother's the four of us went.

Ninth grade in Highland Park was freshman year in the high school, not middle school, and Highland Park High was a huge, sophisticated high school, unlike Longmeadow's small town, provincial school. So as a new freshman with no orientation, I was plopped down in this completely foreign and different kind of school with no help at all. I was lost.

The bottom of the barrel of new-kidism, of course, was gym class. It is the horror for so many pudgy or non-athletic or gay kids, especially back in the unenlightened 1950s. And I was all three. My nemesis was a running track that surrounded the gym on a balcony and to get there at the beginning of every gym period we had to climb ropes. Every day I tried, every day I failed to drag my over-weight body up the rope and had to walk up the stairs, humiliated by the sadistic, gym teacher. I cut gym whenever I could and failed the class. On top of that, I even acquired my own new bully. He would walk me to an assembly, grabbing my hand and bend my little finger in a sort of squeeze that was excruciating, but unnoticeable to the teachers; I was helpless.

I wasn't prepared academically either. At my old junior high, our beginning French class was just about getting to, "La plume es sewer la tab-luh."   But when I walked into the beginning French class at Highland Park High School, I learned that everyone, including the teacher, was *charged a penny for every English word spoken after the bell rang*! Although the teacher tried to assimilate me into this class, I was totally lost; I had to transfer to a Spanish class. I regret this to this day because I wish I'd studied French, which I certainly could have used in my many trips to France.

The one bright spot in this short Highland Park stay was getting closer to my cousins, Marianne and Charles. Full of early teen high jinx, one afternoon, we snuck under the porch and retrieved some bottles of liquor that Charles had appropriated from the country club where he caddied. We got stupidly plastered on stuff like Drambui and Crème de Menthe. Having dinner that night with my Grandmother, who was an ardent teetotaler, was not a pleasant experience.

But we three high school cousins had great fun together, and we are still good friends. They were also the first people we knew with a television set, so many happy hours were spent watching Sid Ceasar and Milton Berle on a their snow-covered screen.

My closest cousins: Marianne and Charles Guyot

My parents were well aware of my misery at this new school, so they planned yet another move. My father was back at Lewis Melind, but he was assigned to supervise the building of a new factory, in a tiny, farm town between Kankakee and Champaign-Urbana, Illinois, called Onarga. The family couldn't move there for several months, but my parents knew that I needed to get out of Highland Park High School. They sent me down two months early so that I could start at the beginning of the second semester of high school there in Onarga.

And, as they say, it got better.

Two

Happy High School

For once being a new kid didn't have the unpleasant connotations or ramifications of the previous schools I'd attended. In Onarga, I was certainly new to the farming community, but I was from the "big-city" so I was considered exotic and interesting. While Highland Park High School had around 1500 students, Onarga had about 1500 people in the whole town. The high school had only 100 students, with four homerooms: freshman, sophomore, junior and senior. And the senior homeroom had only 10 kids, because many had to drop out before graduating to work on their farms.

This town was certainly different from anyplace I'd ever lived. Since a majority of the Onarga folks lived on surrounding farms, the town itself was quite small. Main Street had only two blocks of stores, and only on one side of the street. Running in front of the stores was a rickety, wooden sidewalk, five feet above the roadway. These stores resembled an old Western movie town, including a dusty clothing store, a lumberyard, an antique drug store and a greasy-spoon restaurant. On the corner stood a movie theater, called The Mode, which featured mostly Westerns. Fortunately, the nearby town of Gilman had a theater that ran more mainstream movies, if not art films, so I ventured there more often.

A two lane highway and a railroad cut through the town which contained tree-lined, residential blocks. Surrounding the town were endless cornfields. Connecting the cornfields were long, flat, straight, single slab roads, with one lane of concrete and two shoulders. When two cars met on the road, both of which were visible for miles, each car pulled over onto the shoulder with two wheels. This eventually served as the road where I learned how to drive.

Before my family arrived, I was placed in the home of the Booth family. It was a loving and welcoming family. The father ran the lumber company, but the home was run by the mother, Ginny, who took me to her bosom and made me feel a part of the family. She had other children in the house, but I will always be indebted to Ginny for making my transition to the small town and new school a smooth and healing experience. My mother and Ginny remained friends to the end of their lives.

My parents and Jonathan moved to Onarga later that semester and we all settled into a charming house in town on leafy Seminary Avenue in the middle of town. The house had a large yard, with a second piece of land behind it where we had a big garden and a small woods. Although we lived in town, the next door neighbors had pigs and an outhouse, but far enough away from everything so as not to be offensive. We loved our house and yard, it gave us a freedom and a joy that we never had before. Onarga and our new home was the perfect place for me to come into my adolescence and completely turn my life around. And my family was the happiest it had ever been, and maybe, ever was.

Our house on Seminary Avenue and my bedroom with sweet Belle.

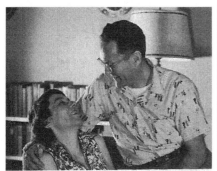

Mom and Dad, happy in Onarga – a Christmas card from that period.

Two important things happened to me in those years in Onarga that played a major role in shaping the rest of my life. One: in my freshman year I shot up to six feet and outgrew my pudginess, so no more husky clothes. Sports were not the be-all-end-all in that school, thus I was no longer automatically an outcast. Two: I was introduced to the study of acting and singing, and so performing soon became a reality for me.

A young teacher in that little school, named Miss Markowitz, had a real love for theater and instilled it in her students, particularly me. When we would read a play in English classes we chose characters, and fully acted them out. This was my first time performing in a real play. She inspired me to join the Speech and Debate team and participate in speech competitions, which were very popular in rural schools. Our team would travel to other schools and my specialty was performing comedic monologues. My most successful monologue was *The Waltz* by Stephen Leacock, which won me accolades and medals galore.

In my junior year, I made my full-length play debut when Miss Markowitz produced, *Fog Island*. This was a small rural school with no budget, so the play was most likely one of those dreadful, no fee, "high school" plays from Samuel French, Inc. We didn't care. It was a pseudo-Agatha Christie murder mystery and to our unsophisticated taste it was a blast to perform.

A hulking, farm boy named Bobby Cox was cast as the sheriff in the play. In the climactic scene, the sheriff is supposed to be hiding in the window seat, overhearing the murderer confess; then at the climactic moment, jump out and apprehend the villain. The none-too-bright Bobby leapt out of the box an entire page too early, and just sat on the box and listened to the confession – then he stood up and spoke his line on cue. My mother told me years later that it was an excruciatingly bad play, but she just loved that I had done it. It was my first real taste of the stage and it set me on the road to my future.

Another fairly new experience at that time for me were the friendships I was able to forge and maintain. There was Herbie Becker, a handsome, blonde farm boy whose friendship was most likely begun due to a healthy attraction on my part. He was also not an athlete, but attended all the games because he was the only boy cheerleader on the squad. Naturally, I decided I'd join him and be a cheerleader, too. This was the first time I gave a damn about football or basketball, and screaming our heads off in support of a touchdown or basket was totally new for me.

Another real buddy of mine was Mary Lou Schultz. Her buck teeth and thick glasses rendered her not much of a looker, but she was a hell of a lot of fun and a loyal friend. We became close because of our love for performing on stage and I remember doing a variety act with her, singing "How Could You Believe Me, When I Said I Loved You,

When You Know I've Been a Liar All My Life". Originally sung by Fred Astaire and Jane Powell in *Royal Wedding,* it remains one of my all time favorite songs.

My social confidence was so high in Onarga, I even went to the Junior Prom. My date was a pudgy, bespectacled girl named Una. The theme was "Under the Sea", and the rest of the prom committee and I made certain colorful decoration evoked an exquisite underwater fantasy. It was 1953, and we were all in bobby socks, laughing and crafting an underwater wonderland with crepe paper, chicken wire and paint. It was like the underwater scene I had drawn in grammar school, come to life. I was in heaven!

At the Prom with Una. Handsome Herbie on the left.

My best friend during that time was Bob Sumrall. He was a townie, from the "wrong side of the tracks". His family lived in a hovel of a house with countless kids running around and with the mother in the back yard making soap in a huge boiling pot. Bob was a very shy boy, tall and gawky, who never said much in school, but in our private conversations he was the funniest person I'd ever met. One day when he came out of the house to meet me, he tripped and fell on the scraggy front yard. He got up and immediately said, "I just washed my feet and can't do a thing with 'em."

Though Bob seemed uncomfortable on our side of town, one day I coerced him to come over to my house to play golf with me. I had constructed a 6 hole golf course on our giant lawn, by sinking tin cans into various places in the ground. On one of the "holes" he stood behind me, and as I swung the club I accidently smacked him right in the mouth. As he slowly spit out chips of his front teeth, he said with a totally calm, straight face, "Dave, you knocked aaaawll mah teef out." Thankfully, my father paid for his dental work, and luckily Bob was never mad at me for this incident.

Bob Sumrall and I, sunning and fencing in our huge yard in Onarga.

I thought I had completely lost track of Bob, but a few years ago I got a Christmas card signed, Bob Sumrall, with no message or return address. I would have loved to make contact with him, but I couldn't respond and never have heard from him since.

Playing the alto sax in the marching band.

Laughter was a huge factor in those high school years. When we would go to other towns for contests, our bus load of kids would laugh our heads off at everything we saw that we deemed unusual. Like a man with a beard – hilarious! A woman with buck teeth – howlingly funny! A girl with an ugly dress – a scream! At school I was a library monitor at the main desk during study hall and I would find a "funny" picture in a magazine, put a marker in the page and Bob would walk up from his seat, take the magazine, saunter to his chair and look at the picture. Then we would silently scream with laughter from opposite sides of the library, with me hiding behind the desk and Bob burying his head in his hands. I'm sure we were more than obnoxious, but this camaraderie was such a new sensation for me that I took every opportunity to enjoy it to the fullest.

My parents were always very funny people and this carefree period of our lives also allowed our family to have a great deal of fun together. This was Small-Town, USA in the 1950s, so teenagers hanging out with their parents was considered normal. We went to parties, movies, and community square dances together as a family. My mother and I performed vaudeville routines in the kitchen like "Ballin' the Jack", featuring our own original choreography. My father, Jonathan and I played games like Monopoly and Battleship, and my mother joined us in the favored game of the era, Cutthroat Canasta.

My parents were also able to make close friends in Onarga. One couple was the principal of the high school and his wife who were a little more cultured than most of the other town folk. One evening this couple hosted a party with some out-of-town company and as a prolonged prank, our family walked through the principal's house throughout the evening, doing outrageous things, with completely straight faces. Some of the antics included: my mother walking into their house through the dining room during dinner in a towel and bathing cap pretending to go for a shower, my father sitting outside the window crooning love songs on a ukulele, my brother running around the table in an Indian costume while chanting, and my walking in and hanging an "I Like Ike" poster on the wall then spouting political gibberish. These antics went on all night and had the guests in stitches.

My brother and I also had a much better relationship in Onarga. Though still in grammar school, he was more mature at this time, and we spent a lot of time playing together in our yard and back lot. One day while we were enacting a scene from a movie he locked me in the shed out back, imprisoning me like the characters in the film. In my attempts to escape, I pierced my foot on a rusty nail. I screamed for him to let me out, but he apparently thought it was part of the movie script. He finally realized I wasn't actually that good an actor and he released me from captivity. As I was rushed to the hospital, we laughed about how real our movie was. Onarga provided a landscape for many moments like this, which caused our family to bond more than before.

As healthy as Onarga was for my development, by my junior year I was ready to move to a more cultured environment. I can't imagine Jonathan shared my restlessness and he would have been happier finishing out his adolescence in Onarga. But our stay in the countryside ended abruptly. My father's completion of the factory, or perhaps another one of his mental episodes, sparked the sudden news that after my junior year we were going back to Highland Park - to my Grandmother's house, yet again. Thus, I would be going back to the hated Highland Park High School for my senior year. Although rushed to leave my friends and my beloved high school in Onarga, I did as I always did, I went along with the inevitable and coped with the disappointment.

* * *

This time my Grandmother moved to the apartment upstairs in her house and we occupied the main floor. Jonathan and I each had our own room upstairs, while my parent's bedroom was downstairs next to the dining room. Even though we now had the larger part of the house, it was still a much smaller space than we'd enjoyed in Onarga. So at first we all felt the restrictiveness of the situation and none of the family was as particularly happy about the change. But soon we learned to adapt and slowly regained the family bond that we had developed in Onarga, which now included my Grandmother.

Back on Glenview Avenue, with Gramma Guyot (and our dog Belle).

The Highland Park High School experience was completely different from my freshman year, mostly because I was now a completely different person. I was tall, thin and my three years in Onarga High had given me a much needed self-confidence. The size and sophistication of the school didn't intimidate me as it had before. It was also comforting that I had my cousins attending the school, so I was able to begin the year with acquaintances who could help me adapt. It didn't take me long to find my own niche in this large, sophisticated school, allowing me to grow much further than I ever would have in Onarga.

Very early on, I stumble upon the Drama Club and immediately became an active member. As an audition for the club, I performed "The Waltz" by Stephen Leacock, the comic monologue that had gotten me all those blue ribbons. The drama teacher and students in the club were very amused by this and I garnered instant acceptance into the group. I also joined the Chorus and was soon elevated into the Elite Chorus, who performed a complex, but kitschy, vocal arrangement of *The Nutcraker Suite* – "Hark to the woodland flow'rs....etc." Here I was singing alongside the best of the singers in the school and so I met many talented students in the Chorus and the Drama Club.

The Bethany Evangelical Church served as another community for me in Highland Park. My family had attended this church in the past, because of my Grandmother's devotion to religion and this was her church. My cousin Marianne was active in the Youth Group and the Choir, which motivated me to become involved there as well. This church was not the chic Episcopal church from across town. Our pastor was a rather ignorant man, who constantly commented after the anthem, "The choir done a good job". My cousin and I, sitting in the choir loft, would hide our heads behind the wooden barrier and laugh hysterically at his poor grammar, much to the chagrin of the choir director.

I made some close friends in that church. Paul Beck, Mo Cimbalo, Marianne and I adventured all over together with the choir. We attended World Convention of Churches in Soldier Field in Chicago, joining thousands of voices and filling this stadium with glorious singing, as with one voice. It was a chilling experience.

My Bethany Church gang.
Mo(left), Marianne (in pink) and Paul (tall)

One awful experience at the high school in Highland Park was upon my returned, the administration told me that because I had failed gym in my Freshman year, I had to take make-up gym, as well as my regular gym class. This happened before homeroom, meaning I had to get to school an hour early, dress for gym, do whatever they told me to do, change clothes for class, attend first period, go back to gym for second period and do it all over again. Fortunately, they only made me do this one marking period, but boy, did I hate it. The good news was that the sadistic gym teacher was replaced by a much more humane one. Regardless, I still hated it.

One exciting, but scary, part of gym class in Highland Park was that once a week was swimming class. And the all boys gym classes did their swimming in the nude! I looked forward to this, but also dreaded it, since I never knew how my adolescent body would react to all this male nudity. I spent a lot of time in the deep end, swimming by myself, for fear that I couldn't control myself. I don't remember any embarrassing moments, so I must have done pretty well. To this day, the smell of chlorine can be quite arousing.

Generally though, I had a whale of a good time. Being a newcomer, I wasn't given leading roles in the plays, but I was exposed to really good theater - unlike *Fog Island*. The drama department did produce excellent shows and I was part of two of them. The first was, J.M. Barrie's *The Old Lady Shows Her Medals*. I had listened to it as a radio play that starred Lionel and Ethyl Barrymore, and playing my role was Douglas Fairbanks Jr.. To be anywhere near the company of Douglas Fairbanks Jr. was an honor and it excited me greatly to perform this role. In the second production that year, I played one of the Three Kings in Menotti's *Amahl and the Night Visitors*. This was the first amateur production of this made-for-TV opera. A line from one of my solos was, "This is my box, this is my box, I never travel without my box....". I still sing it when the right opportunity arises.

Playing another King was Charles Kimbrough, who later went on to become a successful professional actor appearing in several Broadway productions, including the original productions of Stephen Sondheim's *Company* and *Sunday in the Park with George*. Years later while I was teaching drama, Chuck took one of my classes back stage after seeing *Company* and introduced them to the cast, including Larry Kurt, the original Tony in *West Side Story*. Even more thrilling to me was to meet Elaine Stritch, whom I had fallen in love with in *Sail Away!* and who stole the show (as far as I was concerned) in *Company*. Chuck was so gracious to my students and I'll always respect him for that. I have seen him occasionally over the years and we've kept a warm relationship that started being Kings together in *Amahl*.

The "Elite Chorus" *Graduation antics.*

The tall guy on the left   *Chuck Kimbrough is in glasses,*
I have heard is a now transsexual.   *behind the short kid*

    Another famous, or rather infamous, person that I knew well was the pear-shaped, bespectacled Alan Solomon, who later changed his name to Allan Carr. He went on to produce a little movie called *Grease*, and the Broadway musical *La Cage aux Folles*. He also produced the huge flop movie *Can't Stop the Music*, starring the Village People. However, he is most known for producing what is referred to as "The Worst Academy Awards Show, Ever". It's the one where Rob Lowe sings to Snow White.

    Allan became well known in New York and Hollywood for his outrageous parties. His wild exploits are detailed in the book "Party Animals: A Hollywood Tale of Sex Drugs, and Rock 'n' Roll, Starring the Fabulous Allan Carr", in which I am quoted often during the section about his high school and college years.

Alan Solomon in high school, holding Alan Engle

In high school, Alan (before the second 'l' was added) introduced me to the world of adult show business. On his prompting we would often venture into Chicago together to see lots of theater and even some night club shows with famous performers. One night, he took me back stage to meet Carol Channing after her production of *Wonderful Town*. Being a naturally pushy person, Alan forged our way back to her dressing room and knocked on her door. When it opened, there she stood, towering over Alan. She had the brown, short hair that she had in the play, and looked ten feet tall in her orange *schmatta*. She boomed out in her baritone, "Well now, who are you?". Alan quickly mentioned to her that the two of them had met at some party, and since short, squat Alan was hard to forget, she must have believed him. But whether she remembered or not, she was very gracious to these two high school kids, one talking a blue streak and the other struck dumb with awe.

He took me to the Blue Note, a posh nightclub like I'd only seen in the movies. The star of that show was Mae West. She was much more risqué than even in her movies, which was quite shocking to my innocent ears. Though it thrilled me when all the hunky chorus boys, with their backs to us unfortunately, revealed themselves one by one to Mae, and she made appropriate, suggestive responses. Then there was the fabulous, lesbian, jazz singer Frances Faye. "I'm Frances Faye. Gay, gay, gay!" *What? Did she just sing "Gay, gay, gay"?* I was a green kid from the sticks and I ate it up, even if I didn't really know what she meant. Over the years, I've collected many Francis Faye records, particularly loving her jazz version of *Porgy and Bess,* where she sings a baritone Bess and Mel Torme sings a tenor Porgy (or did they switch roles? I don't remember).

I spent my whole college funds savings on these excursions; Alan was loaded, but he didn't pay my way, he simply wanted a friend to accompany him on these evening trips that he took for granted. We were both completely in the closet in those days, but his outgoing personality encouraged me to look beyond the unsophisticated world I'd grown up in, especially my years in Onarga. The possibility of being a part of the world of show business became more than a dream, but an obsession. Who knows if I would have had the chutzpah to come to New York and give it a try, if I hadn't known Alan.

During this time, I also dated a girl, Gail Sloan, who was a dark haired, glamorous Jewish girl from a big house on the lake. I had just gotten my first car, a black "gangster" Plymouth, like in the old movies. It was a wreck. It had one back fender off with a wheel exposed, a missing running board, and a front bumper held on by only one of the two braces, causing it scraped whenever the car went over a bump. The side with the missing fender was always splattered with mud from the uncovered tire.

I often took Gail to the theater in Chicago in this gloriously beat up car. Back then everyone dressed up for the theater, so we always looked quite smart. After a play, we would wait in the parking garage for the attendants to bring the cars down. All the playgoers in their furs and tuxedos would wait for their Cadillacs and Mercedes along with us. Suddenly everyone would hear "Bang Bang, Scrape, Scrape, Bang, Bang" and my car would appear, with the fender-less, mud-strewn, running board-less side of the car toward the awe-struck crowd. The people would look around, wondering whom this dreadful car belonged to.

I would let them speculate for a moment and then, keeping my dignity, I would walk to the car, elegantly open the door for Gail, upon which she would haughtily step over the missing running board into the passenger seat. Then we would drive away like we were in a Rolls Royce, laughing hysterically.

The one boy who I remember for a different reason was Robbie LeClerc. He was beyond handsome and I had such a crush on him, of which I was certainly aware this time. He knew it too, but he condescended to be friends, allowing me to come to his palatial home, sit in his plush living room with him, and listen to records of Frank Sinatra's crooning and Jackie Gleason's schmaltzy orchestra. I would just gaze at him and he allowed it. I always knew he was taking advantage of the situation, but I didn't care.

My heartthrob, Robbie, and my glamour date, Gail.

My senior year at Highland Park High School proved to be one of the best years of my life. Who'd a thunk it?!

Now I had to choose a college. This became one of my life's primary turning points. Though I was unaware of the gravity of this decision at the time, the college I chose would determine my future and I had two options. My parents said that since we lived commuting distance from Lake Forest College and Northwestern University, I could go to either one. Northwestern is, and was, a huge university with a renowned drama department; Lake Forest a small, but prestigious college, with an intimate drama department which left much to be desired.

This was the first major decision in my life that I had to make by for myself. However, I was influenced by a young man and woman from Lake Forest who were student teaching in my drama class at Highland Park. My high school drama teacher was altogether forgettable, but these two college kids remain vividly in my mind. They were enthusiastic about acting and theater and impressed with my work in class. High with their praise, they strongly urged me to come to Lake Forest and join the drama department there. They brought me to the college and introduced me around, and greatly pushed for me to enroll there. I knew no one at Northwestern, so their hospitality and support was powerful incentive. I chose Lake Forest College.

Five years later when I moved to New York, I found that the theater world was filled with Northwestern graduates. My acting education at Lake Forest was minimal, if not negative, which put me far behind all the other striving young thespians. Who can say where my road would have led had I chosen Northwestern instead? Would I have made connections that might have pointed toward a different path? Who can say? We make the choices that we make. And keep on truckin'.

I've always considered this our Family Motto

Three

Hi Ho, The College Life

No matter what kind of education I got from Lake Forest College, it was a smashingly enjoyable time for me socially and creatively. In the drama department I was a very large fish in a small pond (whereas at Northwestern I would have been a tiny fish in a huge pond). This suited me just fine. Over my four years, I would perform in numerous plays, playing the lead often and winning TWO Best Actor Awards. I was always proud that the only well known actor who graduated there, Richard Widmark, only got one.

The main problem with our drama department was that the Head of the Department, John Converse, was an alcoholic, talentless, has-been, who didn't really know (or at least teach) anything valuable about acting. He was a lackluster director who, unfortunately for us, directed all the plays. So the students were forced to rely on instincts and talent to make whatever good theater we could.

I was fortunate that there was plenty of high quality theater in the Chicago area that I was able to experience during these years. There were two professional theaters that yearly resided in my hometown of Highland Park, which offered me the chance to see excellent theater right around the corner.

Tenthouse Theater was a repertory company that came to our town every summer, which included excellent actors like Barnard Hughes and his wife Helen Stenborg, who one summer played brilliantly in *The Matchmaker*. Tenthouse produced one great play after another, with the actors switching character types from play to play. I remember one fine actor, Tim O'Connor, playing Stanley in *Streetcar Named Desire* one week and Tom Lee in *Tea and Sympathy* the next. Seeing so many of their fine productions taught me what good acting should be, if not a method to achieve it, and how a play should be directed. I'm sure I subconsciously absorbed this knowledge and used it during my college career.

Then for pizzazz, there was Music Theater, another tent theater that ran musicals all summer, with "big stars" from New York City in every show. They did *Out of this World* and *Wonderful Town* both with Kaye Ballard, *On the Town* with Helen Gallagher and Jack Gilford, and *Kismet* with Monique Van Vooren (the "va-va-voom girl"). Big splashy musicals were staged in-the-round by the brilliant David Tihmer.

One summer I worked backstage in this theater as a sort of a "gofer". Several times I was asked to pick up the stars at the train station, which I, of course, was delighted to do. I particularly remember my ride with Kaye Ballard because she was such a funny and warm lady. Another excruciatingly funny comedienne whom I delivered to the theater was Jori Remus. None of us had ever heard of her, but she had everyone in stitches as Helen Gallagher's sickly roommate in *On the Town*.

That summer Carol Lawrence, a Northwestern student, was in the dancing ensemble, until the last show and they gave her the lead in *Guys and Dolls*. I didn't think she was very good, particularly as an actress. But the first year I went to New York she was cast as Maria in the original production of *West Side Story*. Thus, my Northwestern conundrum and curse.

In Chicago, I also attended numerous performances of Broadway national tours. The first big Broadway tour I saw was "South Pacific" in 1953, with Betsy Palmer. Now I had watched endless movie musicals depicting Broadway shows with vast marble floors and lavish sets, so that's what I expected to see in a live production. From my high up balcony seat, I was terribly disappointed, at first, that it was just a wooden floor with taped spike marks all over it, and with rolling platforms that brought out somewhat tacky, traveling bus'n'truck sets. But, needless to say, I was soon seduced by the live theater and it became a totally enchanted evening.

Thus, in my theatrical life at Lake Forest College I was not starved for good theater. Therefore in my head I had a sense of what to strive for, even if the head of our department was not capable of always achieving it. I'm sure that I would not have accomplished the acting experiences I did, were it not for the quality of acting I was able to see in the Chicago area.

* * *

At Lake Forest, I hung out with an unusual group of students who regularly socialized with a group of faculty members, so it ended up that my most influential and longest lasting friendships were with two professors, Prof. Franz Schulze and Dr. Marvin Dilkey. I have remained friends with both of these brilliant men over many years.

Franz was the head of the Art Department, and I first encountered him teaching Art Appreciation class. I was blown away by his extensive vocabulary. He was able to show endless slides of art works and come up with a string of different and perfect descriptive words for each painting. And he seemed never to use the same adjective twice. He was a brilliant painter at the time, but later in his life he turned writer. He wrote art reviews for the Chicago Tribune and definitive biographies of architects Mies Van Der Rohe and Philip Johnson.

Franz trying to teach me something about painting.

After I moved to New York, I was lucky enough to buy two of his huge paintings. One, called *Angel Comforting Man,* remains in my bedroom, but the other one was too large for my house so that I had to give it back to him years later.

I wasn't much of an artist, so I don't recall how we were connected socially exactly, but we certainly hit it off. He adored folk music and was the one who taught me how to play the guitar, which would certainly prove instrumental in my later years. Our group of drama students and professors, including Franz, would often party into the night, singing Woody Guthrie and Odetta songs.

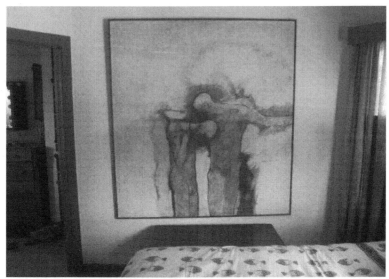

Franz's painting "Angel Comforting Man", in my bedroom today

Dr. Marvin Dilkey, or just Dilkey as he was known to his friends, was not part of that group, but he became my closest friend at school, even though he was in his sixties, I think. He had replaced a sadistic German professor I had, and also taught an Opera Appreciation class. I became his DJ in these opera classes, playing the arias as he was lecturing about them, mostly from his collection of 78rpm records, but some on the new 33rpm recordings. It was my first exposure to opera.

His bachelor apartment became my second home in my last two years at school. I can visualize the Beethoven death mask hanging on his wall, beside a Dutch master's painting, and the walls of books in many languages. What he taught me outside of the classroom was vast, including the love of classical music, a yearning to travel to Europe, social behavior in a sophisticated world, an understanding of the adult gay society, and how to make a great martini which was notoriously called the "Dilketini".

To be frank, I am sure he was in love with me, but being a gentleman, and me being a student, he never pushed the relationship. And I, being rather ignorant of those things, just soaked up his knowledge, advice, and culture; I know I am a much better person for it.

Dr. Dilkey in a classroom and in his ironic Halloween costume.

At the end of my Junior year I wanted to throw a party at my house in Highland Park and I asked my parents to join the party, to prove to them that my friends could drink liquor at a party and not have it turn into a drunken brawl. I was under the illusion that my parents didn't drink at all, but of course, they had gone to college in the Jazz Age, so this was a false assumption. I invited everyone in the drama crowd as well as several of the faculty, including Franz and Dilkey.

That summer Franz was about to leave on a sabbatical for a year and Dilkey was on his way to Europe for the holiday. The rest of us were all celebrating the end of the school year so everyone was ready for some serious partying.

After some congenial folk singing sessions, the party got rowdier and rowdier until it turned into a real Bacchanalia. Sedate drinking turned into guzzling. Amorous couples were making out all over the floor. In the wee hours of the morning on our little porch, where a rickety upright piano was housed, someone was pounding out loud popular music with a bunch of rowdy singers howling off-key. At one point Franz fell off the back porch and broke his glasses. This was not what I had hoped for - it was a disaster.

At about 3:00 AM, Dilkey and I staggered out onto Glenview Avenue and down to the corner, where Manony's pony lived. As we were leaning on the horse's fence, a police car rolled to a stop next to us. I guess two strange men on the street at this hour was suspicious. "What are you guys up to?" calls the cop. Dilkey pulled himself off the fence, standing to his full 6' 2", his distinguished gray hair framing his Mephistophelian face, and sauntered over to the police car. He said in his plumiest, professorial voice, "We are talking to the horse!" The policeman nodded and slowly drove away, and we collapsed in hysterics.

I was terrified at what my parents, who had stayed to the bitter end, thought about this debacle. But when I apologized to them the next day as we were cleaning up the mess, they told me that their college days had been pretty wild, as well, and they had quite an enjoyable evening.

Two high school friends of mine, Alan "Poopsie" Solomon and Rob LeClerc also went to Lake Forest College, but after awhile we drifted into our separate circles. I had given Alan the nickname "Poopsie" the year before when he and I saw *Pajama Game* in Chicago. In the number, "Hernando's Hideaway", a character wanders around in the dark calling, "Poopsie". I started calling Alan, "Poopsie", and he loved it; it stuck. It was his popular name in college, and when he wrote his notorious, college gossip column, he called it "Poopsie Tells All".

Poopsie soon changed his social circles and it didn't include me. He began hanging around with the athletes (who he was attracted to) and the society girls (who gave him social position). He even joined the "jock's" fraternity, Phi Delta Theta, who treated him like a mascot. *Charlie's Aunt* was the only play he participated in at school; he had the drag-wearing, title role and his comedic campiness was perfect. But he wasn't so much a performer as he was a big party thrower, foreshadowing his later years in Hollywood and New York.

My old heartthrob, Rob LeClerc, was in the fraternity that I eventually pledged, Tau Kappa Epsilon, but we weren't close friends, since I didn't live on campus or join the fraternity until my Junior year.

My gang was primarily the drama students, but also to some degree the music students. I almost majored in music, but because I never could pass the required piano tests, it was only my minor, even though I had more music credits than drama credits.

One of my favorite extracurricular activities in college was the Madrigal Singers. This choir was the reason I spent so many hours in the music department and took so many music courses. We sang beautifully arranged Renaissance music *a cappella*, while sitting around a table, because it was the dinner table entertainment in that era.

The Madrigal Singers that I was so honored to be a part of.

My senior year I found that I needed to take the freshman course, Music Appreciation, in order to get a major or minor in music. So when my friend, Tom, another senior, and I took the class we found ourselves in a room full of gullible freshmen and the teacher, who was an old fashioned, unmarried woman and the head of the music department.

During one class she was teaching about the castrati singers of the 17th century and she said, "These males sang soprano because they had an operation on their vocal cords." *What?* Tom and I looked at each other in shock, but the rest of the class blithely wrote down this "fact" in their notebooks. After the class, we went up to the teacher and tactfully mentioned to her that the word "castrati" comes from "castration" which is an operation on something other than the vocal cords. She turned red, packed up her things and left the room, and hopefully never taught about castrati singers again.

My other minor was in education, but that was only because it was a requirement at Lake Forest College for all Arts majors to take teaching courses. Both of those minors played important roles in my future, but that's certainly not what I expected. I was first and foremost an actor and I seriously intended, from first grade, to make that my profession.

During the first two years of college I commuted from Highland Park, so my social life was primarily involving the theater department. I acted in several plays and even though the quality wasn't excellent, I had wonderful experiences.

In Elmer Rice's *The Adding Machine*, I played opposite Roz Chernof, who was also in the Madrigal Singers. Roz was a large girl, with a large personality, with whom I became good friends. She came from a wealthy, eccentric family in Chicago and one day we visited her brother's outrageous bachelor pad. He was obese, truly huge. But he had lots of money, so he proudly showed off the beautiful women he'd dated and shagged – though I couldn't imagine how. He also had a large room full of obviously expensive, working firearms that he collected.

Roz and I were both in the production of Elmer Rice's *The Adding Machine*, where we played couple #1. Although we didn't have the leading roles (couple #0), she and I dominated the "adding machine". Never having been a smoker, I refused to smoke the cigars we were given (even though that was perfectly acceptable in those days), therefore none of the other "numbers" were able to light up. The director told the other "numbers" to do just what Roz and I were doing throughout the whole play, and it was my first sense of power on stage.

Roz (far right) and I (far left) dominated The Adding Machine.

My first leading role was in the play *Claudia*. A Brazilian boy named Alex Tapia played the "lover", and later turned out to be my first lover. Also in the cast was Sheila Hawkins and Paula Ernst, both of whom were great friends and party-goers.

Cruising my first boyfriend in the plaid shirt, in Claudia.
Paula is far right and Sheila in the center.

Although I was only the Assistant Director for *Dark of the Moon*, it turned out to be an important learning experience for my future career, although I didn't realize it at the time. The lead character, Barbara Allen, was played by a good friend from Bethany Church in Highland Park, Sue Brehmer. She was a sweet, beautiful, blond girl, who also happened to be Franz Schulze's girlfriend at the time. And handsome atheletic, Mike Dau, played the male leading role, Witch Boy. An ex-ballerina from Ballet Russe de Monte Carlo, Veda Belshaw, played a witch-girl in that play and was a sexy delight. She had quit the ballet to go to college "because ballet dancers are so dumb! They don't know anything but dance." She was bright and wanted an education.

As I have said, director John Converse was, even sober, rather unimaginative to say the least, so being his assistant allowed me to be creative. I enjoyed staging this fanciful piece about Witchcraft and Revivalists in the Appalachian mountains. Along with Barbara Allen, Conjur Man, Witch Boy, the Preacher Man, and witches all over the woods, there was the loveable old codger, Uncle Smelicue, who played the guitar and sang folk songs. To play the role we'd been lucky to cast an actor who played a mean guitar. But unfortunately he was pulled out of the cast because of grades just two weeks before we were to open.

John Converse looked at me and said, "You better learn to play the guitar, real fast."

Since I'd been to many parties where Franz had played the guitar, I went to him for help. He taught me three or four cords to go with the simple folk songs in the play, and I went on with white shoe polish in my hair, cackling Uncle Smelecue's hillbilly accent, singing and playing the guitar for the first time.

Over the next 2 years I would become a pretty good folk singer, even performing at The Gate of Horn on the same bill as Odetta (she was at the top and I was way at the bottom). This achievement made a huge difference in my life, years later.

Playing guitar as "Uncle Smelicue", with Sue as "Barbara Allen"   *Mike Dau as "Witch Boy" with Veda as the right "Witch"*

* * *

It would seem pretty obvious to the modern observer that from childhood I was a budding Drama Queen. But in the 1940s and 50s, this was not a subject that came up often in conversation. Therefore I was completely ignorant about my inclinations, or at least what they meant, until my college years. The summer after my junior year, following the aforementioned Spring Break to New York City, I worked back stage at Music Theater. I was now cognoscente of my feelings and aware of the gay world as I was told by my "teacher" on the ride back. But I had no real experience with sex of any kind.

One night a costume designer cornered me behind the tent and introduced me to gay sex.

OH! I thought as I drove home, *Now I get it! So that's what all the feelings I've had were about. OK. Good, I'm glad that's cleared up.* No angst. No remorse. No hysteria. No problem. I didn't really come out to anyone else. I just understood myself better and proceeded on with my life.

I did have another assignation with the costume designer. Dilkey and I went to the Chicago Opera one night to see *Tosca*. I had a lousy seat in the back of the orchestra, and at the first intermission I met the costume guy. He told me that I could come up and sit with him in his box seat, and Dilkey thought I'd enjoy that, so he said to go on. It was a private box, with no view from other seats, and during Tosca's big scene, I was receiving a blow job. To this day, I chuckle every time I hear *Tosca*.

At school I didn't have any kind of active gay life, just the awareness of its possibilities. I certainly had my crushes, but nothing much came of any of them, as they were on straight boys in the fraternity mostly. Then the Brazilian in *Claudia* made himself known and I had an off-and-on romance with him for the remainder of the year. Dilkey's tutorials on the sophisticated life began to make more sense, since now he included the international gay scene.

At the end of my Sophomore year, I convinced my parents to let me move onto campus for my last two years, since I was pledging a fraternity and I wanted to live in the fraternity house. Tau Kappa Epsilon was the only national fraternity or sorority on campus that did not have a clause forbidding the pledging of black students. Having been brought up a liberal, I considered this the only fraternity I would join, on principle, and it was definitely the "artsy" fraternity, as well. Several friends of mine were members, so I too, became a Teke.

This fraternity handled initiation in a more mature manner, too, so that instead of the ridiculous, sadistic hazing, TKE pledges spent hours doing community service. Our pledge group repaired and painted a local nursing home. Of course, there was the usual silliness, partying, and rituals as well, including a secret handshake, but generally I'm glad that I joined this particular fraternity. (As an aside, not long after I left school, the Lake Forest College administration banned all the national fraternities that had any discrimination laws, leaving TKE the only national fraternity on campus.)

Living on campus, in the Fraternity Quad, was a very new experience for me. I had a large room on the first floor that looked out over the campus, which I shared with one roommate. The first year my roommate was Billy Mitchell, a black guy from Chicago. He was the only black member of the fraternity at the time, and I was very pleased to be able to share the room with him. We were never close friends because we had different interests, but we got along quite well and it was a wonderful learning experience for me. A few years later I went to his wedding on the Southside of Chicago, where we fraternity boys were the only white faces for miles.

The TKE fraternity in 1957, with me in the far back behind the piano and Billy Mitchell, the only black member while I was there, in the center.

Billy and I, outside our dorm room.

Typically, the room was never tidy, but the floor of our room was particularly filthy, because it was often covered in shorn hair. My father had taught me to cut his hair several years before to save money on haircuts, and so I found myself giving haircuts to students for pocket money. I charged $1.00 (instead of the $2.00 in barbershops) and became wildly popular, even having some professorial patronage. I remember cutting Teke brother Paul Cheng's hair and he was the first Chinese person I ever knew. His black hair was like wire bristles, so that the scissor cut each individual hair separately – click-click-click-click. Sweeping up afterwards wasn't a priority, so hair clippings were usually under foot in our room.

My ink drawing of our college room in the TKE dorm.

Gary Madderom was my senior year roommate. We were good friends, although we had little in common. He wasn't in the theater or music department, he was from a wealthy suburban, Republican family, he studied politics, and he certainly wasn't gay, but for some reason he liked me a lot. One day I felt it was time to be honest, so I confessed my homosexuality to him. He got extremely upset, asking me to go to a psychiatrist to fix it. I didn't particularly want to, but because of his adamant coaxing, I went to a doctor and told her I was homosexual.

She asked, "Do you want to change?"

I said "Not particularly."

She said, "Why did you come?"

I said, "My roommate wanted me to."

She said, "Go back and tell him to get over it."

But Gary and I were friends for many years and I even introduced him to his wife in New York City. I did get him into one play, where he played my "homophobic" roommate in *Tea and Sympathy* – go figure.

The other tense situation caused by my new openness of being gay, happened with a girl that I was rather seriously dating during my Junior year, Gretchen. I guess she was counting on this as being a lasting relationship, so when, in my Senior year, I told her that I was breaking off our relationship – and I told her that it was because I was homosexual – she freaked out. She not only screamed and yelled some pretty horrible things at me, after she was done, she didn't speak another word to me for the rest of the school year. The following year when I lived in New York City, I received a package in the mail of one dozen, dead, dried, black roses, with a card reading "Happy Anniversary....Love, Gretchen".

Gretchen and I, in happier days.

* * *

Leading up to my Senior year of acting, which culminated with *Tea and Sympathy*, I was cast to play many roles, both big and little. As I said, I was a big fish in a little pond. I got a great deal of drama department notoriety when I played drunken Uncle Sid in *Ah, Wilderness* and it got me my first award for Best Actor. It was a fun role, but I've seen great actors play it since (like Wallace Beery and Jackie Gleason) to much better results. I was working on pure instinct, because I wasn't getting any decent acting training or good direction to back up my own abilities.

My first Best Actor award for "Uncle Sid"

It was in my junior year that I got to play the "wacky" (read queer) playwright in Agatha Christie's *Mousetrap*. With no conscious effort on my part, my inner campiness came flying out and I played the character like a silly queen. This made the part hugely popular, getting great laughs, which of course I loved. This was before my Spring Break New York trip, so I didn't really know what I was doing, it just seemed right.

I had no idea what "camping" was, but I sure got the hang of it.

The following year, when I got the great role of Tom Lee in *Tea and Sympathy* the director asked me if I was going to play him like the guy in *Mousetrap*. I couldn't imagine what he was talking about, "Of course not!" I said. But I realized later that he was afraid that I would play Tom Lee "gay", which in this 1950s play he was not supposed to be. He was just "artistic and sensitive". I loved that role, and I think I did it justice. I got my second Best Actor award for it and it felt much more deserved than the first one.

It was a treat acting with two friends, the beautiful Paula Ernst as Laura and her boyfriend the football star, Mike Dau, as the student who tries to teach Tom to "walk more like a man". They would later marry and Mike became the head of the athletic department at Lake Forest College. A few years ago, they dedicated a lounge in the new athletic building to Mike. One of the pictures they put up of him was from *Tea and Sympathy*, a huge blow-up of Mike and me. Franz took me over to see the building, and there I was, hanging in the athletic lounge – how ironic.

My best performance at Lake Forest College,
Tom Lee in <u>Tea and Sympathy</u>

The students make fun of "Tom Lee"
(my roommate Gary Madderom is on the left)

Mike Dau teaches "Tom" to walk
(this now hangs in the Athletic Dept.)

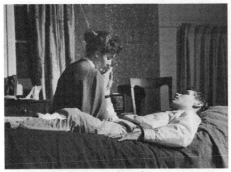 

Paula Ernst (Dau) saying, "If you speak of this, and you will, be kind."   *John Converse gives me my second Best Actor Award.*

Inspired by Franz, I continued to take art classes, doing ink drawings and even a few oil paintings. I wish I still had the "cubistic" painting I did of a guitar on a checkered tablecloth – the guitar had two necks, and could be seen from several sides at once – it was horrible.

But I'm quite proud of one of the paintings that I made my senior year, of the leading characters in *Tea and Sympathy*. I began it the day I got the role of Tom Lee and painted it during the time I rehearsed the part, and finished it when the play closed. I describe it as "one-third Picasso Blue Period, one-third Modigliani, one-third Franz Schulze – and the rest me." Now it hangs in my guest room.

One of my ink drawings. Being what I consider a non-artist, it's pretty good.

59

My painting of Tom and Laura from <u>Tea and Sympathy</u> painted during the time I rehearsed and performed the play.

    My fraternity brothers wanted me to run for Class President, but I was sure there was no chance of me getting elected. So my drama friends and I decided to run a "humorous" campaign, hoping to get the "ironic" vote. So we took a bunch of silly photographs of me in various situations, and put them on posters with equally silly captions.
    Needless to say, I didn't win.

Vote For DAVE for CLASS PRESIDENT

Here are some of his ideas:

"My time is always efficiently spent"

"Fine literature is a must"

"A full wardrobe is a necessity"

"I've car with room for all my friends"

"Athletics is very important"

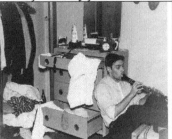
But the Arts are important, too"

"I often have friends in for Bridge"

I graduated from Lake Forest in the Spring of 1958, but I don't remember a single detail of that day. I know that I had wanted to move immediately to New York after graduation, but I needed some funds, so I stayed the summer working on a mink ranch. The ranch was about an hour from our house, and my mother drove me there every morning and came to pick me up at night. I don't know why I didn't drive myself, but I think it's because she needed the car during the day. I recall that she read to me as I drove the car to pass the time – a funny book called, *Barefoot Boy with Cheek* by Max Shulman – and we laughed all the way to the ranch and back.

The ranch itself was a barren field, with no shade, covered with large cages, each holding one mink. My job was to feed them, going from cage to cage wearing heavy, elbow length, leather gloves, because the little bastards would snap at anything that opened their cages. I worked just in shorts, so I had the darkest tan I've ever had. It was a horrible job, but it paid my way to New York and it inspired me to write the only poem I've ever written.

> You can damn all minks with their precious fur
> Who ever said they were sweet and demure?
> They bite at the slightest provocation,
> Why can't we send them to some other nation,
> Like Russia, India or Tibet,
> Or England, who thinks we owe them a debt?.
>
> A mink's screech is like the Confederate Yell,
> Or like the poor lost souls screaming from Hell.
> It's louder than a thousand sirens,
> For their rebellious nature is worse than Lord Byron's.
>
> Oh, I hate all mink, but I hate even more so,
> The women who buy them to cover their torso.
>
> By David (Ogden Nash) Umbach

* * *

During my college years, even when I lived on campus, I spent a lot of time back in Highland Park on Glenview Avenue. I would take college friends there all the time for dinner, because they couldn't believe that I had such a wacky and fun family. I called my parent's repartee at dinner, "The Bob and Mary Show", because they were so funny. My friends had normal parents that they couldn't wait to get away from, and so they were delighted at my parent's comic routines, and in awe of my loving rapport with them.

I've always had a special fondness for the play *You Can't Take it With You*, because I felt that the family in that play mirrored my family to a tee.

Examples:
1. My father studied Mandarin, so weekly a Chinese priest would come over, taking off his priestly attire with a wrinkled Hawaiian shirt underneath, and they would practice, speaking Mandarin and drawing calligraphy.
2. My Grandmother lived upstairs and being slightly deaf, always had her TV up full blast, primarily showing Westerns.
3. My brother was a '50's rock-n-roll fan, so across the hall he would compete with Gramma, playing Elvis records at top volume. He had a guitar, which held, but never learned to play.
4. I was only into classical music at the time, so whenever I was there, I loudly played Tchaikovsky on my record player to drown out the other two.
5. My mother was studying Comparative Religions, so she had rabbis, priests, professors and monks visit our house for discussions, with stacks of textbooks everywhere.
6. I was striving to create "Art", so I had easels and canvases all around the house to work on.
7. My bother had a "zoo" in the back yard, with cages for a skunk, a raccoon, a possum, a couple snakes, a turtle, a rabbit etc. He walked his skunk, Mam'selle Hepzibah, around town on a leash.
8. There was a piano on the front porch, that I used to practice playing, trying to pass my piano tests, but failing miserably.
9. My father took pictures of nature, so he had dried weeds and things hanging around the house to photograph.
10. The TV was in another room from the dining room, so my father rigged a string, that hung from the light above the table, to a stalk attached to the TV knob, so he could adjust the sound from the table – pre-dating remote controls.

Congenial chaos seemed to reign in our house all the time, as it did in *You Can't Take it With You*, and it was a total joy (especially when I actually lived elsewhere).

Four

On The Town

I guess it took a lot of *chutzpa*, because I arrived in New York without knowing a soul, but I felt no trepidation because I knew it was what I wanted and needed to do. Dilkey had arranged a temporary room for me with a friend of his on Bank Street in Greenwich Village. It was on the ground floor of an ugly apartment building with a room facing the alley, but I didn't care because it seemed "hip" and exotic. I had never lived in a city, so the sounds and smells were totally new to me, but I felt at home right away.

It only took me a week to find my own place, which I got from an ad in the local free paper, *The Villager*. The ad that read: "Village Apartment to Share". The guy looking for a roommate was named Frank and he was an actor, so it seemed like it might be ideal. The apartment was a dingy little place at 157 Seventh Ave. South, third floor walk-up in the back. Entering the apartment from the grubby hallway, I was immediately confronted by the bathtub, which was predominantly placed in the kitchen. It was covered with a hinged piece of plywood that was used as the kitchen counter. I also noted that cockroaches ruled the kitchen, which to my suburban eyes were pretty creepy and disgusting, but I was determined to get used to it.

I had a miniscule bedroom, to say the least, while Frank slept in the only other room, which was slightly larger and served as the living room. On the first night, Frank invited me into the living room and proceeded to seduce me. *Omigod!, Live-in lover! How sophisticated! How New York!* It was just how I'd dreamed it would be and I was in heaven.

However, a major problem soon became obvious: Frank was off-the-wall nuts! I did not understand that in the 1950s, "Apartment to Share" meant looking for a sex partner. Frank just assumed that that was the reason I had answered the ad. He became completely possessive of me, violently jealous if I stayed out late, or auditioned for a role he might be right for, or god forbid, made another male friend.

I began dreading going back to the apartment at night. The upside of avoiding my unexpected, jealous lover, was that it forced me to wandered the streets of Greenwich Village for hours and I became familiar with the hodgepodge street system. Needing a place to stay before venturing home, I would spend evenings in cafés like The Bitter End, nursing one coffee, reading Jack Kerouac on ill-matching couches while listening to jazz. I quickly became a denizen of The Village.

Despite the crazy roommate, I was actually felt lucky. I was living in the heart of Greenwich Village. What could be better? The grimy entryway to my apartment building is still adorned with an Erotica Store on one side, and a jewelry store on the other. A couple blocks downtown is Sheridan Square and Christopher Street, and a few blocks uptown is famous jazz club, The Village Vanguard. Across town are Washington Square and MacDougal Street with the Café Wha?, Bleeker Street with Figaro's Café, and 8th Street with the basement nightclub the Bon Soir. And gay bars scattered secretly all around, including the Ninth Circle, where I had my first encounter with a gay man, Joey. Also nearby was the Stonewall Inn, where the gay rights movement got its jumpstart years later.

I was in the center of everything and anything could happen in this neighborhood. Like one night, I walked down those fabled stairs of the Bon Soir to see a chanteuse named Felicia Saunders. We were sitting at our cramped table waiting when the announcer came on and told us that Miss Saunders was ill but that we should welcome a newcomer. Onto the tiny stage walked this homely girl, with long hair in her face and a large nose protruding out of it. We began gathering our things to leave, but as she opened her mouth to sing "Happy Days are Here Again", we decided to stay and listen. Hilariously funny with a powerhouse of a voice, we ended up rising to our feet screaming for more. At the end of the evening, I made sure to get her name. I wanted to see this new girl, Barbra Streisand, again. We all predicted that she would be star. I was a huge fan from that moment, and I did see her perform again and again. I even got to see her in *Funny Girl* when it first opened.

As exciting as it was living in the Village, I was getting exceedingly uncomfortable sharing the apartment with violently jealous Frank. I had met David Bradshaw, an interesting guy who was a pianist studying at Julliard and we became good friends. We plotted together and decided, much to Frank's vehement protestations, to get our own place on the Upper West Side, where we hoped Frank would not find us. To avoid a dramatic scene where Frank would go berserk and cry and blame me for breaking his heart and ruining his life, I packed up and moved out of the apartment while Frank was at an audition.

David Bradshaw and I found a basement apartment at 6 W. 75th Street, right off Central Park West. The address sounds elegant, but it was directly next to the alley behind the huge San Remo apartment building. Every morning at 6:00 the garbage men would crash and bang the multitude of trash cans into a truck and then fling them back on the cement right outside our window. And even though the apartment was almost as small as the Village place, it was our new home, there was no Frank, and we grew to loved it.

David Bradshaw introduced me to a whole new world of classical musicians. I met pianists, violinists and opera singers, Julliard students as well as established performers. I became a regular at the Metropolitan Opera, which was then on 41st Street, not Lincoln Center. We would squeeze into the infamously gay standing room in the back of the sumptuous auditorium. During the opera, many of the group of men who were in this standing room area paid little attention to the music and actual sexual liaisons were taking place. I even heard about a guy who had a pair of pants with an extra zipper in the rear that he called his "opera pants". But most of us just cruised and listened to the singing, and it was an exciting way to go to the opera.

This was during the heated rivalry between divas, Renata Tibaldi and Maria Callas, with armies of adamant supporters on each side. The verbal battles I witnessed defending or criticizing these two great singers were countless and ferocious. But our favorite soprano was Regina Resnik, who taught at Julliard and was David Bradshaw's friend. We heard her sing at every opportunity and even visited her several times in her beautiful apartment, overlooking Central Park.

David Bradshaw went on to be a concert pianist and became quite successful as a dual piano team with his longtime lover, Cosmo Buono. Sometime in the '90s Cosmo died of AIDS, and David died soon after. But I was fortunate to hear them play a concert at Lincoln Center before this and was thrilled at how wonderfully they played together. Our reunion afterwards was a happy event and it brought back our early days in New York, causing much laughter. I was very lucky to meet David Bradshaw and he played a defining role in my life.

* * *

My employment during these "Acting Years" was supplied by Office Temporary Services. They would send me to various office jobs, then once a week I had to go to their seedy offices on 34th Street to pick up a check. One of the jobs I was assigned was at Pacific Mills, in a classy deco building near Madison Square on 23rd Street. I remained in this job for a long time, pulling swatches of wool suit fabric and sending them to various customers around the world. It was a pleasant job, and my strongest memory is of a co-worker, a tough guy from the Bronx, who exclaimed every morning at his cup of coffee, "Ah, Ambrosierrrr". I waited every morning to hear him say it, and it started my day with a smile.

So that's how I made my living, but my acting career was going nowhere. Since I had brought my trusty Gibson guitar, from my folk-singer days, with me to New York, I tried to get some gigs with it, but without much success. Somehow the word of my guitar playing got out to a powerhouse of a woman named Isabelle Stevenson, who was the president of the American Theater Wing. She contacted me and asked me to volunteer to sing for nursing homes and hospitals around the city. Well, I wasn't doing anything else interesting so I agreed. It was a rather gratifying experience, except for the one time I played in a mental hospital.

She booked me to go to a Veteran's Mental Hospital up in the Bronx. I arrived with my trusty guitar in its case, prepared, I thought, for anything. However, none of the other places I'd played prepared me for what I would encounter there. I was led into a vast room full of beds, wheel chairs and folding chairs, scattered randomly around the room. I was placed in a chair somewhere in the middle of all this. Surrounding me were a frightening-looking bunch of men, some staring angrily at me, as I sat there all dolled up in cheerful garb looking completely out of place.

Some of the patients grumbled loudly and shouted obscenities, demanding to know what I was doing there, while others just glowered. I did my best to don my cheeriest smile and told them that I was here to entertain them with some folk songs. I heard shouts about wanting dancing girls, followed by horrifying laughter from surrounding beds. Since I was in the center of the room, there was no way I could face everyone and it was very scary having my back on these ferocious patients. There didn't seem to be anyone to control them, as all the wards in the room just stood on the outskirts, finding their patients' commentary and my terrified look to be comic relief.

Bravely, I took out my guitar, to hoots and whistles. The noise in the room made it hard for me to be heard, but I began what I hoped would be a rousing song that would make them forget their troubles, a union song by Woody Guthrie. It seemed to get the veteran's attention, and the room quieted a bit. Pretty soon there was some stomping and clapping to the rhythms of the song. When I finished, there was a smattering of applause, but more hoots and whistles, too. I immediately barged ahead with another more melodic song, this one not so strong in angry union sentiments. It was the tale of Barbara Allen, and the room hushed. They all just stopped talking and actually listened.

In the middle of the song, a man with a frightening, scarred face got up from his chair, and approached me. Not knowing what else to do, I kept on singing, but he seemed fascinated with the strings of the guitar, not the song. As I strummed the guitar, he reached out and strummed the strings with me. He was so serious and seemed to be completely involved with the guitar, I continued singing and forming the chords with my left hand, but let this man do the strumming for me. He kept up with the beat of the song and as it continued (folk songs have many verses) he seemed to smile, as much as his mutilated face could. When the song finished, he straightened up, faced the other soldiers, and bowed. The applause was deafening.

The rest of the time I was there, the audience was attentive and appreciative, without a bit of the anger and hostility with which I was originally met. They requested songs, many of them I actually knew, and the rest of the session was a huge success.

Although working for the American Theater Wing didn't ever help me in my acting career, it was a part of my training that gave me a sense that my performing talent was sufficient to entertain even in The Big Apple.

To pursue my acting career, I enrolled in classes at HB Studios, run by husband and wife, Herbert Berghof and Uta Hagen. Many fine actors have gone to this school and there were dozens of teachers to choose from. Only the select few got into Uta's classes, and as I didn't know anyone, I was lucky to choose a darling man, named Bill Hickey, for my first teacher. In his gentle way, he more or less told me that I sucked! All my training and experience at Lake Forest College had been worthless, because I was never taught "to be, not to act". The whole "Method" concept was completely foreign to me. I was a "performer" and they didn't want that at all. *I had received TWO best Actor awards, damn it!* But I couldn't walk across a room to Bill's satisfaction. So for an entire year, it was like being back in Kindergarten, struggling to please my teacher and totally failing. It was dispiriting to say the least.

One day I did a scene from *Our Town* – the famous soda fountain scene – and *BAM!* it clicked. Bill Hickey gave supportive, positive comments, and I understood what "being in a role" meant. And it felt so good! I have to say that I don't think I would have lasted a whole year if it weren't for Bill's kindness up to that day. I had heard that Uta ate actors for breakfast, and even the best who survived, many of whom went on to be stars, had a hard time enduring her harsh criticism. But Bill sweetly guided me from the dark into the light and I will always be grateful to him for that.

Soon after that, however, I switched to one of Uta's protégés, Irene Dailey, who became my favorite teacher, my mentor and my friend.

Irene's classes were definitely more advanced and rigorous than Bill's, so I grew a great deal under Irene Dailey's brilliant teaching, doing more and more complex scene work. A particular favorite was an infuriatingly abstruse scene from *Jack, or the Submission* by Eugene Ionesco. The thrust of the narrative involves Jack's arranged marriage to Roberta. The play contains nonsensical exchanges and strings of clichés, similar to *The Bald Soprano,* and chock-full of surreal conceits, like Roberta's multiple noses and talk of burning horses, which were common in many of his later plays.

Trying to figure out what the hell it meant and how bring it to life was an extreme challenge for my partner and me. One rehearsal we grasped upon the idea that the entire scene was representing THE SEX ACT! So we ran the lines, while going through emotional sexual experiences, "foreplay", "stimulation", "violent passion", "climax" and "afterglow". We never touched each other, but did it all with Ionesco's crazy words. It was the multiple noses that simulated foreplay and the "burning horses" that simulated the climax. Every night that we rehearsed, we only "reached climax" once a night, because we couldn't do it twice (or at least I, the man, couldn't).

When we showed this scene to the class, Irene was ecstatic! She not only praised us, but insisted that we perform the scene for all her other classes. This was quite a difference from my first year at HB. It was like getting the Best Actor award again, but this time really earning it.

For one class I was preparing a scene from "Catcher in the Rye", where the two guys were sitting at a bar having a conversation about life. To get the feel of the ambiance my partner and I actually rehearsed the scene in a bar, much to the amusement of the other patrons. We had worked very hard to make the characters come alive, although I don't remember whether I played Holden Caulfield or the other guy. We walked into class excited about doing our scene for Irene.

But sitting in her chair was Uta Hagen. Irene was sick and Uta was substituting – *Oy Veh!*

My partner and I were posted last to do our scene, so we watched as one scene after another was decimated by Uta, one actor after another humiliated, one ego after another crushed. When our turn came we were utterly terrified. What on earth was she going to say to us afterward? We got through the scene somehow and sat down. She took a breath, we held ours, and she said, "That's all for today, Irene will be back next week, Goodbye." We were flabbergasted, we didn't know whether she liked our scene and so she had nothing bad to say about it, or we were completely beneath her contempt because we were so bad. I left the class with that question and I would never find out the answer.

Irene Dailey, who was the sister of Hollywood, musical comedy hoofer Dan Dailey, was a truly gifted teacher, and a great actress, too. I always felt that she was one of the top three actresses of the time, Kim Stanley and Geraldine Page being the other two. Sadly however, she had the misfortune of being acknowledged for her talent everywhere but in New York. She won top acting awards in Chicago, Philadelphia and London, but never really had a personal hit on Broadway. I so loved her and her work that I traveled to those cities to see whatever she did, and I was always overwhelmed at what an extremely talented actress she was.

Her one successful Broadway play, *The Subject Was Roses*, co-starred Martin Sheen and Jack Albertson who incidentally received most of the credit for it's success, because Irene's role was the least showy. This dynamic actress had to work extremely hard to create the repressed Nettie, by stifling her strength, so that we who knew her talent, appreciated how brilliant she was. But those who weren't familiar with her work just figured she was "mousy" by nature. It was a major disappointment that Patricia Neal got the role in the movie, even though the playwright had promised the whole cast that he wanted them for the film.

What saved Irene from poverty in her later years was a soap opera, *Another World,* where she got the role of Aunt Liz. She became so famous for this role that anytime I mentioned her to people who had never heard of her, I would add "She's Aunt Liz on *Another World*", and they would go bananas! And it made her lots of money so that she could retire in comfort. Without that I think she would have ended up a bag lady, or supported by the rafts of her students who loved her.

My friend and mentor, Irene Dailey

Irene in her dressing room for "The Subject Was Roses"

Irene with James Patterson in her London hit "Tomorrow With Pictures"

* * *

Soon after David Bradshaw and I moved to 75th Street, some people on the top floor of the building invited us up for a party. In this crowded, smoky apartment I had my first "across a crowded room" experience. I caught sight of a pair of blue eyes, surrounded by a pretty, young face topped with blond hair – these eyes connected with mine and it was honestly, love at first sight.

The face belonged to Reynolds Lash Callendar, and we were instantly attracted to each other. I think we left the party right away and got to know each other more intimately, in many ways. It was a whirlwind romance, and I remember thinking, "Oh, what a relief to know that I am capable of 'falling in love', just like in the movies."

Reynolds Lash Callendar

Those days are a blur now, but Reynolds and I spent as much time together as possible. He soon moved into our cramped apartment on 75th Street, and David B. moved to his own place with his boyfriend at the time, John Atkins. So between working temp office work, studying with Irene Dailey, auditioning for Off Broadway parts, gallivanting with Reynolds and other friends, they were giddy, happy, love-filled days. I even acted in a couple plays with the 1010 Players, on Park Avenue, playing God in some Medieval play, and Papa Yoder in *Plain and Fancy*.

One day during this period, Dr. Dilkey came to New York, back from a trip to Germany. He brought us a roll of *pfennigs*, which were coins that were worth ¼ of a cent, but Dilkey told us that they were the exact same size as a NY subway token at the time. Reynolds and I were delighted and blithely used them every day going to and from our work.

One morning, they wouldn't go into the slot, and as we tried shoving them in, two plainclothes policemen came up and arrested us for *pfennig pfraud*. Evidently this was rather common, and once we readily admitted that we had used them, the cops were quite pleasant.

They even took us out for coffee and donuts before taking us in, most likely because they wanted their breakfast. Over coffee they confided in us that they had arrested lawyers and doctors who adamantly refused to admit that they had used the "slugs" and gotten violent in their denial. So they liked the fact that we freely admitted it and even turned over some extra *pfennigs* to them, glad to be rid of them. They told us that at some point the police had put a gizmo into the turnstile that played a loud "Deutchland Uber Alles" when *pfennigs* were inserted, but it gave people heart attacks, or something, so they had to remove them.

After our jolly breakfast, they dragged us way uptown where nighttime arrests were tried, and some bully of a guard threw us into a bullpen. We found ourselves in a smelly cell with all the charming folks that had been rounded up during the night – drunks, pimps, hookers, thieves, etc. One guy looked fairly normal, so I asked him what he was in for, and he croaked, "raping little girls".

The cops had told us that we were lucky, because the morning judge was known for giving a verbal rap on the knuckles and letting first offenders go. But as we awaited trial, we heard that another judge was now in place who didn't let anybody off. Disapproving of his predecessor's leniency, he look down his cruel nose at us and said, "Take them to be booked and finger-printed!" But our nice policemen came to the bench and pleaded that we were decent, young guys who'd been unaware of their serious offence. So the judge paused a moment and then said, "OK, the fine is $100 each (a fortune for us) to be paid immediately (impossible), OR a day in jail, which ends (and he kind of smiled) when court was over today".

So, we were led back to jail, but our friendly cops pulled one more favor for us. They asked the jailor to put us in a cell by ourselves, which he did – way at the end of the hall where we had total privacy. As soon as they lock the cell door, I asked for a piece of paper and pen, and proceeded to write Dilkey a letter, starting, "Dear Dilk, I am writing this from jail…….." I understand that it became quite a popular letter around Lake Forest College campus.

As the long day wore on, Reynolds and I began to feel more relaxed and a bit bored. So at some point, sensing that we would be left alone, we followed our baser inclinations and had sex – right there in the cell – and it was hot.

It was around this same time that my mother came to visit me in New York. I was playing Papa Yoder in "Plain and Fancy" and she wanted to see me in an actual Off Broadway play. She stayed in a hotel near where Reynolds and I lived on the Upper West Side, while the play was across town on the East Side.

In those days Central Park was not a safe place, especially at night. Muggings were frequent. But I knew parts of the park very well, especially the "Brambles", which is a wooded section around the Delacourt Theater that was very *cruisey*. I knew of a well-lighted path across the park through the Brambles that I used often, even at night, because it was always crowded with single gentlemen trying to hook up with other single gentlemen.

After the play, my mother and I intended to go to Greenwich Village for supper and some sightseeing, so we waited on Fifth Avenue for a downtown bus. We strolled a bit downtown waiting for the bus, but it got to be after midnight and it seemed that buses weren't running that late at night. Giving up our Village excursion, we decided to make our way back to the Westside and go to bed. We weren't near a crosstown bus and we were definitely not near the place I was used to entering Central Park. But we forged ahead on foot and I was certain that I'd find the way across. As we got deeper and deeper into the park I realized that I was totally lost and wasn't even sure what direction we were going after awhile.

I kept telling Mother that I knew exactly where we were and that the Park was safe and that we'd be home any minute – but that was a completely, fabricated lie. I don't know how long we wandered, but suddenly with great relief, I viewed the towers of the San Remo, so I knew the way home. It wasn't until years later that I admitted to my mother what a dangerous situation we had been in that night. She laughed and said that she had an idea of the truth, but didn't want to frighten me.

So Reynolds and I were living the high-lives of struggling New York actors: office-temp work, acting classes, auditions, with very little money, but lots of enthusiasm and the giddy innocence of youth. Somewhere along the line, I decided to get a stage name. In those days, actors rarely used ethnic names like Al Pacino, Arnold Schwarzenegger or Meryl Streep, so I felt that Umbach was too "foreign". My father suggested David Brookside, which is sort of Umbach translated from German, meaning "beside a brook". I've often wished that I'd taken his advise.

But one night Reynolds and I were riding the Staten Island Ferry, which was a romantic thing that we often did on summer nights, and there was a little boy singing and dancing for all the passengers. He was a charmer so I asked him his name, and he said "I'm Christopher".

I took this as a sign and David Christopher was born.

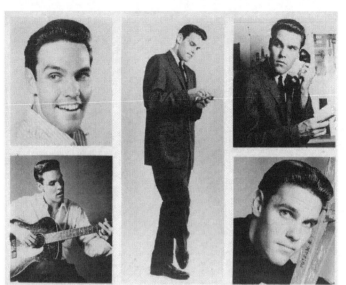

My composite head shots when I was a New York actor.

While we were still on 75th Street, my brother, Jonathan, came to New York. When he was a freshman at Highland Park High School, a scandalously incompetent guidance counselor told him, "You are not college material, so you should take vocational courses". In a school of primarily college bound kids, this completely discouraged him and he rebelled against school and home.

So my parents sent him to a private school down South, where he didn't last a year, and was thrown out for a roll-in-the-hay with some local girl. He insisted that he didn't want to go back home to Illinois, but wanted to move to New York City where David lived and live on his own. With great trepidation they agreed and brought him to New York.

Well, I was glad to see him, but I certainly didn't want to take care of him. I felt if he wanted to be "independent", he should be just that. Reynolds and I couldn't have him living in our little apartment, so we rented him a room, got him a job as a messenger, and insisted that he, indeed, support himself. Jonathan quickly learned the city by running around delivering things, and did quite well on his own. He easily adjusted to his brother having a male lover, and the three of us got along very well. It was a major growing up period for him and I think it did him lots of good.

*Jonathan rebelling as Jon Elvis (see signature)
though he never really played the guitar*

One summer Reynolds and I decided to take a posh summer sub-let on West End Avenue, where we both got crabs. One of us noted the itching in our pubic hair and discovered the little moving critter, which completely horrified us, because we had no idea what it was. Enclosing one in a tissue, we showed it to a doctor, fearing we had some deadly venereal disease. The doctor assured us that it was a common occurrence and gave us the unpleasant cure, but we were determined to get out of that sub-let as soon as we could.

We then moved to another basement apartment on 81st Street, off West End Avenue. This one was in the back of the building, but a much larger place and it had a cement garden. This was when I got my first cat. I'd always had dogs, but they are such a bother in the city, I decided to try a cat. My mother had an aversion to them so we never even considered having one. I thought it would be a good idea to get the cat for Reynolds as a birthday present.

There was a place that advertised free cats so I went to that address, which was in an apartment on West End Avenue where a woman lived who saved strays. When she answered the door, I was confronted by a plump, squat little woman holding two cats in her arms. She welcomed me in and when I entered her living room I saw at least twenty cats lounging around on all the furniture, each tending to their own business and very contented. She told me to look around and find the cat that appealed to me, that they were all up for adoption.

As I wandered around the apartment, I found most of the cats ignored me. Then I went into the bedroom and on the bed was a calico cat, rolling around on the bed. When I went in, he perked up and looked me straight in the eye. I tentatively stroked his head and he leaned in and began to purr. Then he stood up and I realized that something was wrong – he only had one back foot. One of his legs had been amputated. *Oh, dear! That's no good.*

I left the bedroom and look for another cat, but none of them paid me the least attention. Going back in the bedroom, the calico cat leaped off the bed and hopped over to me, rubbing my leg. He seemed to get around without any effort, he just hopped on the one good leg, instead of walking normally. The woman told me that this cat was very affectionate and had no trouble getting round.

So I ended up bringing a three-legged cat home as a birthday present to Reynolds. We named him Pseudolus, after the lead character in *A Funny Thing Happened On the Way to the Forum*.

I have been a "cat person" ever since.

The front apartment was empty and my college roommate, Gary Madderom, came to New York and he rented it. Soon after, I introduced him to a dear actress friend of mine, Marilyn Morris, they fell for each other and lived in the front apartment together – eventually marrying. The four of us quickly became a happy family.

My dear actress friend, Marilyn at the 79th Street Boat Basin

Marilyn and Gary's wedding.

Five

Of Ships and Planes
and Eurail Pass

Early in our relationship, a relative of Reynolds left him a small inheritance. At the time, we were both studying under the actress Irene Dailey when she landed a leading role in play on London's West End. So Reynolds seized the opportunity to use this money to take a trip to London to see Irene's play and to tour Europe, and he brought me along. It was the first trip abroad for both of us and we took a whole summer traveling to England, France, Germany and Italy. The trip had its traumas and it's pleasures, making it a thrilling experience that gave birth to my love for Europe and for travel in general.

Our trip had a rather scary beginning and thinking about it, even today, makes my knees weak. Ocean liners were still a common method of travel to Europe in those days, so we decided to take a ship across and fly back. The ship we took was the *Amsterdam* on the Holland-American line, which set sail out of Hoboken. To get onto the ship from the pier there was a long metal staircase going over the water, with open space between each stair. I was carrying a large, leather wallet that foolishly held all our money, our tickets and both our passports. As we were ascending the stairs, I attempted to put the wallet back into my inside coat pocket, but unfortunately I missed my coat pocket. The wallet fell down onto the stair tread. It landed right on the edge, half on the tread and half over the water. It rocked back and forth like a seesaw for a long couple of seconds before I reached down between my legs and grabbed it, before it plunged into the Hudson River. This was how our trip began.

It took almost seven days to make the crossing, but we found the ride quite an enjoyable time. We led two completely different social lives on board. One was with the fellow, straight passengers that we met and chatted with around the dining table and danced with in the evening. Many single female teachers were on their summer holidays and they flirted with us a lot. We played their game, dancing with them all and Reynolds and I had quite a nice time with everyone.

But it was later in the night that we really partied. The crew of stewards and waiters were all Dutch boys, who loved to socialize long into the night after they finished work. Many were gay and welcomed us into their group, so we crammed into their tiny state rooms, drinking, talking and laughing. They of course spoke English with us, because we certainly didn't speak Dutch, nor did we speak any other foreign language, for that matter, which is dreadfully common for American tourists, even today.

One charming steward took us under his wing, since we were taking our virgin trip to Europe. He showered us with advice and wrote down suggestions for us that would end up being enormously helpful in two of the cities we visited, Paris and Zürich.

We began our tour in London, so initially there was no problem with a language barrier. I suppose we did the usual sight seeing things and went to some theater, but the most memorable part for me was seeing Irene in *Tomorrow With Pictures*, which was playing at the legendary Duke of York Theater. It was a rather dreadful piece of melodrama, but Irene was magnificent in it. The British were not accustomed to American Method Actors, yet, and she blew them away and actually nabbed herself the Olivier Award (or whatever it was called back then) for Best Actress that year. She was so grateful that we had traveled across the "pond" to see her performance, being her only students who had that pleasure. We went out on the town after the play with her and a host of celebrities, most of whom we didn't know. Needless to say, it was just a glamorous and glorious night.

Reynolds, singer Jane Morgan, Irene and me,
out on the town after seeing "Tomorrow With Pictures.

The billboard outside the Duke of York Theater

Before we left the British Isles, we wanted a glimpse of Scotland, so we took the train to Edinburgh for a day, stayed overnight and returned the next day. We were heading to Paris and wanted to get there directly without stopping at another hotel, so it was a tortuously long trip. The eight hour train ride to London was then extended to another train to the airport, a flight to Paris airport, then a bus into Paris, all in one day.

It was an extreme culture shock for both of us when we arrived in France and for the first time in our lives heard and saw nothing in English. When we boarded the bus that took us from the airport into the city, I just held out my hand to the bus driver to take whatever it cost for the trip. We looked out the windows of the bus in terror at the utterly unintelligible billboards. We were so relieved that the bus would drop us off at the American Express office, and we hoped that someone there could guide these two weary travelers to a friendly hotel. But when we got there, it was just after 5:00 PM and the American Express office was closed.

It was then that our kindly cabin steward from the *Amsterdam* saved the day for us, the first time. On the slip of paper he had handed us on the boat, he wrote down the suggestion for a hotel in Paris. As we stood bleary-eyed in front of the American Express building, with our heavy luggage, I remembered this piece of paper and found it in my wallet. It said "Hotel de Lille, 40 rue de Lille, Paris". I had no idea where rue de Lille was, it could have been far on the outskirts of the city for all I knew, but I showed this paper to a taxi driver, he nodded and we got in. It turned out to be very close, just across the Seine on the Left Bank.

So we got out of the taxi, paid the driver some unknown amount, and stood in front of this charming, modest hotel. The two of us must have looked like drowned rats as we rang the bell. A *très sympathique* woman named Madame Denise answered the door, and much to our relief she spoke English. We asked her if she had a room for us. She puffed out her cheeks in sympathy and said that the last room was reserved for a married couple, who were supposed to arrive an hour ago. Observing our bedraggled state, she told us to take a seat in the small parlor. Taking pity on us, she said that if the couple didn't arrive within the next hour, the room was ours.

As luck would have it, we got the room and soon found out that this was more than just a place to stay. The Hotel de Lille was a haven for gay travelers visiting Paris and Madame Denise was a French angel. She introduced us to many of the English speaking guests, from around the world, who gladly guided us to the joys of the city, either by suggestions or actually taking us places. Everyone we met encouraged and helped us navigate through the intricacies of Paris.

Madame Denise was quite a character, lovingly catering to all "her *garcons*" even trying to romantically hooked them up sometimes. At *petite dejeuner* she might comment to a single guy at one table that "Ze new boy in Room 323 is *très agreable* and you may wish to meet him." Staying in the Hotel de Lille heightened our Parisian experience and alleviated my fear of foreign cities, all thanks to our sweet Dutch steward.

We stayed in touch with Madame Denise and years later she visited New York. Reynolds and I escorted her around the city because we simply adored our French angel.

Thanks to the trusty Eurail Pass, the rest of our European vacation was a whirlwind of many cities in many countries. The Eurail Pass is purchased in the USA for a comparatively smaller amount than if purchased in Europe, and gives the traveler unlimited First Class train travel all over Europe, except the British Isles. We would often use the train as a hotel, traveling to different cities overnight. Since we could get into the First Class compartments, which were quite expensive for the European travelers, we often had them to ourselves and could stretch out on the comfy seats to sleep. Or we would meet some interesting people to chat with and sometimes they would even help us when we arrived in new city or country.

I can't say that the trip was hassle-free for our relationship. Missing trains or boarding a wrong one, not being able to read the time tables, and sometimes getting lost, caused Reynolds and me to often lose our patience with one another and even escalating in some momentous, shouting matches, and usually in train stations. I had always played a "teacher" role in our relationship, so I was responsible for knowing what to do at all times. But here in the middle of Europe, I was pretty much as ignorant as he was, but nonetheless, he still expected me to have all the answers. Thus: friction.

My parents were living in Amersfoort, Holland for a year during this time, so this was one of our destinations. My father had been transferred to this small city to set up a factory, like in the one he did in Onarga, Illinois. Though unlike anywhere they had lived before, my parents seemed to enjoy their time living in this quaint, Dutch town. Since I was not "out" to my parents about being gay, I made like any closeted gay and referred to Reynolds as "a good friend and roommate. (It wasn't until I was in my 50s that I found out that they knew I was gay even before I did.) All the time I was with Reynolds, they called and referred to him "Rey", finding his name pretentious, I think. They didn't like him much, but they covered it well and were always pleasant with him. Fortunately, Amersfoort is a suburb of Amsterdam, so that's where Reynolds and I spent most of our time while in Holland.

During our time with my parents, my father wanted to buy a Volkswagen Beetle in Germany, because they were not yet being sold in the USA. He wanted to go to the factory where they were made and pick it up, intending to drive it back to Holland, then ship it to America. So the four of us got on the train to Wolfsburg, Germany where Volkswagens were manufactured.

It turned out to be more of an adventure than we had anticipated. While relaxing in the dining car in the front of the train, the rear of the train, including the car that held all our belongings, was switched off and connected to another engine that would go to Wolfsburg. The dining car, however, was headed to another destination: East Germany. We didn't realize this until we walked back to our car, and came to the end of the much shorter train.

Fortunately, my father spoke pretty good German, so he immediately reported the loss of all our luggage to the conductor. We were put off the train right at the border of East Germany. Had we taken much longer at the dining table, we would have ended up in East Germany, without visas, which was a dangerous thing to do at that time. After haggling with many overbearing, self-important German officials, we were put on a train back to Wolfsburg, where our luggage was being held for us. Once we retrieved our belongings, Reynolds and I set off south, while my parents dealt with the automobile purchase. I don't believe my father was successful sending the car to the States, but they did enjoy it during their stay in Amersfoort.

*   *   *

Using our Eurail pass again, we headed off to Italy, nervously preparing to tackle another foreign language problem. Sitting in a First Class compartment, we struggled to make conversation with some very friendly Italians who didn't speak a word of English. When finally we all found a common interest, it turned out to be the movies. It began with my mentioning Italian actress Gina Lollobrigida by saying, "Va-va-voom!" with the appropriate hand gestures. Everyone understood this and a lively discussion ensued about Hollywood stars, with each of us trying to express how we felt about them, using gestures, sounds and facial expressions. Our charades-like game had us all howling with laughter, and by the time we arrived in Rome, we felt relaxed and welcome.

We took bus tours around Rome to be sure to see the sights. Our favorites were the Coliseum and the Roman Ruins where we spent hours and hours, despite the heat. On that tour we met another American gay couple who appeared quite amusing, making it seem like they could be fast friends. The four of us took silly pictures all around the ruins, laughing and camping it up. Afterwards we all went out for an enjoyable dinner. These guys asked to see us the next day, and we thought it was a good idea, so we met up with them again. After a day or two of this, however, we started getting fairly tired of them because their sense of humor was all gay and sophomoric. One of them had a horrific, horsey laugh, which became quite embarrassing, particularly in restaurants. They started booking things for the four of us without asking, that we'd rather have done alone, and we couldn't seem to get rid of them.

Getting desperate to escape these two guys, we said we were going to Naples the next day, to which they replied that they'd get tickets to go too. The next morning we snuck off to the train station, grabbed the first train to Naples, in hopes of ditching them, and we did.

In the Roman coliseum with the two obnoxious Americans

In Naples we found a charming, out-of-the-way *pensione* where we felt safe from discovery. It was even hotter in Naples and I proceeded to get quite sick with some flu-like illness. The kind concierge of our *pensione* was a wonderful grandmotherly type who brought me hot soup and some horrible, hot, salty brew that she insisted I drink. But it was nice to be nursed and cared for, since I felt so rotten in the middle of a noisy, dirty city.

When I finally felt better, we scheduled a tour of Pompeii, which was not far away. When we got on the bus, of course, the American couple we'd tried to ditch was on the same tour. However, we found Pompeii fascinating, especially the pornographic wall drawings. We decided to leave Italy the next day, to avoid any more meetings with those obnoxious guys, and we hopped a morning train to Austria.

We loved Italy, but never quite realized while we were there how noisy it was until we travelled overnight and got off in the Vienna train station in the morning. At first we couldn't tell why it seemed so odd, almost frightening. Then we realized that nobody was shouting! It was just completely quiet. What a difference from the Italian train stations, where it was always a cacophony. Interestingly, my feelings for Vienna were similarly bland. All those long boulevards, huge buildings, and reserved people, left me pretty bored by Vienna. I loved the pastries and anything *mitt schlag* (with thick whipped cream).

The next highlight of the trip was a complete surprise, again thanks to our dear Dutch steward from the *Amsterdam*. When our Eurail Pass took us to Zurich, we didn't really know what to do there.

It's a pretty, but rather boring, city and we were getting tired of travelling at this point. Our cute steward had given us the name of an old boy friend of his in Zurich, so we called him. The guy met us at a café and he spoke perfect English, introducing himself as Nico Odermatt. He was a very handsome young man, obviously well off, and he couldn't have been nicer to a couple of Americans he'd never met. One of the first things he said to us was "I just purchased an Alp. Do you want to accompany me while I inspected it?" *Purchased an Alp*?

It turned out that he had wanted to buy a stone farm house on an alp to remodel into a summer home. He'd found out that the owner of this house was an old woman dying in the hospital, and she didn't know which property number her farm was on the map. So he just bought all the numbers, which meant he bought the whole damn mountain.

The trip up to the farmhouse was extraordinary. First a short, scenic train ride to an tiny Alpine village, then a rented car up the mountain as far as there were roads, then onto a frightening aerial tramway that resembled a rickety fruit crate with two boards to sit on, and finally walking the rest of the way to the stone hovel.

This area of the Swiss Alps, reminded me of the Appalachian mountains in the States, and it would have been considered "hillbilly country". The folk of this village and the surrounding mountains were very poor. Nico told us that most of them had never been down from the mountain in their lives. As we rode up the tramway past all these farms, we noted that the women were doing the work, while the men sat on collapsing porches smoking. Since the old woman that had owned the farmhouse was dying, her neighbors had inherited its contents and were periodically lugging items down to their own houses. We saw women carrying tables, chairs, chests and kitchenware on their heads, walking down the steep inclines like mountain goats.

The house was empty now and entirely made of stones - walls, floor and roof. Nico said that city dwellers, like himself, were buying these houses for places to retreat in time of nuclear war. Modernizing them for more civilized habitation.

It was all fascinating, but the real glory of the trip came when we were told to continue up to the top of the mountain on foot. We were expecting the Alps to be craggy with cliffs like we see in mountain climbing films. But this was a "Heidi Alp". The top was round, soft, warm and covered with heather and other wild flowers. The view of all the other mountains in the area was breathtaking! It was one of the most glorious vistas I have ever seen. We silently thanked our dear cabin steward once again, for enhancing our trip.

Our flight home was uneventful, but I know that we were exhausted, although very happy to have made our first trip abroad at such a young age. It would be Reynolds' last trip to Europe, I believe, but I would return many times, under many different circumstances, and always be enriched by the experience.

Six

The Traveling Troubadour

Back in New York, our lives as struggling young actors continued. Irene Dailey had had some sort of split with Uta Hagen, so Irene started her own school, The School of the Actor's Company. She rented a loft on 14th Street, brought over all her students who loved her dearly, and built a fairly successful acting studio. Reynolds also studied with Irene at the time, so this became our home away from home, with Irene as our Earth Mother.

In these advanced classes we did some rather heavy acting exercises. For one of them we were asked to spend some time delving into our subconscious and conjuring up an "image". Then we were to "ask" that image questions and have it "show us" a scene of its life. I had some trouble finding an image at first, so Irene told me to start with a shape and see what happens.

I imagined a diamond shape, which grew into a harlequin who turned out to be a marionette. No matter how many questions I "asked" it, it refused to speak. I must have looked pretty crazy "talking" to my imaginary image while sitting on the subway or in a coffee shop, since this was long before everyone talked into their hidden Bluetooth earpieces. But finally the harlequin did show me a personal scene from its life.

The puppet was in a vast throne room of a king, with a throne at one end. In the scene the puppet was trying desperately to sit on the throne, but hard as he might, he never was able to make it. Nor, since he was a puppet, was he able to speak. Irene told us to make a costume and props and do the scene in class, but not rehearse it, just do it as an improvisation in class. So I cut out diamond shaped, red and black material, and sewed it together to make a harlequin costume.

There were no props in my scene except the throne. So in class, I put on my costume, set up a chair on a platform, and did what the puppet did in my mind, try to get onto the throne. But this time, I actually reached the throne and triumphantly sat on it. Now I swear that what happened next is absolutely true. As I was sitting on the throne feeling proud of myself, the "strings" yanked me off that throne and I threw me across the room where I landed motionless on the floor. This was not planned, or even consciously decided upon in the improvisation, it just happened. Those damn strings yanked me so hard that I landed on the other side of the stage, but had no awareness of my legs doing anything to make this happen. And I actually bruised myself quite badly. Irene had to come over and touch me to see if I was all right. When I got up, I just shook my head indicating that I was fine, got up and sat down, stunned.

Years later, while telling someone about this exercise, I concluded my narration, "It seems my subconscious was telling me, 'Don't be a puppet, you can't survive as an actor, this isn't the life for you!" That was the first time I consciously had made this connection.

I looked at the person I was talking to and said, "I never realized before what a meaningful exercise that was. It seems that my subconscious knew more of what I was feeling than I did. When I did it in class, I just thought that it was a fascinating acting experience."

And it was soon after I had that eventful acting class that I came to the shocking and troublesome decision to quit acting professionally. It dawned on me suddenly that I wasn't enjoying my life. I hated just going to classes, rehearsing scenes and auditioning, being rejected time and again, being poor, and not being able to even go to the theater. The uncertainty, the rejection, the instability, the lack of control of my life... I wanted something different, although I had no idea what that was.

A good friend of mine was a "gypsy", a singer/dancer, who played mostly in Broadway musical choruses. During that time, more musicals and plays opened on Broadway in a season than today, and of course not many were hits. In one season, my friend was in EIGHT Broadway shows – auditioning, being cast, rehearsing, opening, getting bad reviews, closing, and starting the whole process over again. This was no way to run a life, for me at least, and I wasn't even getting into any Broadway shows.

One day as I slaved away typing in an office, I realized that I actually had training for something else. Since, I was forced to take Education courses at college, I was close to having a teaching degree.

Hmmm? I thought. *Anything would be better than this damn office temp work.* And though I didn't feel like teaching theater, because it was too close and painful then, I could use all those music credits I had and teach music. I knew I would have to work on my piano playing, but since this was January, I could look for a September teaching job and prepare for teaching vocal music in the months ahead.

Upon some investigation, I was disappointed to find out that I could never get a teaching job in New York State, because they had a record of my draft examination, where I declared myself homosexual, and they didn't hire homosexuals in the New York school system. But for some reason, New Jersey would not see this record, so I could apply there.

Thus, on a Monday morning in January, I went to a Teacher's Employment Agency to apply for a September job teaching vocal music. After filling out the forms, they asked me if I'd like to go on some interviews for replacement teachers right now. *What the hell*, I thought, *it might be fun and it's better than going back to the office.* So they arranged three interviews for me that week, the first, being the next day in Waldwick, NJ.

Knowing nothing about New Jersey and not having a car, I took a bus out to Ridgewood and a taxi to Waldwick Junior High School to meet with the principal. He seemed interested, but after our interview, I told him I had two more interviews that week and would let him know of my decision after those interviews.

Then as I returned to the parking lot to wait for my taxi, the principal ran out of the school and urgently pleaded, "We really want you to take this job. Please don't go on the other interviews, we have no one to cover our music classes and we'd like you to start right away." Slightly taken aback, I mentioned that my piano playing was not up to par and I needed to work on that, but he indicated that it didn't matter, he wanted to hire me on the spot.

So in that instant, I weighed the two alternatives, going back to temp-typing or coming out here to teach, and again said, *What the Hell!* and took the job. The principal told me that another teacher drove in from New York, and he arranged it for him to pick me up at the bus terminal near the George Washington Bridge the next morning.

Dazed, I got into my taxi for the bus station and return to our apartment to break the news to Reynolds that I was leaving acting and taking a teaching job – in New Jersey – the next day! He wasn't thrilled.

So on a bitter cold Wednesday morning at 6:00 AM, I took the subway to the George Washington Bridge and waited for this teacher to pick me up. He never came. I found out later that he was kind of flakey and had just forgot about me. I called the principal and he told me to take the bus like I had the day before and someone would meet me in Ridgewood bus station.

I arrived at Waldwick Junior High at about 10:00, expecting to be instructed on what I was to teach, having absolutely no clue. But the principal said, "Well, you've missed your first class, but your third period class starts in 3 minutes in Room 12."

"What should I teach", I asked.

"I don't care, just don't let them throw the furniture out the windows", he said as he closed his office door.

So off I went to Room 12 to begin an entirely new career.

The classes that the principal was desperate for me to cover were Eighth Grade General Music classes. The original teacher had left to have a baby and none of the substitute teachers had lasted very long. When I walked into Room 12, I was faced with about 25 sullen, hostile, but curious 8th graders. They obviously hated music class and had evidently terrorized the substitute teachers into leaving, and I was their next victim. Having no plan, all I could do was wing it.

First, I asked what they had been studying and they held up a hideous, green booklet entitled, "The Lives of Famous Composers". Looking inside I found that each page had the history of a different classical composer. "So, who have you studied so far?", I asked.

They grumbled, "Palestrina and Bach".

"Have you heard any of their music?"

"Yeah, we heard some Bach and we hated it!"

Then I made a quick decision and I told them to hand up their booklets. When I got them all, I dropped them in the wastebasket, saying, "In my class, you will never have to see these books again!"

A cheer went up. I quickly realized that my job here was to make these children love music, any music, and not make General Music their most hated class.

Then I questioned them on what kind of music they did like. This was the early '60s, pre-Beatles, so they tentatively told me about the Rock-n-Roll singers of the day. They also mentioned some Folk singers like Pete Seeger, The Kingston Trio, and Peter, Paul and Mary, because "Hootenanny" was a popular TV show at the time.

I did pretty much the same routine in my other two classes that day. At closing bell, I went to the principal and asked him if he cared if I brought in a guitar and didn't use the piano. He repeated the line about not caring as long as the desks stayed in the room. My idea was that since I was a folk singer during my college years and I had brought my Gibson guitar to New York with me, this could be a perfect use of it in my new job.

The next day, just three days after I stepped into the employment agency, I brought in my guitar and had the office run off some mimeographed pages of lyrics to some folk songs. And so it began that in the General Music classes I started by getting the kids to sing to my guitar playing. Slowly, their attitudes turned around, so that they started enjoying music class, and much to my surprise, I became a teacher.

The following week I began my Roaming Music Teacher gig in some of the lower grades, and brought my guitar from the beginning. The elementary teachers were happy to have their once-a-week free period, while I came into their room with my guitar and got the kids to sing songs.

A favorite song, in all grades, was "Ragtime Cowboy Joe", and I still hear from former students about their memories of that song. Music classes were a big hit and by the Spring Concert, I got entire grades up on stage singing with me sitting on a stool in front strumming my "git".

A Waldwick Grammar School Spring Concert with the Fourth Graders doing "Chim-chimminy" with my guitar accompaniment

By the next year, I started teaching private guitar classes after school as well. There were around eight students to a class at $5.00 a student, which was a bargain for them, and I was able to go to Europe that year on the proceeds.

Soon, seen all over town, were kids carrying guitar cases and Waldwick became the "The Guitar Capital of Bergen County". The vocal music section of all concerts took over in popularity from the band sections, with parents filling the auditorium for the first half, since everyone in the school was in the choral section, and then leaving for the second half when the band performed. Needless to say, the band teacher, who was not very good, was not happy. All the kids wanted to be in the choruses; it was amazing to see this transition in music appreciation. Music became popular, just as I had hoped after the first class I taught.

As the years progressed, I taught less elementary school and added high school vocal music to my schedule. Peter Paul and Mary were changing folk music, with more complicated harmonies (and guitar chords) and they became favorites of my students, like "Puff the Magic Dragon". And along came the Beatles, legitimizing Rock 'n' Roll. At one concert I got three other teachers to put on Beatles wigs and we sang "She Loves You, Yeah, Yeah, Yeah", to the delight of all the kids and the horror of some of the parents.

Of course many students didn't have the dedication to become true guitarists, but some stuck with it and ultimately got better than I was. A boy named Joey Wanco, who started playing guitar with me in 8th Grade, became quite good, moving on to classical guitar, which I couldn't teach, let alone do. We became friends when he was in high school, along with several other kids who were interested in theater, as well.

Another student, Andy Wentink, who was in one of my first classes, was obviously gay and surprisingly came out to me, so I befriended him and helped him through the difficulties of being a gay adolescent. Andy became a devotee of the world of ballet, intimate with the members of the New York City Ballet, about whom he has written several biographies. He is now a professor and the curator of the vast archive collections at Middlebury College in New Hampshire, living with his partner Judah, and we have remained good friends.

One day while teaching in the Middle School, I passed the auditorium during the lunch hour. I heard piano music coming from the grand piano in the pit. I peeked in and saw Joe Handy, a quiet eighth grade boy who I had in class, and I was amazed at how beautifully he was playing a classical piece. I asked him if this was something that he was working on, and he told me that it was an early piece he'd learned. I asked him to play something else for me and as he played, I thought *This kid is really special!* The sensitivity of his playing was astounding, especially for one so young – and frankly for any age.

After a few weeks of hearing him play every lunch break, I arranged to have him meet my old Julliard friend, David Bradshaw, who had become a concert pianist and also taught piano. I felt like a Proud Papa when Joe played for him, and David's mouth dropped open in admiration. He immediately asked if Joe could get his parents to allow him to come into Manhattan for lessons. Joe's New Jersey piano teacher was adequate, but Joe needed someone with David's Julliard training to further his natural abilities. David was convinced that Joe Handy could be a major concert pianist, if he had the drive.

So for many years Joe took piano lessons from David Bradshaw, getting better and better, but for whatever reason, Joe never became a professional pianist. He lives in California now with his partner Mark, and we've kept in touch over the years. When I have visited them, Joe has played for me several times on his enormous, Bösendorfer grand piano, playing solo or in duets with Mark. Joe only plays for his own enjoyment now.

One of those little disappointments in the life of a teacher.

Andy and his partner Judah

Joe (bottom) with his husband Mark

Even though I wasn't teaching theater in school, my love of theater couldn't be repressed completely and I started preaching theater to some favorite students and taking them into New York to see plays. Unfortunately, the Waldwick High School drama teacher, Mr. Brush, was horrific and my drama-loving kids hated him and his classes.

Mr. Brush and I drove back to New York together occasionally and I concluded after talking to him on these trips that if he liked a Broadway production, I would hate it, and vice versa. So at the pleading of my students, I began teaching acting on Saturdays, in one of the student's homes, trying to undo the wretched theater classes my students were getting from Mr. Brush.

An art teacher, Ari VanEverdingen, who was a tall, blond Dutch guy with whom I had a brief affair, was an ardent theater lover. So he, another teacher named Joan and I started a community theater called

Theater Three. Several of my enthusiastic high school students, who were smitten with live theater, got involved and we produced a number of plays on the high school stage. I made my directorial debut with our first play, Albee's *Sandbox* and *American Dream*. I always thought those two plays should be paired together, since they have the same basic characters. Oddly, I've never seen anyone else attempt to put them on together, but I think it worked rather well.

The next production for Theater Three was *The Miracle Worker*. The high school stage that we used was more of a concert or lecture hall than a theater. The front of the stage was in the form of a 'V', so that the wings were way upstage. *The Miracle Worker* has need of a front door into the house, and two doors going into the dining room stage left and the living room stage right, but also a large front lawn with the pump downstage. I solved this set problem by constructing a large three-door unit, with the front door connected to the two side doors leading into the living room and the dining room. But sightlines into these rooms were obstructed when the door unit was downstage. So it rolled forward into the 'V' and back out of the way as needed, lumbering back and forth throughout the play.

The critic for the local paper, who I think was Mr. Brush, wrote, "No one could watch the actors because they were constantly being attacked by a big door". Thereafter, this became our name for that production, "The BIG DOOR".

Theater Three's last production was *Time of the Cuckoo*, the play that was adapted into a movie with Katherine Hepburn, called *Summertime*. Playing the lead was a woman named Mary Kleban, who became a lifelong friend. Mary was a suburban housewife with two boys and a sweet, tall, husband. She was working backstage in some of our productions and I thought she'd be perfect for the lead, even if she hadn't acted much before. It turned out that I was right. She was terrific, though she never acted again.

As I got to know her, I found out that she was lovers with another suburban housewife, Thelma Cavellero, who also had a husband and one son. They had led this double life for years and seemed to balance the two extremely well. The two families were very close. The husbands and sons, who were kept unaware of the other situation, seemed happy with their wives and mothers, and the women were exceptionally happy with their lesbian relationship.

Relations with my Theater Three partners at this time became very strained, so we dissolved it. Mary, Thelma and I, along with Reynolds, formed a new theater group we called Theater World Four.

The four of us fit together well, Mary and I had the same sense of humor also became close friends, and Thelma and Reynolds, both having fiery, emotional personalities, also became close. With Mary and Thelma's strong affinity for producing, TW4, as it became known, really started cooking. Since Reynolds and Mary were up for directing, I was now off the hook to do some acting, and our team produced some powerful pieces of theater.

Reynolds, Thelma, Mary and I form Theater World Four

We used other, more suitable venues to mount our shows, so they had a much more professional look to them. Our first production was *Stop the World, I Want to Get Off!* and I took on the Anthony Newley role of Littlechap. This was a huge step and challenge for me, but I was young and fearless so I tackled the part with innocent vigor. The play was a terrific success, but I've always love to quote my first review: "Mr. Christopher was an actor first, a singer second, and a mime fourth". In later years when I did this role two more times, I worked diligently on my mime.

For TW4, I directed the avant-garde *The Physicists* by Friedrich Durrenmatt, working with the fascinating actor Ed Thom. Ed was half Chinese and half Russian Jew, and a wonderful actor who was used in many productions over the years.

The most challenging production we produced, starred Reynolds and me as "Cocky" and "Sir" in *The Roar of the Greasepaint, the Smell of the Crowd*. Irene Dailey came out to New Jersey to see that one and she made an awkward remark afterward. Talking to me, but within Reynold's hearing, she said, "The wrong one gave up acting." I know that Reynolds was terribly hurt by this, since he revered Irene's opinion, but we never discussed it.

As our final production I directed *The Fantasticks*. This experience introduced me to a girl that would play many major roles in my life story, as well as my theatrical history. Her name was then Lisa Minogue and when I cast her she was a 15 year old high school girl. During one of the performances she had her 16th birthday, and so when she said, "I'm sixteen, and everyday something happens to me....", it was true. She played opposite one of my high school student/friends, Joey Wanco, and I loved it that they were both the right age for the roles, which is not usually the case.

Reynolds and I, as "Cocky" and "Sir"

"The Fantasticks, with Lisa, Joey and Ed Thom (on the right)

Now that I was a fully employed teacher, I had more money to play around with, so life became different. I bought my first car to make commuting easier, which was a Volkswagen Bug – I loved that car. Reynolds and I took real car trips, like a Christmas in Highland Park, Illinois. We brought along a crazy actress from Irene's class that we'd befriended, Arlene Udoff. She was Jewish and had never had a real Christmas, so the three of us packed ourselves into the "Bug" with luggage and presents for the trip. Of course, there was a blizzard all the way to Chicago and VW bugs don't do well in the snow. But we got there and my parents gave Reynolds and Arlene a riotous Umbach family Christmas. They both saw a different view of parents from their own – the Mary and Bob Show revisited.

Another road trip we took in the bug was with Irene Dailey, when she was cast in the play *Night of the Iguana* in a prestigious summer theater in Philadelphia. We offered to take her down to the theater and she accepted, but since she was going to stay for over a month, she had lots of things to take with her. The VW was not big enough for everything, so we strapped a laundry basket on the roof of the car full of various items. Somewhere along the NJ Turnpike, it flew off the car, spreading her stuff all over the median. We retrieved most of it, but it was an arduous task, though we laughed all the way through it.

When Irene, Reynolds and I got to the theater, we found that she was booked into a boarding house with actors from the current play, which included Celeste Holmes. Reynolds and I were also able to get a room there, which was great fun boarding with all these professional theater-types. One day, Irene's play was rehearsing and the other actor's wanted to go swimming, but Celeste said that she'd stay back to make chili for everyone's dinner. I said that I'd stay and help her, being excited to spend some personal time with this great actress. She was absolutely lovely to me as we sat in the kitchen chatting about things while she prepared the meal.

Now, a trend that was happening in New York theater at the time was that modern, absurdist plays were becoming more mainstream. Non-realism and profanity were becoming much more common, but some actors who were more traditionalists were not happy about this turn of events. The current hit Broadway production of Albee's *Who's Afraid of Virginia Woolf* was a prime example of the direction that theater was headed. Irene's ex-mentor, Uta Hagen, was the original "Martha", so I saw the play several times and I fell completely in love with it.

So as Celeste Holmes was chopping vegetables for the chili, I was nattering on about how much I loved *Virginia Woolf* and everything it stood for. She was putting up gentle arguments against this kind of theater, but I continued on blithely stating my opinions, oblivious of how they were affecting Miss Holmes. She must have felt threatened by the new wave of dramas that she didn't quite fit into, but she remained quiet in her objections. However, the large knife that was chopping veggies started going faster and harder and more violently, as her body revealed how adamant she felt about this new direction taking over her style of theater. At some point, I realized how upset she was, just by the physical actions of her chopping, though she never raised her voice.

Years later when I ran The Acting Studio, I used this example many times in acting classes to illustrate that "Objects Are Good for You" (a slogan on the wall), showing how actors could use their physical life and objects to reveal what is going on beneath their words. Thank you, Celeste, for the valuable acting lesson.

One summer Reynolds got a job as an apprentice at Allenberry Playhouse in Pennsylvania, a small town near Harrisburg. Their season ran from May to October and the VW got a workout that year because I drove out every weekend I could to visit him and see the shows that he did, although I can't remember a single one. But some of the other apprentices were interesting actors that remained our friends for many years. They included David Christmas who later originated the male lead in *Dames At Sea* with Bernadette Peters. I remember meeting her in their tiny dressing room Off Broadway, and she seemed a bit snooty to me; I never imagined she'd become the star she did. What do I know?

Jane Farnol, an English actress who was another apprentice at Allenberry, played quite an important part in my life. First of all, when she returned to New York, she began dating my brother Jonathan, who was quite a stud and a ladies man by that time. She basically transformed that rough, crude kid into the intellectual, polished and creative man he is today.

She also introduced us to her RADA (Royal Academy of Dramatic Arts) teacher, Peter Barkworth. He was in New York to perform in John Guilgud's production of *School for Scandal*, playing Sir Benjamin Backbite, with a cast that included Guilgud, Ralph Richardson, Geraldine McEuan and Richard Easton. Jane took us back stage after the play and introduced us to Peter and Richard, then we all went to a party. Peter and I hit it off splendidly and he became one of my all time favorite people.

Peter Barkworth was a brilliant actor, who played on West End along side some of the greatest British actors, and was also well known in England for numerous television series. Playwright Tom Stoppard's *Professional Foul*, a TV movie, was specifically written for Peter.

Often over the years I was Peter's guest in his wonderful house in Hampsted, right off the Heath. And it was during one of these visits that I spent more time with Richard Easton, who is still a good friend. Richard since has moved to New York and won a Tony for Best Actor a few years ago for Stoppard's *Invention of Love*. Without dear ol' Jane, I would never have met these two splendid actors.

<u>Headshots from 1963</u>

Peter Barkworth   *Jane Farnol*   *Richard Easton*

While Reynolds was at stock, I found a new apartment for us at 157 West 76th Street between Amsterdam and Columbus. This area of Manhattan had not yet been up-scaled to what it is now. Our building was the first brownstone on the block to be renovated, so it was a pretty shabby neighborhood. There were hookers hanging out the windows and decidedly seedy types in all the surrounding buildings. But our building was spanking new, the only one on the block where the stoop and brownstone front had been replaced by shiny, white bricks.

Our apartment was on the first floor in the back with just a living room, a small bedroom and an even smaller kitchen. However, outside the bedroom was a huge "terrace", which was the roof of the large living room on the floor below. Therefore, in the warmer months we had a much bigger apartment. But it was all new and clean and with terribly low rent. I lived in this apartment until I left New York, and Reynolds lived in it until he died and the rent remained incredibly low.

Below us lived a male couple, Fred and Ben. I never knew what Ben did but Fred Grades was an actor/singer/dancer. He became a big influence in my life because he got me into The Prince Street Players, the only decent acting job I had in New York. Also on that floor lived another couple, Duke and Jeanette, a typical lesbian couple of the era. Jeanette was the "fem", very Brooklyn with teased hair and glamorous clothes, while Duke, the "butch", had a slicked-back man's haircut, tattoos, and drove a taxi. She claimed that was once a "leg breaker" for the mob. We became fond of all our neighbors on the first floor.

Freddie was one of the original "Newsboys" in Ethyl Merman's *Gypsy*" and always related what an interesting time that was for him. One night he was having a party in the apartment below us, and we heard them playing songs from *Gypsy* loudly on his record player. Merman's voice just rattled the windows. I didn't know why Fred hadn't invited us to the party, but I didn't complain. He told me the next day that it wasn't the record player, it was Merman herself. They were having a *Gypsy* reunion, and that's why I wasn't invited.

Although handsome, charming and charismatic, Reynolds was quite neurotic. Most of his problems stemmed from his misplaced love of his monster mother. She had put him into a military school when he was very young, because she was a "party girl" who didn't want to be saddled with a child. On occasions when she would allow him to visit her, he would fanaticize about this beautiful, loving mother while traveling on the train to wherever she lived, but the reality always shocked him. She turned out to be the opposite of his "dream mother", uncaring and dismissive of him. He would return to school hating her. But as the months passed before his next visit, she would develop in his imagination back to the loving mother – and it would happen all over again. This fantasy of his mother still occurred when Reynolds was an adult.

One Christmas, the year after we had visited my mother, we drove in the VW to Ohio to see his mother – the trip was a disaster. Again Reynolds was excited about seeing her again, talking about the glamorous woman and the beautiful times he'd spent with her in his youth. When we arrived at the hovel of a house, the reality was an impoverished bitter, drunken, slob of a woman, living with her two young children and no man in the house.

One morning we got up about 10:00 AM, finding these sweet little kids sitting in the kitchen, hungry, waiting for their mother to get up and feed them. She was passed out from a night of drinking and wouldn't get up until afternoon. I poured corn flakes in a bowl for them, but there was no milk in the fridge. We left the day after Christmas, with Reynolds mumbling, "Why do I always get fooled". It was a gloomy trip home.

I always felt that so much of what Reynolds did, or tried to do, in his life was subconsciously to please his mother and get her love. It never worked. He even got married to a woman later on and this was long after his mother had died.

That certainly didn't work.

Reynolds and I, as the "Dynamic Guitar Duo"

Seven

Europe, *sans* Reynolds

It was the best of vacations, it was the worst of vacations. The summer after I made some extra money teaching all those guitar classes, I decided to travel to Europe on my own. The thrust of the trip was to visit Peter Barkworth in his house in Hampstead. I had no particular plan in mind, but visiting Peter would allow me to experience London for an extended period of time and see some in other European cities as well. Reynolds was working on some job, but I was a teacher with my summer free and I was ready for an adventure.

Peter's home was a charming, old English house right near Hampstead Heath, on a picturesque street called Flask Walk. At one end of the short road were tiny shops, like a green grocer, butcher and of course a pub. On the other end was a path leading into the Heath, which is a large, wild park in the middle of London. Peter offered to give me a room on the third floor of his house for as long as I wanted to stay in London. All the rooms in his house were small because the house was very narrow, but each one was beautifully furnished with many small oil paintings, bookcases and theater memorabilia. The first floor had a quaint living room with a gas fireplace in front, and a tiny kitchen in the rear, which led on to a garden behind the house. The dining room was in the basement, and I had to duck my head before sitting at the table. Two floors above included a bedroom each, with one bath.

A portrait someone painted of Peter in his picturesque garden.

Lovely evenings were spent in that tiny parlor listening to classical music and discussing the world of London theater. Peter had acted with some of the great British actors, like Ralph Richardson, John Guilgud and Penelope Keith, but the actress that intrigued me most that summer was Irene Handl (pronouned the British way, "Irenee"). Famous for her wild and funny characters, she had only a small following in the states, but I had grown to love her after seeing her play David Warner's mother in the film *Morgan*. I liked to fancy myself as the "President of the Irene Handl Fan Club in the USA." Peter thrilled me with stories about her and other people he had played with on the West End.

When I took a day trip to Stratford-upon-Avon to see some Shakespeare, Peter got me an invitation to have tea with a *grande dame* of the theater (who's name escapes me) after the matinee. It was on the lawn behind her house, right on the Avon where the swans were swimming. A butler brought us tea and little butter sandwiches with the crusts cut off. I felt that I was in *The Importance of Being Earnest*, especially since this actress had often played Lady Bracknel at Stratford and in London. Sheer Heaven!

One night during my stay with Peter, he threw a party in my honor with some young actors that he had taught at RADA. Two of them were John Hurt and David Hemmings, before they became famous movie stars. As part of the evening's entertainment, we were all asked to draw an ink caricature of one of the other guests. David Hemmings had the task of drawing me, which I have framed. John did a picture of David, which I had for a long time, but alas, things disappear. The entire evening I was treated like a celebrity, being the "American Actor", and it was a jolly, drunken, joyous party.

David Hemmings before he made "Blow Up"

John Hurt before he made "Man for All Seasons"

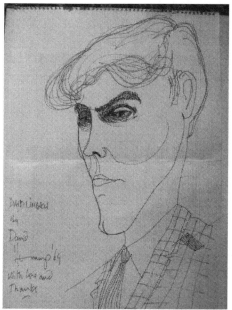

The caricature that David Hemmings made of me at Peter Barkworth's party.

At the end of the party, David Hemmings insisted that he take me to his favorite restaurant. I was excited to be going on a date with this handsome young actor. So the next evening I eagerly awaited his arrival on the curb in front of Peter's house. A half an hour later, David roared up in a tiny, two seat MG convertible with the top down. I was quite disappointed, however, to see that he had brought a girl with him. There was no room for me in the two seats, so I was perched up on the back, sitting precariously on the "boot" with my feet in between David and the girl.

He then took off like a bat-out-of-hell through the streets of London, out into the suburbs, then beyond to the countryside, with me clutching desperately to the back of the seat trying not to slide off as he whipped around the curves. He chatted noisily to the woman sitting next to him, and paid very little attention to the terrified passenger behind him. It was an unmemorable meal in the picturesque country pub, but the time spent in that beastly little car remains the scariest ride of my life. I often wonder if Mr. Hemmings was sadistically playing this prank on the naïve American Actor. Perhaps he was proving that he was straight and showing off to the girl, or maybe he was just self-centered and unaware. Happily, the return trip was more subdued, but I was never happier to see Peter's adorable house in Hampstead.

The other lovely part of my London stay was Geoffrey, a handsome, blond Cockney boy I met in a pub and with whom I spent many a pleasant night. I was having a pint when I heard this great Cockney dialect from the guy next to me and I thought, "I just have to get him into a conversation just to hear him talk". Geoffrey was a charming photographer who had pulled himself out of the slums of London by his love of photography. He was as fascinated by my American dialect as I was of his Cockney one. This was not a gay bar, since I didn't know how to find them back in the 60's, so I didn't expect anything to come of it, I just wanted to hear him talk. But as our conversation went on, I realized that he was interested in a more intimate relationship, and I was completely happy to go along with this. So over the remaining weeks of my time in London, I spent many nights at Geoffrey's flat.

Fortunately, Reynolds had insisted that we have an "open relationship" so I had no need to feel guilty – I even reported my liaison to him in a letter.

Geoffrey, in a picture he sent me later.

One night I did bring Geoffrey to Flask Walk and Peter was not pleased about this, since he wasn't free of class snobbery, I fear. It was at this time, when I had been staying at Peter's for about a month, that I felt it was time to move on. I think I had outstayed my welcome, though Peter would never have said anything. We parted on excellent terms and I was to visit Flask Walk many times after that, but never for such an extended period of time.

The day I left I realized that I was getting a canker sore on my lip, and my stomach was giving me trouble, too. Therefore, I was not feeling very attractive and in some discomfort as I boarded the boat to France, en route to Paris. The only contact I made was with a French girl named Yvonne, who was a university student. She spoke very good English and wanted to practice it by talking to an American. Although we had a lively conversation, I didn't think much of our encounter, however I would be grateful that she gave me her phone number and an invitation to visit her, later on.

When I reached Paris, I went immediately to the Hotel de Lille, to my friend Madame Denise, the owner. Seeing that I was not very well, she gave me the whole garret floor of the hotel, and pampered me with soup and sympathy. But there I was in Paris and my stomach hurt so much I could only eat soup and yogurt. Spending most of my time in the hotel, I became depressed and lonely, wishing I could go home earlier, though my flight back was still a month away. I wrote long, sad letters to Reynolds, feeling very sorry for myself.

I finally realized I had to take some action about my stomach pain, so I decided to go the American Hospital in Paris. I looked up the address and found it to be on Victor Hugo Boulevard, which was across town, but looking on the map I saw that it could be reached by the Metro with several complicated exchanges. So feeling pretty lousy, I made the long journey to the hospital, but when I finally arrived at the address, there was no hospital. Asking a nearby pharmacist, I was told that I was on <u>Rue</u> de Victor Hugo, and Victor Hugo <u>Boulevard</u> was on the other side of Paris. I had misread the map.

So, with more Metro changes, I finally reached the hospital. And after waiting over an hour in the waiting room a pleasant American doctor examined me. His diagnosis was an ulcer at the entrance to my stomach, which was why it hurt so much to eat anything rougher than yogurt. I was given medication and sent on my way, relieved that it wasn't something more serious.

The other event that led to my recovery, came from a rather surprising source. While I was in London, I met an actor friend of Peter's for whom I developed an instant dislike. I thought he was a snobbish, self-centered egotist. But one day in Paris, he showed up at my hotel and I couldn't have been more surprised. Evidently Peter gave him my address and he decided to look me up while he was in town.

He got one look at the sorry state of my living conditions and morale, and immediately took it upon himself to get me out of my slump. He persisted to encourage me leave my little garret and enjoy Paris. He talked me into going to the river barge swimming pool in the afternoons, and when my stomach was feeling better he took me out to dinner. He turned out to be a knight in shining armor and I felt guilty for writing him off in England as a "rotter".

At last I felt well enough to leave my haven and desired to move on again. I had the phone number of Yvonne, the girl I had met on the boat who had asked me to visit her in Normandy, so I figured that would be a nice way to leave Paris but still stay in France for awhile. When I called her, she was thrilled and instructed me on how to get to her town by train. I said goodbye to Madame Denise and Paris, regretting that I hadn't enjoyed it as much as I should have, and vowed to return soon for a more pleasurable visit.

When I arrived in this small town in Normandy, Yvonne met me at the station and we proceeded to her house where she told me *déjeune* was about to begin. I wasn't aware that she lived with her family, so when we came to her charming, stone house I was surprised to find at least ten people sitting at the table awaiting my arrival. From grandparents to little sisters, they all scrutinized the American with suspicious smiles on their faces. No one but Yvonne spoke a word of English, and my French was extremely minimal, so she had to translate everything for everyone.

When the food arrived, it was a huge platter of some French version of corn fritters. I politely took two fritters onto my plate, smiling, then the platter was passed around the table and everyone took one or two fritters. From my first bite, I realized that this was something special, and grinned my approval. The platter was passed back to me and I gladly took a couple more, complimenting everyone on how delicious they were. They kept smiling and passing me the platter, and I figured, *Why not? they were so good.* I didn't notice that no one else was taking a second helping.

When I really couldn't eat another one, I thanked them and said, "I'm stuffed!" When Yvonne translated this to the family, they broke into hysterical laughter. I looked confused, she told me that to be "stuffed" meant to be pregnant. This broke the ice with the family, and we all smiled and nodded at the joke. I sat back and told them that it was one of the most delicious lunches I'd ever had, but they all looked at me with a knowing smirk. Then the Main Course, a gigantic platter of meat and potatoes, came out of the kitchen. They took one look at my face and broke into more laughter. They all knew that I didn't realize that the fritters were just the first course appetizer.

The family were warm and gracious to me the whole time I stayed, wanting to show the "Yankee" all the sights in Normandy they felt I would find interesting, like the Nazi bunkers on the site of the Normandy Invasion. They were excited to take me to the American War Memorial Park. Yvonne told me that I would be standing in the United States when we went there, because the grounds were officially designated U.S. soil. I thought this would be a thrilling experience until I got there and saw the miles and miles of crosses and Stars of David lined up in perfectly straight rows, stretching as far as the eye could see. These marked the graves of thousands of the U.S. soldiers killed in World War II that were either memorialized or buried there if their remains had been found. It was shatteringly sad.

They also took me to see the Bayeaux Tapestry, which was made by Queen Matilda, the wife of William the Conqueror, who embroidered it over many years, while her husband was away conquering places.

The tapestry is 1.5 feet tall and 230 feet long, stretching around the huge room of the museum. It was like a long cartoon telling the story of all his travels and battles. It was very impressive.

American WW2 Cemetery in Normandy

William, the Conqueror

A few feet of the 230 foot Bayeaux Tapestry.

But it wasn't all sightseeing. On my last day in Normandy, Yvonne told me that we were all going on a *pique-nique*. For their version of a picnic, the whole family piled into several cars and drove out to a cow pasture, complete with cows. They set up a long table and tablecloth, with full silverware service for all, with china and wine glasses, and ten folding chairs. Then, with the cows chewing their cud and silently observing, we proceeded to have a three course dinner, exactly like it would have been in their home. And it was, of course, simply delicious. Thanks to this generous family, Normandy was one of the highlights of my summer.

* * *

It was time to move on and visit some other places in Europe, so Berlin was my next destination. It was late afternoon when I pulled into the terminal in West Berlin. Every train station in the major cities of Europe has agencies who specialize in finding tourists accommodations, at no charge. I went immediately to the travel bureau, only to find that the hotels in the city were completely booked up because of a medical convention. But these agencies are determined to find tourists places to stay, at their desired rates, even getting rooms in private homes. So they sent me to the house of a family who would rent me a room. It turned out that no one in the family spoke English, but since I had studied German in college, I was able to do some primitive communication. I was relieved and happy to settle into this charming German home.

On that first night, I went out to explore the neighborhood and found a *Bier Keller* nearby. Curious, I went down the stairs, following the music into the cellar, where I found rows of tables, with jolly Germans linking arms, singing and guzzling steins of beer. I was a bit intimidated by it all, so I sat by myself, ordered a beer and observed the raucous merriment. Not long after I arrived, a group of guys at a table beckoned me over to join them. They were all German, but when they found out that I spoke English, they all switched effortlessly to my language. They were welcoming and jovial, so the conversation and beer flowed easily.

I found out that one of the fellows has just escaped from East Berlin, by running through a subway tunnel being shot at by soldiers. The West Berliners were very happy for him, congratulating him and buying him more steins of beer. At one point, the ex-East Berliner pulled me aside and asked if I planned to visit East Berlin. I didn't realize that I could, but he said that Americans, and only Americans, were allowed to cross over into the East via Checkpoint Charlie. I told him that I would try so he gave me a letter with an address, telling me that it was close to Checkpoint Charlie. He asked me to deliver the letter to his family, letting them know that he had survived the escape. Spontaneously I said, "Sure", not realizing how dangerous this would be, and I took the letter. He drew a little map showing me how to get to the address, and telling me that I could slip the letter into the mailbox outside the door with no trouble.

Somehow, in my drunken state, I found the house where I was staying and staggered up to bed. The next morning I had the mother of all hangovers. When I made it to the kitchen for some coffee, my landlady was waiting for me with the mother of all breakfasts. German breakfasts are not like the French or English; they give their clients a smorgasbord of cheeses, wursts, headcheese, breads, fruit, jams, etc. My landlady wanted to impress the American with how lavishly she served her guests. Given my hangover, I didn't want to eat a thing, but to be polite, I picked at some bread and cheese, smiling with appreciation and nausea.

As I was just about to leave the table, she stopped me with her *piece de resistance,* steak tartar! As I was about to turn green, I croaked out, "*Danke*, madame, but *nein*. In America ve *kucken de fleisch – kucken de fleisch!*" and groped my way back to my bedroom. Despite this faux pas in etiquette, the family and I became quite friendly and I was surprised at how much German I was able to remember from my college days. It was the only time I'd ever completely communicated in another language, and I was rather proud of myself.

After I recovered, I found the letter that the East German had given me to deliver, so I decided to make my way through the Berlin Wall and explore the Eastern sector. The scariest part was when I handed over my passport to the East Germans at the beginning of a long building and was told to go to the other end of the building to wait for its return. There were soldiers everywhere with machine guns, guarding the wall, which was really two walls, covered in barbed wire with a "no-man's-land" section in between. So for about 10 minutes I was in the Communist Block without any identification. My passport was finally returned, much to my relief, and I began to wander around East Berlin.

What a huge difference from West Berlin. The West side was colorful, energetic, and the people were fashionably dressed, friendly and bustling about with purpose. The Eastern sector was bland, colorless, subdued, and the people dressed alike and wouldn't even look at me for fear of being considered collaborators. The West had innumerous restaurants and entertainment centers. I wandered for a long time in the East looking for somewhere to eat, finally found a restaurant and went in. No one was talking, everyone was just sitting eating with their eyes on their food. If there was conversation, it stopped when I came in. On the wall was a portrait of Lenin, and my impression was that it was the only color I saw in the whole city.

While I was in East Berlin, I wanted to see what the famous Pergamon Art Museum had on exhibit. I had read that it held some of the greatest European Art anywhere in the world. Westerners were saddened that it had fallen into the hands of the Communists and therefore out of reach by most of the world. The building was immensely impressive and I eagerly looked forward to what was inside. However, all I found was room after room of hundreds of dreadful propagandist paintings. The purpose obviously was to show the East Berliners how badly off they were before the war, and how much better their life was now under the current regime. Where all that great art was hidden I have no idea, but I certainly hope that it was returned to the galleries after the Wall had fallen.

After a pretty horrible lunch, I took out the map and the letter that I had promised to deliver. I retraced my steps back to Checkpoint Charlie and followed the directions to where the apartment building would be. To cover my covert and scary operation, I took out a big tourist map of East Berlin and became a casual tourist just looking around the area. Without too much difficulty found the address. No one seemed to be on the street in that area, that I could see, at least. I felt like James Bond as I approached the apartment building and saw the mailbox on the front. I quickly slipped the letter in the appropriate slot and scurried away, trying to look inconspicuous. I sauntered, with my heart thumping a mile a minute, back to Checkpoint Charlie and over the bridge to the West. I was probably foolish to have attempted this, but I'm very glad I did, and I hope it gave comfort to the family of that polite young escapee.

After this adventure, I felt the need to move on. I'd found that traveling on my own was not much fun. I was getting homesick and missed Reynolds, but I couldn't go back to the states until my return flight from London. Despite our open relationship, it wasn't easy for me to hook up with anyone else. I've never been good at "cruising" and the people I'd meet at tourist attractions were pretty boring and usually paired up already. I would wander through the museums and tourist locations, hoping to find a friendly face, but it never seemed to happen. I ventured to Vienna and a couple more places, but I was not really enjoying myself anymore, I just wanted to go home.

My final foreign destination, before going back to London, was Copenhagen in Denmark. I knew nothing about this city so I didn't know what to expect. The gay life in the Germanic cities that I'd been visiting was very closed and secretive, at least to the uninitiated. But in Copenhagen, I was surprised and delighted to discover that gay men were walking around holding hands in broad daylight and friendly cruising was open and warm, and seemed to happen everywhere. The whole atmosphere was completely different from anything I'd ever experienced. This was still the early 60's and back in the states everything was heavily closeted.

On my first afternoon, I was sitting in a cafe, admiring a pretty blond kid, who seemed to be admiring me. A guy sitting with him suddenly walked over to my table and said that his friend was shy, but he thought I was cute and would I join them for coffee. Stunned, I quickly agreed and moved to their table and it was then that I met Eric Jensen. The others at the table spoke fluent English but Eric was less fluent, making him shy to introduce himself. However, he and I hit it off immediately and his friends were happy to translate whenever needed. These guys took me to dinner, then to a gay club for dancing and finally left Eric and me alone. He told me that I could come up to his house for the night, and even though I had a hotel room, I readily accepted his invitation.

The next morning we were lying naked in his smallish bed, when there was a knock at the door. "Come in" said Eric (in Danish) and I was horrified to see his mother step into the room. I hadn't realized that Eric lived with his family and I certainly hadn't expected his mother to join us when we were naked under the covers. Expecting a screaming, angry scene, I cowered behind Eric, but mama just said something about breakfast being ready, and welcomed me to join the family for it.

Flabbergasted, I asked Eric why his mother wasn't upset finding me there, and his reaction was something like "What would she be upset about? She knows I have boys up to my room." So, we went down to the kitchen and there was papa reading the newspaper, making my heart skip another beat. But we were all introduced and sat down to a lovely breakfast. It was an experience I never dreamed could happen.

I spent my remaining days in Copenhagen in a haze of enjoyment. Eric and I were quite fond of each other, but knew that our time together had to end when I went back to the states. He and his friends took me on many excursions around the city, including a ferry ride to Malmo, Sweden and back. The closer we got to my departure, the harder it was. Mama even asked if I couldn't stay longer, as I was so good for Eric. It was actually a tearful separation, with promises to write faithfully. We did write for a while, but of course, the letters petered out after a couple of months, because Eric's English was so minimal, but this romantic interlude made my European adventure end on a beautiful blond high note.

My Copenhagen romance with Eric.

Eight

Look, Ma, I'm a Professional Actor

During this period I was lucky to have two long-run, professional acting gigs that were great fun. The first came from my downstairs neighbor Freddie Grades who worked with The Prince Street Players. This was a highly regarded and popular children's theater company, that produced successful musicals of classic children's stories. Jim Eiler and Jeanne Bargy wrote Broadway-style music with delightfully campy scripts, beloved by kids and adults alike. The Players toured around the East Coast, playing in summer stock theaters from New York to Boston to Albany to Philadelphia, doing our shows in the afternoon on the sets of the adult plays that would play in the evening. Freddie was able to get me an audition and I was fortunate to gain a spot in the company. I worked with this company for two years and learned more about being a professional actor in that time than any school had ever taught me.

We rehearsed in a loft on Prince Street in the Village and on the night before we left on tour with a new play, friends and local denizen would bring their children for the dress rehearsal. The audiences went wild for these hilarious and sophisticated shows. My initial role was Mr. Stitch, one of the two tailors (the other being Mr. Sew) in *Emperor's New Clothes*, singing, "Stitch and Sew, Sew and Stitch, who is who and which is which....". Later I played Gepetto, in *Pinocchio*, which was a nostalgic trip for me, The Prince in *Sleeping Beauty* and The Emperor-of-All-China, in *Aladdin.* I played them all in repertory for two exciting and exhausting seasons.

"Stitch and Sew, Sew and Stitch, who is who and which is which....".

Freddie as Aladdin with The Emperor-of-All-China

One summer we toured all the New York City parks with *Pinocchio*, and we discovered that the audiences in each of the five boroughs had completely different personalities. In Central Park we got mostly sophisticated, white audiences from upper-middle class families, with children who were theatrically savvy. They got all the subtler humor and treated the story as a serious drama. In Prospect Park in Brooklyn, the children were ethnically diverse and the reactions were confusing. The kids seemed to love the story, but were much more vocal about it, yelling encouragement to Pinocchio and laughing loudly at the slapstick.

But it was playing Gepetto for the children in the Bronx that was the most heart-warming for me. It was evident that a number of these children had harsh family lives, so they adored this good-natured father figure, who seemed to me to be the real hero of the play for them. When we did our "meet & greet" after the play, these kids, most of whom had never seen live theater before, were amazed by the fact that we were not cartoons. They were dumb-struck as they passed us and would reach out to touch our costumes, making sure we were real. They had no idea about asking for autographs or making comments. And the circle around Gepetto was the biggest, which I loved.

After a performance of <u>Pinocchio</u> in Central Park with great comedienne, Marcie Stringer

I had hoped to play the Emperor-of-All-China in the CBS-TV presentation of *Aladdin*, but Jim Eiler's lover got the part and I was just a guard and a magic tree in the cave. I also was one of the black hooded figures that change the set pieces, who in "kabuki theater" are supposed to be invisible. These were not the most exciting parts in the play, to say the least. We spent three grueling days rehearsing and filming the musical under the hot studio lights needed for television in those days. It was my first experience doing this kind of work, and with the hours of waiting and sweating, it formed my dislike of movie/TV making that I have felt my whole life. Give me live theater any day.

The cave tree costume was hot, heavy and horrible. Once I was in the costume, I had to stand the entire time covered in black material except for my head, which had a tree mask and headdress. One arm was exposed, which held up a heavy branch. The other hand was under the black cloth holding onto to a bar, which was my only means of support. At one point during the long, long shooting of that scene, my nose began to itch unbearably, but I had no hand free to scratch it. The director, who was a well known TV director at the time, came by and I squealed, "Help, please scratch my nose!" So he reached up under my mask and did so. Quite embarrassing.

When the black and white show was finally aired, the whole cast gathered in our grubby loft and huddled around a tiny TV set to view the first Prince Street Player's TV show. We were pretty pleased with how it came out. Freddie looked great as Aladdin, Jim's boyfriend was good (if not great) as the Emperor-of-All-China, and Victoria Mallory (who went on to play the original role of Anne in *A Little Night Music*) was beautiful as the Princess. Regrettably, the woman they cast as Aladdin's mother came off as a man in drag, which she wasn't, and I was recognizable only once, when I walked in front of the camera as a guard. That was my one and only time on National Television, and I never had any inclinations to audition for TV work after that.

As much as I loved my time touring with Prince Street Players, it wasn't all fun and games. We were picked up by a van as early as 5:00 AM and drove to the various venues for the show, sometimes 4 hours away. All of us would set up the stage, perform two shows in a hot tent, and then drive back. The major entertainment on those drives was reading, and one summer I finished the entire "Lord of the Rings" series.

One year we did a production of *Snow White Goes West*, the only fairytale that was updated, but it worked quite well. The "dwarves" were all tall dancers, playing the miners, and they were given energetic and difficult choreography. It was a running joke with the company that I was a non-dancer. I told everyone that during the TV shoot of *Aladdin* that I was tapping like crazy under the cave tree costume. So although I really wanted to be one of the dancing dwarves, I had to be the Cowboy Narrator instead. I had to watch the great dance routines in rehearsal, standing with my cowboy boot on the barrel, waiting to narrate. I would jokingly say as they whirled past me, "I wanna be a dwarf, I wanna be a dwarf."

The choreography was done with lots of circles, because we staged it primarily for tent theater, in-the-round. When we got to our first theater, we found that we were to perform on the set of *On a Clear Day You Can See Forever*. The set designer had placed on the circular stage a small, circular platform, *off center*, and it was immovable. So the poor dancers, doing the circular routines, had to jump up and around this inconveniently placed platform, trying desperately not to trip on it. As they whizzed past me at my barrel, I whispered, "I'm glad I'm not a dwarf, I'm glad I'm not a dwarf."

The year that CBS bought the Prince Street plays for television, Jim Eiler felt that much of our silliness was getting too gay. A lot of the humor that we put in for the adults involved camping it up, and my Mr. Stitch was no exception. One rehearsal when I was being particularly silly with Mr. Stitch, Jim said to me "More balls, David, more balls!" At which point the hilarious comedienne and fellow cast mate Marcie Stringer yelled, "PROPS!" This got a huge laugh from all of us, but I was particularly delighted one night in Sardi's to hear someone tell that story in the next booth. Proudly I turned around and said, "That was me!"

Aladdin was by far the most fun to play, partially because of the brilliant actor, Will B. Able, who most often played the Genii. This 6' 6" vaudevillian-pro never said the same jokes twice on stage and was screamingly funny. Trying to keep a straight face when playing opposite him in a scene was almost impossible. Also the trips to and from the theaters were non-stop laughing, if you got to travel in Will's car. I don't think I've ever known anyone who was "on" all the time, like he was. My friend Vince Tampio played the Genii sometimes, and he was also a hoot. Plus I got the chance to play the Emperor-of-All-China with my black shoestring mustache, so it was definitely my favorite of the Prince Street musicals.

* * *

The other professional acting job I got was in a production of *The Fantasticks*, which turned out to be the first of ten productions of *The Fantasticks* I would be involved with over the years (so far). I had seen the original production on Sullivan Street in the Village many times and I fell in love with it. Baritone Jerry Orbach played the original El Gallo and I certainly didn't see myself in that role at the time.

It was in June when Reynolds auditioned to play Matt in some out of town production. He was to replace an actor who had to leave in August. They cast Reynolds for August, but also they asked him if he knew of anyone who was free to play El Gallo - right away. He recommended me, believing that I wouldn't be cast or that I wouldn't be able to go. I don't have the low a baritone voice that is needed for El Gallo and I was definitely too young, but they were desperate so they cast me.

The production was in San Juan, Puerto Rico and I had to leave *immediately*. I had just begun a new teaching job and I needed to get permission to leave a week before school was out. Fortunately, this job was to teach drama, so when I told the principal that I was cast in a play in San Juan for the whole summer, he was impress and released me. So off I went, alone, to Puerto Rico to begin rehearsals for my first adult professional industry gig.

The Fantasticks was scheduled to open only two weeks after I arrived, in the Peacock Room of the Caribe Hilton Hotel. It was a basement dining room, which they half-heartedly converted into a theater, that looked out onto a garden with real peacocks strolling around. Our rehearsals were held in a gorgeous house in the suburbs, up on a mountain. We rehearsed in the "music room", a glass enclosed structure that overhung the jungle on tall stilts and looked out at the blue-green ocean. The view was magnificent, particularly at sunset!

It wasn't an easy musical to learn in two weeks, and our director had never seen the production in New York or anywhere else. He was also a radio director, so he listened more that watched, and those of us who knew the show were easily frustrated by many of his choices. He didn't like any pauses, even though we filled them with acting that he didn't see. But, as contracted, we worked hard and all too soon we moved into that beautiful hotel on the Condado, a sandy strip with many luxurious hotels. We were only allowed two dress rehearsals in the theater. All of us extremely nervous, we opened on a Friday night, to a small, but very enthusiastic crowd of American tourists. Everyone seemed to accept my youth and tenor voice, and I got excellent reviews in the local papers. And so my fabulous summer in the tropics began.

The Caribe Hilton Hotel, where I played El Gallo for the first time.

I rented a small bungalow on the beach, a short bus ride from the hotel, but I spent most of my days at the Caribe Hilton in their pool or on their beach. We would do the show at 8:00 PM, go out partying, sometimes until dawn, sleep until noon, go to the pool, do the show and start all over again. *This was a job? What a life!* And this went on all summer. Reynolds joined the cast in August and it was the vacation of a lifetime – and we were paid for it. There was an airplane strike that summer, so many tourists were stranded and looked for more entertainment, so they came to our show. Our poster was up all over town with our picture, so we became sort of celebrities around the pool or when we went out at night. This was the life of a professional actor - sheer heaven.

An amusing thing happened during that run. One night while Louisa was saying in her opening monologue: "One morning a bird woke me up, it was a lark or a peacock…", a peacock outside in the garden gave a loud squawk, and the audience (and cast) got a huge laugh out of that.

At the top of the hotel was the "big room" where real celebrities performed, and we were able to go up and see their late show for free. I loved hearing Jose Feliciano, the blind guitarist/singer, whose "Light My Fire" was a big hit at the time. But my favorite entertainer that summer was Dionne Warwick, who was also one of our passions back in New York. Her show was extraordinary and Reynolds and I watched it every night. She saw us there and after the show one night she asked us where we were going. There were lots of gay clubs and bars in the Old Town section of San Juan where we usually spent our nights. We told her this and she asked if she could come along. *Of course!* Dionne Warwick travelled with us on the city bus into Old Town and bar-hopped with us all night. It was quite a high watching the queens of San Juan react when we brought Dionne into the clubs with us. She was even gracious enough to sing in a couple of them. That was easily the highlight of the entire *Fantasticks* experience.

We became friends with guy who would become quite well known, Danny Apolinar. He and his lover worked in a club in San Juan, singing his original material that was utterly delightful. They went on to write the first "rock musical", called *Your Own Thing*, which was loosely based on *Twelfth Night* and opened Off Broadway in 1968. Danny played in cabarets and piano bars all over the world for the rest of his life. But that summer in Puerto Rico, we all just hung out in his club and had a ball.

Danny Apolinar, his lover David and a friend in their apartment in San Juan

Although I have acted and directed in several professional companies over the years, Prince Street Players and *The Fantasticks* in San Juan are the only long running professional jobs I've ever had.

My Top Ten memories from these experiences are:
1. The reaction of the Bronx children to Gepetto.
2. Learning and singing "I Can See It" for the first time.
3. Attaching my long, black shoestring mustache and twirling it like tassels.
4. Being able to improve *The Fantasticks* after the ignorant director went back to New York.
5. Singing "Stitch and Sew, Sew and Stitch" to the preview audience, and getting a wild applause.
6. Dionne Warwick……
7. Marcy yelling, "Props".
8. Lounging around the pool at the Caribe Hilton, signing autographs.
9. Watching the poor "dwarves" trip over the circular platform.
10. Meeting Danny Apolinar and singing with him in his club.

Nine

The Drama Club

One of the basic philosophies in my life has been, that when a situation is not making me happy – I change it. I've not been afraid to step into the unknown, leaving an unhappy status quo to see if a completely different situation will work better for me. Getting stuck in a rut is not the best policy for me and I've always strived to avoid it. Leaving professional acting and jumping blindly into teaching, for example, is a decision I've never regretted.

While I was teaching music in Waldwick, both high school and middle school, I was also coaching drama, off the record, on Saturdays to some of my favorite students. I was also busy producing, directing and acting in Theater World Four productions. Obviously, my love for the theater was coming to the fore again, and teaching music was getting tiresome and uninteresting. When I realized this, I easily made the decision that I should be officially teaching drama not music.

So with little trepidation, I quit my job in Waldwick that year even though I had no specific job awaiting me. I began looking for drama teaching job during the summer but there weren't any available, so I was out of work when September came. Then in December, much to my relief, the teacher's employment agency found me a position that would begin in January. This brought me to Roselle Park, New Jersey, where a whole new era of my life would begin.

Roselle Park is a suburb south of New York, so my commuting changed from the elegant George Washington Bridge to the seedy Holland Tunnel. Waldwick and Roselle Park were about the same distance from Manhattan, but the commute was much more stressful to Roselle Park. I travelled on the Westside Highway, the Holland Tunnel, Route 1-9, the Pulaski Skyway, Route 22, and the Garden State Parkway, any one of which could be screwed up with traffic jams, going either direction.

I still had my VW bug and it was often a long and harrowing trip coming home or going to the new school from our 76th Street apartment in New York. The one pleasure of these drives was seeing beautiful ocean liners, like *Queen Elizabeth, Queen Mary, France, Normandie,* parked on the Westside piers every day. I became able to recognize them by their smokestacks.

The makeup of the two towns were also very different. Waldwick was primarily made up of middle class, New York commuters, while Roselle Park was predominantly working class families of Italian or Polish decent and was considered more a suburb of Newark, New Jersey. Sports was big in this school particularly football and the wrestling team, which won many championships.

But at least the school had a fairly active theater program, although I was not officially a part of it yet. They produced a Junior and Senior play every year, directed by one of the English teachers. My job was teaching Public Speaking to every kid in the high school, taking groups out of their English class for six weeks during their freshmen, sophomore and junior years. It was also a fairly new program, which I was asked to develop. That first semester I struggled because it was the middle of the year and I didn't really have a plan yet. But by the next year I had a healthy program going and became quickly acquainted with the whole student body.

Although I wasn't able to direct any of the plays right away, I did start a Drama Club, which became a popular hit and grew every year. In my first year, I had about 20 enthusiastic students in the club. We worked on short plays and since most of the Drama Club kids were trying out for the school plays, that got me involved. The director was blond bombshell English teacher, Darlene Mangold, and she had produced successful work thus far. I asked her if I could help out with the play and she was happy to have me do so. The play was *Arsenic and Old Lace* with a large cast comprised of many Drama Club students which made working on it great fun.

When Darlene saw how well I worked with the students, she asked me to direct the musical the next year, which she never really liked to do. So I helmed my first school production, *Bye, Bye, Birdie.* And my career as a high school Drama teacher went into full swing.

My first two plays at R.P.H.S., <u>Arsenic and Old Lace</u>

and <u>Bye, Bye, Birdie</u>

Although my teaching job was in Roselle Park, Theater World Four was still functioning up in Northern New Jersey, so I continued to have this extracurricular theatrical project to work on as well. I believe we were doing *The Physicists* that year. Since I was teaching in Roselle Park, Reynolds became more involved with the people in the Theater World Four group, which I had originally been directing. Mary Kleban and I saw things the same, but Reynolds and Thelma had other ideas, so it caused awkward tension between us.

After ten years together, my relationship with Reynolds was beginning to crumble. His neurotic, passionate and sometimes unstable personality was getting harder and harder to stand. That, combined with the hateful commute, gave me reason to move out of our Upper West Side apartment to a place by myself in New Jersey. It was a hard decision for me to leave Manhattan. I hated not being "a New Yorker" but it seemed a good decision for my functionality as a teacher in Roselle Park and a calmer home life. I wasn't "officially" leaving

Reynolds, and we worked together for many years after that, but in reality, the move meant that I had broken up with him as a life partner. We were together ten years.

In my second year working in Roselle Park, I met the next person who would affect my life profoundly, though I certainly didn't realize it at the time. One afternoon this short, energetic Jewish boy (the only Jewish person in the school), came striding into my Drama Club, stuck out his hand to me and announced, "Hi. I'm Gary Cohen – I make movies!" He was a freshman at the time and was avidly using a Super 8mm movie camera to make his movies.

We welcomed him into the club and it was amazing how his forceful personality soon had the club under his spell. He encouraged the drama club kids to spend their afternoons and weekends making "movies". Here were juniors and seniors, asking this little freshman kid, "Where do you want me, Gary? What should I do now, Gary?" He even convinced me to be in one of his movies that first year, recreating El Gallo's death scene on the roof of the high school. He was just amazing his first year, and continued to be a creative powerhouse for all four years at RPHS. Gary was the heart and soul of the Drama Department, acting in many plays, including the lead in *The Music Man* his senior year. In addition, we became friends in his freshman year, a friendship that has lasted to today, with him becoming my director and producer as well.

Some of Gary's high school performances:

Snoopy in *You're a Good Man, Charlie Brown*

Mr. Stitch in
Emperor's New Clothes

The Harp in Prince Street's
Jack and the Beanstalk

Mr. Dussel in
Diary of Anne Franck

Harold Hill in *The Music Man*

A constant help with all the high school productions that I helmed was my good friend Ed Williamson. Ed was a Texan who was a beloved, master English teacher (his friends called him "Massa E'ward) and he was also gay and an ardent theater queen. He took this teaching job in the New York area to be near the Broadway shows. He loved musicals most of all, *Hello, Dolly* being his favorite, and had a great understanding of scenic design and construction. So as I got more and more involved in directing the plays at the school, he became my creative partner, designing the set and organizing the backstage crews with aplomb.

Ed and I were also great theater-loving friends, going to lots of theater together. We discovered Stephen Sondheim one day in New

York because we liked the purple and orange poster of "Company". We chose not to go to *Sugar*, because the ticket price went up to an exorbitant $45.00. We travelled to Boston to see Angela Lansbury in *Mame* for the out of town tryout and almost fell out of the balcony when Bea Arthur sang "The Man in the Moon is a lady...".

Massa E'ward, with his dog "Party"

Ed and I caught in a follow spot, this picture made the yearbook

Since he didn't know Edward Albee's *Who's Afraid of Virginia Woolf,* I chose to share my favorite play with him. I had obtained the original cast recording of the whole play, which took four 33rpm records. I took them over to his apartment one night and we played the entire play non-stop. Like George and Martha, we drank bourbon (or "bergen" as George tells it) the entire evening, consuming an entire bottle as we listened to the recording. Unfortunately, it was a school night, so we staggered into school the next day still a bit drunk, until the hangovers started. It caused a difficult day – but the night of drinking and Edward Albee was worth it.

Drama Club regulars, Gary with the guitar and Ed Williamson sitting on the right

Massa E'ward really worked miracles on the RPHS stage and was a major part of why our shows were so successful. And successful they were! Over my 11 years in that school, our drama department became famous in the area, packing the houses for our musical and dramatic productions and winning all sorts of awards. Some highlight productions were: *Mame, Skin of Our Teeth, Hello Dolly!, The Music Man, Pajama Game, Up the Down Staircase, Damn Yankees, Bells are Ringing, The Diary of Anne Frank, and You're a Good Man, Charlie Brown,* as well as the many children's plays we produced.

Damn Yankees

The Music Man

The Skin of Our Teeth

Hello, Dolly!

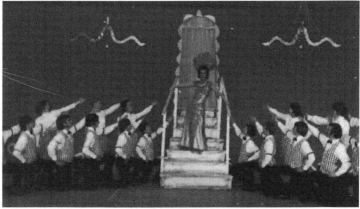
Hello, Dolly!

The Drama Club established a Children's Theater program, which performed plays for the elementary schools. It became a tradition that every spring our auditorium was filled with all the grammar school children, who got their first glimpse, and I hope a love, of theater. I introduced the Prince Street Player's musicals, which were extremely popular. I'll never forget Gary as the Golden Harp in *Jack and the Beanstalk*.

During Gary Cohen's senior year he and another student, Paul Kaye, wrote a musical they called *Hello, Dragon!* It was based on "The Reluctant Dragon" and had clever, parody lyrics to Broadway show tunes. The townspeople of Tea-and-Crumpet, upon hearing there is a dragon in the hills, sing, "Oh, oh, we got Trouble, right here in Tea-and-Crumpet" (*Music Man*). And St. George sings, "I'm, the greatest Knight, I love to fight...." (*Funny Girl*). And of course the big Dragon number, with all the "Dragonettes" was "Hello, Dragon!" When we took *Hello,*

Dragon! to Buck's County Playhouse High School Drama Contest, where we had won many prizes over the years, the other schools scoffed because we were competing with a children's play. But it took everyone by storm, taking top place in all categories.

St. George and Dennis the Dragon, in <u>Hello, Dragon!</u>

The year I directed *Mame* at Roselle Park, it was the Senior musical and tradition had it that a senior would play the lead. Many of the senior girls were licking their chops and sharpening their claws over the title role – competition was fierce. Before auditions, a student that was a friend and a very active actor, Peter Adams, told me that his sister was trying out for the musical. I recalled his sister to be a quiet, shy junior in my speech class, Judi Adams, who hid in the back row behind her hair. "Okay," I said, expecting very little.

At auditions while we struggled through short solo songs from every girl auditioning, I was looking down at the table when suddenly my ears perked up. I said jokingly to the music director "Did Barbra Streisand just walk into the room?" There on the stage was Judi belting out some Streisand song with power and superb musicianship. I immediately had her sing one of Mame's songs and it was like hearing a Broadway show right there on our stage. "Wow," I said, "If she can act like she sings it will be phenomenal." But I knew how shy she is in speech class, so I didn't expect much, again. She took the script and suddenly transformed on stage into a mature woman – Mame!

I didn't know what to do. She was obviously, by far the best Mame, but she was a junior. A few years earlier I had insisted that all classes could be in all shows, but the leads were always from the class that sponsored it. Well, much to the anger and disappointment of my senior girls, I cast Judi as Mame. As rehearsals progressed, everyone in the cast started to realize how special Judi was and how powerfully she played the role. I'm happy to report that the seniors got together on opening night and presented Judi with a huge bouquet of flowers, thanking this talented junior for making their play such a wild success.

Judi Adams as Mame in her junior year in high school

Right after she graduated high school, Gary Cohen got out of college and wanted to start a theater company. He asked me to repeat my role of Littlechap in *Stop the World, I Want to Get Off*. I said "Sure!" and told him I knew who would be perfect for the demanding, multiple role of Evie/Anna/Ilse/Ginnie: Judi Adams. Gary was a couple years ahead of Judi and didn't know her, and condescendingly said, "Have her audition".

Well, she not only got cast as Evie, but the leads in three other shows that season. Judi is maybe the most talented actor I've ever known, but after doing a number of shows with Gary's theater for many years, she decided to get out of show business, get married and be a housewife and mother. Fortunately I recently tempted her out of a 15 year retirement with the role of Mrs. Meers, in *Thoroughly Modern Millie* and in classic Judi style, she knocked 'em dead - again.

Judi Adams in <u>Philemon</u> soon after high school

And years later as Mrs. Meers in <u>Thoroughly Modern Millie</u>

    Over the 11 years I taught in Roselle Park, I directed many productions that I am still extremely proud of today. Many of those talented students are still my friends, such as Gary Cohen, Peter and Judi Adams, and Paul Kaye, (and many more thanks to Facebook).

    As I look back on my 17 years of public school teaching, I realize that overall it was a scintillating and gratifying part of my life. I think that I was a born teacher, and that acting and directing was just part of that package. I intuitively, with no real training, figured out what students needed, and more importantly, wanted. I was a popular teacher not because I was soft, but on the contrary, I demanded that students look in new places in themselves and stretch themselves, striving for their best.

    My music students in Waldwick hated music when I arrived, but ended up reveling in singing and even playing the guitar. The children I introduced to theater in Waldwick, who had hated their acting teacher, were excited when I introduced them to authentic acting experiences, albeit not in an official classroom.

    The mandatory speech classes in Roselle Park were unpopular at first, but as the students were goaded into expressing themselves in ways they hadn't before, they grew to be proud of their improvements and enjoyed their classes. Putting in a faux radio booth in the classroom and making them give news reports and commercials on a microphone was a clever way to make them use their voices to express themselves. I found that classes which the English teachers found difficult to control, were some of my favorite classes. I insisted that they toe the line, but with humor, so they respected me and were able to perform. I always believed that respect was the best way to gain discipline and it proved true again and again.

The plays I directed were successful, and so many of the students loved their experience in them, because I strove for Broadway quality and demanded students work at their personal best. And, consequently, we achieved high quality high school theater, which can be very good indeed.

The crowning academic class that I am most proud of creating was called Communication. It was a senior elective, in which I taught the many ways to communicate beyond simply writing. In every English class since grammar school, students only read literature or wrote papers, but in my class we would study visual art, music and musical lyrics (not just poetry) and film most particularly. They devised drawings and collages that had a message, they played records they felt spoke a message and they often performed original songs. A large component of the class concerned the concepts of film making, which led to students to watching, analyzing and even creating their own movies.

One day in that class, I taught a lesson that was completely extemporaneous, but it demonstrated the art of communication better than any other lesson I'd ever taught. It was a lovely spring day, a few weeks before graduation. Nobody, including me, wanted to be in a classroom. So I got an idea how to use the concepts from my acting classes and I made the spontaneous decision to take the class outdoors into the sunlight.

"What are we going to do?" the students asked me.

"We're going to have a game of baseball", I said.

"What?" they cried. This being the "intellectuals" of the senior class they had little love of sports.

"We don't have any bats or balls", they exclaimed.

"Precisely", I told them, as I led them out on to an unused baseball field.

I divided the class up into two teams, giving each team their positions on the field. I said that they would play a complete game of baseball, but without any ball, gloves or bats, that these had to be in their imagination. One of the boys was on the baseball team, so I told him that he was the umpire. It would be his job to be sort of God, deciding everything about the game, determining whether a pitch was a strike, ball or a hit, and where the ball went if it was a hit. He would determine if the ball reached the player's hands in time for an "out", or if the running player was "safe". He would control the whole game, but the players had to follow and react to whatever he determined. I called it "Invisible Baseball" and it was a perfect lesson in communication.

Dubiously, they began an inning, but as they saw how the game worked, and how they had to imagine where the ball was at any given time, they started getting into the game. By the second inning, they were cheering on their teammates and groaning when a player would swing at the "ball" and the "umpire" would call "Strike". And they would cheer on a player to run, when the ball was "a long fly ball into left field", then groan if the Ump would say that the ball was caught, causing an out. They would scream and holler when a run was made for their team, and I knew that most of these kids had rarely attended any of the real baseball games, let alone cheered for their team.

The key to this typical improvisational acting exercise was that the students had to watch the imaginary ball at all times. They had to listen carefully to the umpire and follow his every call. I had never seen a group of students work so closely and with such determination in such a short period of time. It was the epitome of teamwork.

The exuberance of our class was so noisy, classes in the school began coming to the windows of the their classrooms and watching the game. Cars stopped along the road to watch our game, marveling at the Invisible Ballgame. It was a highlight for everyone involved and I'll never forget it.

Recently, I attended the 1972 Roselle Park High School class reunion and a man came up to me who was obviously a jock, that I didn't remember at all. He said, "I was in your Communication class. I bet you didn't think I was listening, but that class changed my life. I made a collage in your class (like this was a big deal). I'm a union organizer now and I use what you taught me every day. I'm glad that I got to see you because I always wanted to thank you."

Thanks to Google and Facebook, I hear from students from the past all the time now. Years ago, in early email days, I received a message from a Waldwick student who found my address somehow and wanted to tell me that she still sings *Ragtime Cowboy Joe* to her kids and remembers her music classes with me all the time. It has been extremely gratifying to often hear this kind of testament from students who appreciated the learning as much as I appreciated the teaching.

Ten

The Swingin' Sixties

The hippie teacher.

Education was changing in the Sixties, and there was a polarization between the older and younger generations. This occurred in the faculty as well. The younger teachers were trying new methods of reaching the students, but the old guard stuck to traditional methods and that did not always lead to pleasant teacher's meetings. Being the first teacher to not wear a tie, to grow facial hair, and to let my hair and sideburns grow, I became quite popular with the students, but not well liked by all the teachers, particularly not with the longstanding, head of the athletic department, "Puggie" Williams. Puggie was a bigoted, bloated, far right-wing, squat, little tyrant, and he literally hated me.

He hated that I got his athletes to be in the musicals, he hated my long hair and attire, he hated that I was friends with the "hippie" students, he hated all the standards I upheld. On the day that Martin Luther King was assassinated, a number of teachers sat around the lunch room and Puggie actually congratulated the assassin, making light of the situation. Most of the teachers were too intimidated by him to respond, but I immediately protested, proclaiming that it was a major tragedy, that Dr. King strived for peace and harmony, gaining freedom for the black people through non-violence.

Puggie turned red, steam coming out of his ears, he stood up and stormed toward me, fists clenched. He stood over me, glaring down, because even though he was short, I was sitting down. Bringing back memories of the bullies in my life, I was honestly scared. He hesitated for a moment, shaking with rage, then he turned and walked out of the room. One of his young coaches was sitting next to me and he quietly said, "I wish he'd grabbed you, then I could have decked him." Puggie, once a popular coach, was not loved by many anymore. His time was over and it was rather sad.

During those years in Waldwick and even more in Roselle Park, my teacher/student relationships became rather fluid, frequently blurring the line between teacher and friend. I was the first "hippie" teacher so all the "hip" kids wanted to get into my classes, many of them working on the school plays with me as well. When the generational gap was created by the era, I was on the side of the kids, not the parents, protesting the Vietnam war, loving rock music, dressing in "mod" clothes and flashing the peace sign.

My bachelor apartment became a hangout for many of the students. They enjoyed my day-glow bedroom with posters of Jimmy Morrison and Jimi Hendrix lighting up the room with the black light. This bedroom was even being used for teen-sex assignations at times, with Gary bringing over his various girlfriends. In my red-white-blue kitchen, where everything in the room had to be of those colors, I often gave hair-cuts to the boys. They wanted to keep their long hair, so by giving them just a trim, they could tell their parents they got a hair-cut. Pot was smoked in my living room on countless occasions. The musical "Hair" was our favorite show and we all considered it the wave of the future. I was just "one of the guys" and it seemed perfectly natural to all of us.

I had traded in my VW bug for a flashy, yellow, Firebird convertible as soon as I moved to New Jersey. One weekend, Gary and a bunch of boys (all straight, by the way) came over to my apartment. We all got wasted, climbed into my car to drive down-the-shore for some amusement park fun. The effects of the grass made it seem like we drove and drove and drove until we finally reached the end of my apartment complex to see the diner across the street. "That's the BETTY LYNN", we yelled, "we're <u>only</u> at the Betty Lynn!"

Laughing all the way to Seaside Amusement Park, we got onto our favorite the ride that spun around, sticking it's patrons to the sides by centrifugal force. As we rose higher and higher, we sang the opening theme "2001 Space Odyssey", *Also Sprach Zarathustra*, at the top of our lungs. This was a teacher and his high school students! But hell, it was the 60s!

Stoned with Gary and his friend Bobby

Gary Cohen and I developed a close friendship which started even when he was a freshman. I was having a minor affair with one of his buddies at another school, and the boy and I felt bad about lying to Gary about our whereabouts when Gary wanted to do something with one of us. I was terrified to tell him what was really going on, and possibly spoil our budding friendship, but I felt it was necessary to do so. Therefore, one day I took him up to his bedroom, sat him down on his bed and enlightened him about my being gay and the relationship I was having with his friend. Being a nice Jewish boy in a nice Jewish home, he had never suspected this and was shocked when I told him. But he was quick to accept it, and it became an simple understanding in our friendship from then on. This talk and the change in our relationship showed how much I trusted him and how much he liked and respected me.

On my 33rd Birthday, my students threw a surprise birthday party for me in my apartment. Half of the Drama Club was there (the pot smoking half), and I was surprised and touched. The elaborate decorations included potato chips hidden EVERYwhere around the apartment, because I had a penchant for them as munchies. Days later I found chips in coffee mugs, under the sofa, and one taped over the shower-head. There was no alcohol at these parties, just a lot of pot smoking. For such an unforgettable birthday, I don't remember a thing.

The Olympus of our inspiration for life was the revolutionary musical *Hair*. Many of us had gone to see it's original production at the Public Theater, and felt that this was "where it was at!" Then it moved to Broadway, under Tom O'Horgan's direction, and I even took my Drama Club, a secret kept from many a parent. The play became the controversial loadstone between the generation gap.

Right after it opened on Broadway, the summer following Gary's junior year, he and several friends organized a production of *Hair* with high school and college students, along with a couple adults - me - enthusiastically included. They didn't have a script, but knew all the music and had seen it enough times to write their own script. Gary played Berger and directed, his friend Mark (the boy I'd had the fling with) was Claude. I played some small roles, including the Statue of Liberty on roller skates with a Playboy Magazine and a flashlight singing the "Star Spangled Banner", in falsetto. I also played a looter of war corpses singing the poignant duet "What a Piece of Work is Man" as we picked the pockets of the dead soldiers. The irony was so powerful that I had a difficult time not crying as I sang this beautiful song.

The cast was so excited by our rehearsals that we all wanted to actually perform the play for an audience. So Gary went to the office of the Broadway producer, Michael Butler, and pleaded with him to give us the rights. Wearing the guy down with his persistence, Butler finally consented, provided we didn't charge or publicize, a gesture that would absolutely in no way be granted today by any producer. But this was *Hair*, in the 70s.

We had been doing our rehearsing at Upsala College, a conservative, Lutheran school. When the powers-that-be looked in on a rehearsal they were horrified and virtually booted us out for "indecent material". Now we had no venue to do our show and we all were crushed. Fortunately, someone had a connection at Rutgers University, and they, being a more liberal organization, let us use their student recreation room. So that is where we put on our production of *Hair*, and it was an instant smash.

For both scheduled shows, we had so many people lined up around the campus, that I had to go out and tell half of them that the show was full up. They shouted in "protest" so we told them, "What the Hell – we'll do a third show!!" The audiences were so moved by this production that they stood and cheered all the numbers.

And at the end of the show, the cast walked through the audience on their arms of the chairs, while holding their hands and singing "Let the Sunshine In". There wasn't a dry eye in the house, including the cast's. I was bawling like a baby at every performance, as I grasped weeping audience member's hands. I've never had another theatrical experience like it.

I think this production captured and combined the best of the original Off Broadway and Broadway productions. For many years people would come up to me and enthuse that they had seen our *Hair* and it had changed their lives.

Hair directed by Gary Cohen, also center as Berger

 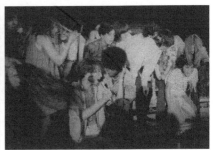

"What a piece of work is man....."   "Hair, hair, hair-hair-hair.."

*   *   *

My own creative juices were inspired by Gary when we made a collaborative Super 8 movie together called *The Peace Trilogy*. The three parts were divided by my making part one, Gary making part two, and both of us working together on part three. Since the Vietnam war protest was a part of our "revolutionary" mentality at the time, each part was our depiction of this idea.

I have always been a lover of animation, starting with *Pinocchio* at age four, so for my section I chose to do a stop-action animation movie. Photographing one frame at a time, I made a cartoon drama about the word "Peace". On my white, sheepskin rug, a pack of colorful construction paper appeared to have each piece of paper slide out and "cut itself" into a P, E, A, C and E. Then they arranged themselves into the word, followed by a cutout of a peace sign and a rose adjusted itself on top of the frame. Then an ominous kitchen knife appeared and slithered it's way to the paper letters, slicing them in half. At the devastation of word "PEACE", the rose shed a single tear.

For Gary's part, he made a still-photo collage with Life Magazine pictures of the horrors of war, political leaders, hippies, rock stars, and most important, symbols from the musical *Hair*. Most shots went from 18 frames to 6 frames, but as a joke, Gary put in a 2 frame shot of Dougie Goger's penis (shot in my living room, by the way). We wanted it to be a subliminal shot, knowing that no one would really register seeing that quick a shot in a movie.

Then for our joint venture, Gary and I took the camera into Manhattan. We spent a cold wintery day filming people holding up the two finger peace sign. Some people were cooperative, but some gave us the middle finger or angrily refused. But we managed to get all sorts of people: soldiers, nuns, business men, school groups of children and Eastside matrons to make the peace sign for us. Then we spent hours selecting and editing the footage, cut and glue style, into a movie.

When we were done with all three parts, we were very proud of the finished product. Since the project came out of the Drama Club, I showed it to the principal of the high school, Dale Springer, and he was quite pleased. He decided to show the movie to the whole school at an assembly. Through our excitement, we completely forgot about Dougie Goger's penis! After the showing, we got enthusiastic congratulations from everyone.

But Miss Wood, an old spinster, who had been head of the English Department for many years and my immediate boss, took the principal aside and said, "I believe I saw a naked penis included in that movie collage!" The principal called me into his office and asked if that was true. I blushed and admitted that the boys had done that short shot as a mini-protest of their own. Dale, a good guy (who I found out later got my ass out of many sticky situations) sat a minute and then let out a huge guffaw. "Why" he said "was Miss Wood, of all people, the only one who noticed it?" After we laughed awhile, he told me that if we were to exhibit this film later, under the name of Roselle Park High School, we had to take the offending frames out of the movie. I sadly agreed and told Gary. I think he held on to those two frames and re-inserted them at some later point, but I don't have that copy. Too bad.

THE PEACE TRILOGY

Part One,
  by David Umbach

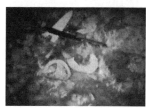  

Part Two,
  by Gary Cohen

Part Three,

by Gary & David

I went on to make two other films on my own after Gary graduated and went off to college. My favorite consists of cleverly shot scenes, some with stop action, that were edited to fit exactly to the lyrics of Carole King's *You've Got a Friend*, as sung by James Taylor. I used my student/friend Peter Adams and my current boyfriend, Alan Tulin as the "friends". I took them all over the place; from Greenwich Village, to "down-the-shore", to a baseball diamond, and to a cemetery. They acted out each line from the song, in an amusingly, literal way.

For example, when it says, "They'll hurt you, desert you, they'll take you soul if you let them." We showed one boy on the beach being beaten with a towel by the other, then he magically disappeared, then come back and steal the boy's sandal. And their clothes instantly changed on "Winter, Spring, Summer and Fall". We had such fun making that film and I still love watching it. Later I over-dubbed James Taylor's singing with my own, with Gary playing guitar, which made it even more personal.

YOU'VE GOT
A FRIEND

a film by
David Umbach
song by
Carole King

The Diner was the last movie I ever made. It was a serious, dramatic story, with Peter Adams as a nasty biker, who robs and terrorizes the proprietor of a small diner. We find out at the end that the boy is the man's son. We used a lovely little diner in Roselle Park as the location, and I got a excellent New York actor to play the father. It's well acted, and for a Super 8 movie, I think it tells the story quite well, even if the camera work is a bit artsy-fartsy.

THE DINER, a film by David Umbach

I've always felt so lucky that I spent my thirties in that '60's environment, because I was able to be an adult, but experience the "youth revolution". The Sixties and Seventies were lots of fun, but they fucked up lots of kids. I hope I helped some of my students wend their way through that tricky era without it harming them.

*   *   *

Of all the "highs" (in every sense of the word) during my high school teacher years, the highest was the cross-country trip that Gary and I took together the summer after he graduated. The two of us, with long hair and "hippie" attire, set off in my yellow Firebird convertible for the West Coast taking the whole summer for the trip, there and back. Gary had never been west of Pennsylvania and I'd never been west of Illinois, so it was an adventure for both of us.

In Chicago we stayed with my parents in Highland Park, but not for long since they didn't have a lot of room in their house and I didn't feel that they really approved of our hippiedom, either. We did tour a little of Chicago and one day, as we cruised down the Outer Drive after finishing a joint, we spotted a billboard with a huge, three dimensional cow sticking out of it. I howled from the open, yellow convertible, "I'm a Yellow Moo-Moo", which caused stoned hilarity for hours. This became a catch phrase for the rest of the trip.

Then at the Chicago Theater we saw the new movie *Start the Revolution Without Me,* with Gene Wilder and Donald Sutherland, in which Hugh Griffin, as King Louis XIV, wandered around a dress ball in a chicken costume, apologizing heartily to everyone through his beak, "I thought it was a costume ball. I thought it was a costume ball." We thought it was the most hilarious movie ever made.

Leaving Chicago we had to drive through the Great Plains of Illinois, Iowa and Nebraska which seemed endless and we weren't even high through most of it. Just miles and miles of straight, flat highways with corn or wheat on either side. It was so boring. Even though Gary had never seen this type of landscape before, it still became tiresome in a short time.

When we got to Omaha, which was at least a city, we got a motel and decided just to take pizza and some beers into the room, crash and watch TV. There was a bar nearby that sold pizza so we went in and sauntered up to the bar to order. Suddenly we realized that the noisy room had gone deathly quiet and everyone was staring at us. We stood there with our long hair and colorful attire (I may even have been wearing my American flag shirt) and we were in the middle of a redneck, trucker bar, at a time before even bikers had long hair.

Although I was scared to death, I croaked out, "We'd like a pepperoni pizza, please and a six-pack." The bartender just stared at us and there wasn't a sound in the room. Fearlessly, Gary plopped down on a bar stool, leaned over to the bartender and proclaimed, "I thought it was a costume ball." I am sure the bartender had not seen the movie, but it seemed to break the tension, and he nodded and called our order into the kitchen. We waited nervously at the bar for our pizza, while the patrons eyed us hostilely. Finally we hastily made our exits and were very glad to have gotten out alive. But in the car we burst into hysterical laughter. I still think that was the funniest quip Gary has ever made, in a lifetime of funny quips.

One of my favorite stories, that defines me, as well as Gary, happened at the Grand Canyon. We were so happy to get out of the plains, going through Denver and being awed by the Rocky Mountains, we decided to visit this great national monument on our way to California. Yes, there is some breathtaking scenery in Colorado and Utah, but as we got into the deserts of Arizona, it got a bit barren for us, so we were looking forward to the spectacle of the Grand Canyon.

When we arrived, in the late afternoon, the parking lot was full, so our walk to the canyon was hot and long. We finally reached the viewing area (predating the see-through Sky Walk), peered out over the vast expanse, looking left, looking right, then looking at each other, I said, "Let's go to Vegas!" Gary nodded in agreement, and we headed back to the car. I fear that is my taste in touring, even today: glitz and show-biz over scenery, any day. As a boy, when my parents would take a Sunday drive with the family just to look at the scenery, I uttered a similar sentiment: "You seen one tree, you seen 'em all."

But Vegas was magic! Gary's father, who worked in the entertainment concession trade, had friends in Vegas so he arranged for us to get free tickets to several big shows. And although neither of us were gamblers, the atmosphere of the casinos, seedy though it was, just thrilled us. We were able to see headliners like Dean Martin, Todie Fields and Tom Jones, but our favorite show was Don Rickles. OMG he was so funny! And to think that he's still insulting audiences for laughs, well into his 80's.

Gary and I were aware of the each other's sexual tastes – blonds (girls for him, boys for me). So we would each keep an eye out for someone that the other might enjoy "cruising". I would nudge him when a cute girl would be coming, and he'd elbow me for a cute guy. We loved it when a pair of cuties came towards us and we'd shout, "Both Great!"

We didn't "hook up" much during our summer together, but Gary befriended a chorus girl from the production of *Hair* in Vegas at our hotel. He waited for her in his room for what he hoped was a "night of love", but she never showed. Depressed by this, he consoled himself with playing a slot machine, and ended up hitting a pretty good jackpot as a consolation prize. I, however, did get lucky in Vegas. I met up with a guy there that I had known on the Jersey shore and he invited me up to his apartment for the evening. I turned out to be less than a good idea, since when I got back to New Jersey, I found out had given me the clap.

After this eventful time in Las Vegas, it was then on to Hollywood, our primary goal. I had written to my Uncle Chuck that we were coming and he said that we could stay at his place in Beverly Hills. We zipped through the roasting desert and arrive at my Uncle's home in "lower" Beverly Hills. By lower, I mean that it was not the "Home of the Stars", by any means. He just had a bungalow in a fairly seedy part of Los Angeles which was officially in Beverly Hills, but way at the bottom of the hill. We got there in the evening, hot and tired from long drive through the desert, and my uncle was nowhere to be found. We ended up breaking and entering through a window, found a room with a carpet, and fell asleep. My uncle came home to find two hippies sound asleep in his den.

Luckily, my Uncle Chuck was a fun, liberal guy, who greeted us in the morning with pancakes and a big smile. He couldn't wait to take us for a tour up into upper Beverly Hills, so after breakfast we crammed into his VW Bug and took off for his tour of the Homes of the Stars. It turned out to be one of the most terrifying rides I have ever taken outside an amusement park.

Uncle Chuck was tall and had to scrunch himself into the driver's seat, while I was in the front seat, desperately holding the dashboard, with Gary in the back clinging for dear life to the back of my seat, because in those days there were no seat belts. My uncle was a brake-clutch-shift-accelerator-brake-again kind of driver, speeding around those curves up and down the hills while he pointed out the sights, never seeming to look at the road. But he was so proud to be able to show us the famed Beverly Hills that we couldn't complain. We just held on tight, trying to keep our pancakes down.

I was excited to see my cousin Marianne, Chuck's daughter, whom I hadn't seen in many years. She was then married and lived in Orange County with a man I didn't know. We spent an awkward afternoon in her home and it was upsetting to see a different woman than I remembered, the Married Marianne. It was a strained visit, and I didn't know if it was because of my "hippie" attire and Gary, or that Marianne was not comfortable in her new life. She just wasn't the same as my dear childhood friend.

Years later, I was happy to see that she was her old self again, the liberated woman, after divorcing her husband, moving back to Illinois and marrying an old flame from high school.

Fortunately, I had a connection into the real Hollywood, because I reunited with an old acting buddy from New York that had moved to the West Coast and made a successful career as a set designer for television. Vince Tampio, who had been an alternative Genie in *Aladdin*, was one of the warmest and funniest people I've ever known. He welcomed us into his apartment for several nights and escorted us around town in style.

The most exciting part of his tour was taking us to the home of famed producer Joseph Pasternak, most famous for introducing Mario Lanza in *The Great Caruso*. His house in Beverly Hills was the kind you dream about, with hundreds of photos and paintings of movie stars, a gilded grand piano and a huge swimming pool. Mr. Pasternak was very old by then and we didn't even meet him, but Vince had the run of his house and pool, so we spent several afternoons with beautiful young actors lounging poolside, drinking exotic drinks brought by a servant. We were told that Mr. Pasternak observed the youthful parade in his back yard from his bedroom window upstairs.

While in Hollywood, Gary and I went dancing in gay clubs on several occasions, heard an excessively loud rock concert at the Filmore West, saw Burt Bachrach at the Greek Theater (with the opening act by The Carpenters), and spent a riotous day at Disneyland on mescaline.

After enjoying the Hollywood sights, Gary and I had a reason to go to San Diego, because a classmate of Gary's, Lisa Flammia, was visiting her family there and we wanted to meet up with her. Lisa was a major force in our high school theater department and I enjoyed her company enormously, so we headed south. After we got to her place, we all thought it would be fun to go across the border to Tijuana. So the three of us hopped into the Yellow Moo Moo and headed for Mexico.

We were told not to bring our car into Tijuana, that parking it there was likely to have it vandalized or stolen. So we parked in a huge lot on the U.S. side, and walked to the border crossing.

Our first obstacle was the United States Customs. None of us had passports, because they weren't needed in those days to visit Tijuana, but you did have to check in with the authorities. Their obvious question was "Who is this under-aged girl you are taking across the border?" "A student, I'm her drama teacher in New Jersey ", I said proudly with my long hair and '60's clothes. Needless to say, they would have none of that and we were denied exit from the States.

So, disappointed, we got our car out of the lot and had to drop Lisa back to San Diego. But Gary and I didn't want to give up our excursion into Mexico, so back to the parking lot we went and easily got through U.S. customs. But now we hit the office of Mexican Customs. They took one look at us and firmly, if not viciously, said "No Heepie!"

"What?" I cried, "I'm a teacher from New Jersey!"

"No Heepie! No long hair!"

Then Gary actually said to this humorless border guard, "I eat tacos....?".

The response was the same, "No Heepie!" So back to the car we went.

Undaunted, we went into a gift shop and bought some leather hats. We stuffed our hair into the hats, changed into less colorful shirts, put the top down on the Firebird convertible, and drove to the border cross-point. We sailed through both customs stops, the Mexicans being more than happy to have rich American tourists come to spend money in their country.

Tijuana was a pretty crappy town after all the trouble getting there. The most amusing thing was how often we were approached by the people with "Hey, Hippie, wanna buy a watch? (or grass? or girls?)" We did buy some stuff, including a red, white and blue, stained-glass ceiling lamp, which went into my red, white and blue kitchen, and even now hangs in my den. Our car was unmolested and we exited Mexico with no problems at all.

Of course Gary and I were always looking for theatrical events and the two that stand out in our trip were both in San Francisco. In a small, Off Broadway-like theater we saw a production of *One Flew Over the Cuckoo's Nest*. I'd seen the play in New York with Kirk Douglas and had not been too impressed with it, although I had loved the book. Unlike Broadway, this production was brilliantly done and was performed intimately, in-the-round. William Duvane gave a stunning performance as McMurphy, but most memorable was a dwarfish, little guy who ran around with hilarious hyper-energy as Martini. He was wonderful, but I thought it was a shame that such a good actor should be so short and therefore probably never make it in the real world – his name, I later realized, was Danny DeVito.

The other great theater experience was Paul Sills' *Story Theater*. Using his now-famous improvisational style, this Chicago-based ensemble troupe told Grimm's stories with actors narrating the story while acting out all the roles. This was all revolutionary to us at the time and made for extremely exciting theater. Among the ensemble members were: Valerie Harper, Linda Lavin, Paul Sand, Peter Boyle and Melinda Dillon, who were all unknowns at the time. In years to come I would direct or act in several productions of "Story Theater" and teach Paul Sills' use of Theater Games in my classes.

The drive back to the East Coast was mind-numbingly boring. We made no interesting stops, just driving long days to get as far as we could. The summer of fun was definitely over and we were anxious to get back to New Jersey, but it left us both with one of the best summers we'd ever know. And it bonded Gary and me for a lifetime of friendship.

* * *

Before he went off to college, Gary and I attended several 70s theatrical experiences in New York. Inspired by *Hair* and the new freedom for sexuality in theater, many Off Broadway plays featured nudity. Gary and my more progressive high school students were excited by this and sought it out whenever possible. So when we spotted the ad in the New York Times for the play *An Artist's Life,* which featured "Frequent and Prolonged Nudity", it sparked our interest.

One Saturday afternoon, lured by the ad, Gary, Paul Kaye and I trekked into lower Manhattan in search of this play. We found the address on 14th Street, with no marquee, just a small sign pointing to a long flight of stairs leading to a seedy lobby. Behind the box office window was a middle aged woman, with a Tallulah Bankhead voice, who eagerly sold us tickets. Tacked up in the lobby were photographs from the play, showing an artist painting a very beautiful model, who was obviously naked. Tallulah-Voice told us to come back at 7:30, when the theater would be open. The boys were excited by the photos and we all went out for a bite anticipating a titillating theatrical experience.

When we returned, we were greeted again by Tallulah-Voice who took our tickets and told us to take any seats we wanted. The intimate stage was surrounded by two rows of chairs and we eagerly took our seats in the front row. On the stage was an easel and a rolling, fold up bed. After about 20 other theater goers joined us, Tallulah-Voice came on stage to make an announcement. She welcomed us and introduced herself as the playwright, Amy P. Bell. She proudly announced that there would be a replacement in the cast, and the part of the model was now being played by herself. Gary and Paul were not happy about this, as the actress in the photos was much younger and prettier.

When the play began, the "artist" discussed with a friend how he was besotted with his new model, describing her as the most beautiful woman he'd ever known. When this exposition finished, in walks Amy Bell, who was definitely over-the-hill and perhaps the worst actress I'd ever seen. Mincing and indicating around the stage, she then proceeded to remove her clothes and drape herself on or around the bed, "posing" for the artist's painting. After some more pretentious dialogue, where the artist professes his love for her, there was an act break.

The three of us went out into the lobby to hear the reactions of the rest of the audience. Even though Amy Bell was now selling refreshments, the comments were as scathing as we were feeling. Being aware that the whole audience felt the same way about the play, and the leading lady, made it easier to go back into the auditorium, because we needed to see what the rest of the play had in store. We all wished that Miss Bell would keep her clothes on for this act, but we didn't have much hope.

The second act continued where the first had left off, and now it came time for the seduction. This of course led to the artist removing his clothes and he was no Adonis either, much to my disappointment. After Miss Bell removed the sheet she was wearing, she sat on the bed, this time in profile for us, and her stomach pouched out in a most unattractive way. The two actors badly simulated sex on the creaky bed. It was excruciatingly embarrassing. But it was also hilarious, and Gary, Paul and I were beginning to loose control of our giggles.

Since we were just a few feet from the actors, I didn't want to hurt their feelings, so I held my pea coat in front of my mouth, biting into it to cover the laughter. I almost bit a hole through the thick fabric. The three of us were silently laughing and shaking the chairs that we were sitting on, trying to hold it in. When the play ended, we applauded loudly and then rushed down the long flight of stairs. When we reached the sidewalk, we collapse on it with hilarity. On our drive home, we had to pull over to the side of the road because we were laughing so hard, as we recalled the most outrageous moments of this ghastly play.

The experience was so special that immediately after I got home, I wrote a letter Miss Amy Bell, complimenting her on her performance and asking her to send an autographed photograph of herself – signing the letter, Gary Cohen, with his address. I wish I'd been there when the picture arrived.

The term "Frequent and Prolonged Nudity" has stayed with me as a catch phrase for truly tacky theater.

But by no means was *An Artist's Life* typical of the theater that we saw in Lower Manhattan during that period. Some of it was absolutely brilliant, like Performance Group's *Dionysis '69*, where innovative and powerful story telling, along with excellent acting (as well as nudity) told the tale of Dionysis' life and death. Or Julie Bovossa's hilarious *Moondreamers*, a bizarre comedy at Café La MaMa, that featured "Dr. Ababa - the first doctor in the phone book" and "a Truly Rotten Chorus".

The "birth" and "death" of Dionysis, in Performance Group's <u>Dionysis '69</u>

The 1970s was an inspirational era for the theater and for the joy of life. I was of an age that I might not have been able to take part in it, being an adult and a teacher. But because I embraced the 70s culture, for good or bad, and joined the students instead of the parents in this generational war, I was able to experience it to the full.

Eleven

First Hippie on LBI

I had two interesting summer jobs during this period. The first was working at the Cape Cod Melody Tent in Hyannis as manager of the concessions stand, a job that Gary's father, Elliot Cohen, arranged for me. I took a boy I'd been dating with me to help with the concession job. We rented an apartment that we were told Elaine Stritch had rented the previous year, and we ensconced ourselves into the world of summer stock.

It was a wild and wacky summer. The job of preparing and selling concessions wasn't exciting, but the fascinating part was being able to observe the goings on at this professional, summer stock theater. One well known star was cast in each show, like Donald O'Conner in *Promises, Promises*, Jean-Pierre Aumont in *Fanny*, and Mitzi Gaynor in her own show, *The Mitzi Gaynor Show*.

Sad to say, at that time of his life, Donald O'Conner had a terrible drinking problem. It showed every night in his erratic performance. Everyone was excited to see Mitzi's show and we wanted to impress her at how professional our theater was. Therefore, the hard working apprentices stayed up all night painting the round stage to look like a tufted, pink cushion. Being theater-in-the-round, the painted pink cushion would be the primary scenery for this one-woman show.

The next morning Miss Gaynor arrived with her entourage, including a husband who's job it turned out to be to follow her around apologizing to the people she screamed at and offended. The scenic designer and the kids who had arduously painted her stage waited to hear her reaction, expecting her to be ecstatic. She shouted, "Who put all that pink shit on my stage? I want it painted over in black!"

After much ranting and raving, her show opened and although nobody could stand her, we had to admire how beautiful she looked and what an entertaining show she performed. I remember her interrupting some song or intro she was making with a spontaneous cry, "I quite smoking!" The audience would cheer her bravery and candidness. Of course, this was part of the act and she made the same "spontaneous cry" every night in the same place.

Every night just before her show her dresser would come to my concession stand with an empty pitcher and coffee pot. She'd ask me to fill each one with ice and then she took them back to Mitzi's dressing room. On closing night I just had to ask, "What does she want the ice for?"

The dresser, who was not any more fond of Mitzi than anybody else, said, "She rubs ice on her tits just before she goes on stage, to make them stand up and out."

Well, I couldn't leave this alone, so I got some masking tape and put a label on each container saying, "For the Right One" and "For the Left One". Forevermore she will be referred to by me as "Titsy Mitzi".

Jean-Pierre Aumont was known in Hollywood as a famous ladies man having had romances with the likes of Maria Montez, Paulette Goddard and Grace Kelly, including several marriages. Now in his late sixties, he was still a handsome man. He was cheerful and charming, and was always friendly with me and my boyfriend in the concessions stand. He would stop and chat every time he passed the stand. Hearing all this Hollywood gossip, I was thrilled, but the boy was shy around any of the famous people. Nearing the end of the run of *Fanny*, Jean-Pierre asked me if I'd like to have dinner with him after his closing show. Surprised, I told him that I would love to and could I bring my friend, to which he said, "Of course". I told the boy about our dinner invitation, but he was too nervous to go, so I went alone.

I took a taxi to the hotel where he stayed and went up to his room where he told me to meet him before dinner. When I came into the room, he was standing by the fireplace, in a smoking jacket, leaning on the mantel and holding a glass of champagne and a cigarette in a long holder. He appeared to have stepped right out of a 1940s romance movie. Then with his charming, but smarmiest, French accent he proceeded to woo and ultimately try to seduce me. I was shocked. I had never imagined that he had any interest in me sexually, just as someone to talk movies with. He was such a famous heterosexual!

I wasn't the least bit attracted to him and I felt very embarrassed for him: *did this corny routine still work on anybody?* After several clumsy attempts, I warded him off with the excuse that I never cheated on my boyfriend. He accepted this with grace. He dressed, and we had a lovely dinner in the hotel dining room, chatting about Hollywood again, without any reference to what had happened upstairs.

* * *

The second summer job was with my two friends from Theater World Four, Mary and Thelma, who decided they wanted to open a hippie/head shop on Long Beach Island, New Jersey. It would be based on the many shops in Greenwich Village that sold rock and movie star personality posters, wildly colored day-glow posters, anti-Vietnam War banners, pro-pot tee-shirts, anti-establishment buttons and bumper stickers, and marijuana paraphernalia. Being that LBI was a rather conservative place, Mary and Thelma knew that the marijuana items would have to be kept to a minimum, but they hoped all the youth-oriented stuff of the era would be popular with the kids on this family vacation spot.

They asked me if I would come down for the summer and handle the poster section of the store. I thought it would be a hoot, and a paid summer down-the-shore seemed like an excellent idea, so I accepted.

Long Beach Island is indeed a long, sandbar island off the coast of New Jersey, with beaches along the entire ocean side of the island. There is only one entry by automobile via a causeway at the middle of the island that connects to the mainland. The bay side is covered with homes and boating docks, where hundreds of sailboats and motorboats are stored. The island has one road that goes from one end to the other, the Boulevard, and the island varies from two blocks to five blocks wide at different points. Thousands of primary and summer homes fill the island, from Barnegat Lighthouse on the north to the town of Beach Haven on the south.

Mary and Thelma picked a prominent location in a new mini-mall right off the causeway and rented a two-story unit, that had a wooden staircase in front leading up to the second floor. The downstairs room would be for Mary and Thelma to sell all the buttons, tee-shirts and fun hippie stuff. The upstairs would be my domain, exclusively devoted to the posters that were so popular at the time. They named the store after our first Theater World Four success, STOP THE WORLD.

We spent time before the season, setting up the place. On the second floor I constructed a raised platform that held the cash register, and was decorated with day-glow paint and posters making it a sort of go-go box for me to overlook everybody and take the money from the customers. A black light and a strobe light was installed to give the room a disco feel, with the controls for the lights and music up in my booth, so that I could change the atmosphere as I wished. The walls were completely covered with all the posters that were on sale. Everything from Paul Newman and Robert Redford in "Butch Cassidy and the Sundance Kid" to bikinied Ursula Andress in "Dr. No"; from Jimmy Morrison to Jimi Hendrix to Mary Poppins to Janis Joplin; and brightly colored day-glo Andy Warhol or Peter Max posters. When it was done, the place had an exciting mod-60's feel that we knew was totally new to Long Beach Island.

This was my long-haired period, so I thought that while selling in this store I should emphasize the hippie look with my clothes and accoutrements. Mary gave me a batik mu-mu that I wore on the cooler days and evenings, or short shorts and beads in the hotter days. So, complete with headband and bracelets, I would fit beautifully into any cast of *Hair*.

Since LBI is more a Philadelphia and South Jersey based resort than New York, the vacationers were less sophisticated and not really familiar with the "hippie" thing. Therefore, Stop the World was a real novelty for most of the vacationers. I'm sure most of the people had never been to Greenwich Village and never seen a "head shop", so they came into our place with fascination and awe.

My upper room in particular was a magnet, especially for all the teenagers. I had rock music playing constantly and I would stand up on my go-go pedestal, turn on the strobe light and dance the frug and mash potato, and the kids ate it up. Sometimes my room was so crowded, people had trouble moving around, but we sold lots of posters. Summer homes need cheering up and the adults liked the personality posters with movie stars, while the teenagers liked the rock stars and day-glow posters. And every evening, when people got off the beach and needed something to do, my poster room was a popular place to come and hang out.

I made two friends that summer that made my work-vacation even more enjoyable. My daytime friend, Timmy, was an 8 year old urchin from a very poor family nearby the shop. He and his family lived on the island year-round and Timmy had to care for his younger, mentally challenged brother while his mother was at work. Having grown up on the island, the beach held no pleasures for Timmy, and his brother wasn't allowed to go there anyway, for fear he would wander into the water. Therefore Timmy, having nothing to do all day but hang around the store, attached himself to me all summer and I thoroughly enjoyed his company.

On the "beach days" when business was slow, we played games or we just talked and joked. He had a sharp sense of humor for a little kid and he kept me laughing all summer. I would also buy his brother and him lunch most days, because it was obvious Timmy didn't have the resource to get it on his own.

My nighttime friend, Scott, was different matter entirely. Long Beach Island is not known for having much of a gay life, at least an obvious one, so I never saw many gay men in the store (at least attractive ones) and very few on the rest of the island either. My shop was often crowded with shirtless teenagers in shorts, so there was lots of eye-candy, but that's all.

One evening I noticed a beautiful blond boy hanging around much longer than the usual customer and he seemed to be looking at me more than the posters. Then he was back the next night and stayed even longer. I didn't want to be the aggressor, as it could cause major legal problems for the store and for me if I was wrong about him, so I contented myself with just watching him when he came in the store.

On the fourth night that he came in, he approached me and asked what I did after the store closed and would I like to go out for a drink or something. *Would I ever!* So we went out that night and found we were quite compatible, and became friends for the rest of the summer.

Scott turned out to be a sophomore in college and was staying with his family for the summer. He basically hated coming to LBI because it had been the family summer vacation place every year since he was young. He was completely out of the closet to himself and his college friends, and was lonely on LBI because it was so straight. He had hoped that I was gay and wondered if we could spend time together. And we did -- almost every night, in fact, we managed to at least take long walks along the beach, if not go back to my rented room to be more intimate. We also had some hot encounters in the dunes, late at night. Our time together in this delightful summer romance, made my stay on LBI much more enjoyable than it could have been.

The front of Stop The World, with Scott on my daisy-covered VW bug

Mary, Thelma and I in the downstairs store

Scott upstairs in my poster room

With my young friend Timmy

    The following year Mary and Thelma moved Stop the World to a larger mall in Beach Haven and I chose not to work there. I had done my summer at the shore. Along with a strobe-lit disco, LBI now had several "hippie" shops, following our influence. The new Stop the World primarily specialized in custom-made Hoppi coats, that Thelma created, and it was not the same exciting place that it was that initial year.

When I visited that summer, I felt badly that I couldn't hang out with Timmy, though I did see him a couple of times. Scott chose not to come to his parents summer house that year, but stayed in Las Vegas where he attended cooking school. I saw him when Gary and I passed through Vegas on our cross-country road trip.

Though I am not a "beach" person, and thus don't go there often anymore, I will always treasure my time on LBI. The thrills, the affairs, the friendships. And although the island has changed over the years with new families, new stores, and new homes, the spirit of the island still remains. Even the tragedy of Hurricane Sandy, which caused immense devastation and destruction for many on Long Beach Island, could never strip it of its spirit and sense of "summer vacation down-the-shore". I will never forget that summer when I was the first hippie on Long Beach Island.

Eight

Look, Ma, I'm a Professional Actor

During this period I was lucky to have two long-run, professional acting gigs that were great fun. The first came from my downstairs neighbor Freddie Grades who worked with The Prince Street Players. This was a highly regarded and popular children's theater company, that produced successful musicals of classic children's stories. Jim Eiler and Jeanne Bargy wrote Broadway-style music with delightfully campy scripts, beloved by kids and adults alike. The Players toured around the East Coast, playing in summer stock theaters from New York to Boston to Albany to Philadelphia, doing our shows in the afternoon on the sets of the adult plays that would play in the evening. Freddie was able to get me an audition and I was fortunate to gain a spot in the company. I worked with this company for two years and learned more about being a professional actor in that time than any school had ever taught me.

We rehearsed in a loft on Prince Street in the Village and on the night before we left on tour with a new play, friends and local denizen would bring their children for the dress rehearsal. The audiences went wild for these hilarious and sophisticated shows. My initial role was Mr. Stitch, one of the two tailors (the other being Mr. Sew) in *Emperor's New Clothes*, singing, "Stitch and Sew, Sew and Stitch, who is who and which is which....". Later I played Gepetto, in *Pinocchio*, which was a nostalgic trip for me, The Prince in *Sleeping Beauty* and The Emperor-of-All-China, in *Aladdin.* I played them all in repertory for two exciting and exhausting seasons.

"Stitch and Sew, Sew and Stitch, who is who and which is which....".

Freddie as Aladdin with The Emperor-of-All-China

One summer we toured all the New York City parks with *Pinocchio*, and we discovered that the audiences in each of the five boroughs had completely different personalities. In Central Park we got mostly sophisticated, white audiences from upper-middle class families, with children who were theatrically savvy. They got all the subtler humor and treated the story as a serious drama. In Prospect Park in Brooklyn, the children were ethnically diverse and the reactions were confusing. The kids seemed to love the story, but were much more vocal about it, yelling encouragement to Pinocchio and laughing loudly at the slapstick.

But it was playing Gepetto for the children in the Bronx that was the most heart-warming for me. It was evident that a number of these children had harsh family lives, so they adored this good-natured father figure, who seemed to me to be the real hero of the play for them. When we did our "meet & greet" after the play, these kids, most of whom had never seen live theater before, were amazed by the fact that we were not cartoons. They were dumb-struck as they passed us and would reach out to touch our costumes, making sure we were real. They had no idea about asking for autographs or making comments. And the circle around Gepetto was the biggest, which I loved.

*After a performance of <u>Pinocchio</u> in Central Park
with great comedienne, Marcie Stringer*

    I had hoped to play the Emperor-of-All-China in the CBS-TV presentation of *Aladdin*, but Jim Eiler's lover got the part and I was just a guard and a magic tree in the cave. I also was one of the black hooded figures that change the set pieces, who in "kabuki theater" are supposed to be invisible. These were not the most exciting parts in the play, to say the least. We spent three grueling days rehearsing and filming the musical under the hot studio lights needed for television in those days. It was my first experience doing this kind of work, and with the hours of waiting and sweating, it formed my dislike of movie/TV making that I have felt my whole life. Give me live theater any day.

    The cave tree costume was hot, heavy and horrible. Once I was in the costume, I had to stand the entire time covered in black material except for my head, which had a tree mask and headdress. One arm was exposed, which held up a heavy branch. The other hand was under the black cloth holding onto to a bar, which was my only means of support. At one point during the long, long shooting of that scene, my nose began to itch unbearably, but I had no hand free to scratch it. The director, who was a well known TV director at the time, came by and I squealed, "Help, please scratch my nose!" So he reached up under my mask and did so. Quite embarrassing.

When the black and white show was finally aired, the whole cast gathered in our grubby loft and huddled around a tiny TV set to view the first Prince Street Player's TV show. We were pretty pleased with how it came out. Freddie looked great as Aladdin, Jim's boyfriend was good (if not great) as the Emperor-of-All-China, and Victoria Mallory (who went on to play the original role of Anne in *A Little Night Music*) was beautiful as the Princess. Regrettably, the woman they cast as Aladdin's mother came off as a man in drag, which she wasn't, and I was recognizable only once, when I walked in front of the camera as a guard. That was my one and only time on National Television, and I never had any inclinations to audition for TV work after that.

As much as I loved my time touring with Prince Street Players, it wasn't all fun and games. We were picked up by a van as early as 5:00 AM and drove to the various venues for the show, sometimes 4 hours away. All of us would set up the stage, perform two shows in a hot tent, and then drive back. The major entertainment on those drives was reading, and one summer I finished the entire "Lord of the Rings" series.

One year we did a production of *Snow White Goes West*, the only fairytale that was updated, but it worked quite well. The "dwarves" were all tall dancers, playing the miners, and they were given energetic and difficult choreography. It was a running joke with the company that I was a non-dancer. I told everyone that during the TV shoot of *Aladdin* that I was tapping like crazy under the cave tree costume. So although I really wanted to be one of the dancing dwarves, I had to be the Cowboy Narrator instead. I had to watch the great dance routines in rehearsal, standing with my cowboy boot on the barrel, waiting to narrate. I would jokingly say as they whirled past me, "I wanna be a dwarf, I wanna be a dwarf."

The choreography was done with lots of circles, because we staged it primarily for tent theater, in-the-round. When we got to our first theater, we found that we were to perform on the set of *On a Clear Day You Can See Forever*. The set designer had placed on the circular stage a small, circular platform, *off center*, and it was immovable. So the poor dancers, doing the circular routines, had to jump up and around this inconveniently placed platform, trying desperately not to trip on it. As they whizzed past me at my barrel, I whispered, "I'm glad I'm not a dwarf, I'm glad I'm not a dwarf."

The year that CBS bought the Prince Street plays for television, Jim Eiler felt that much of our silliness was getting too gay. A lot of the humor that we put in for the adults involved camping it up, and my Mr. Stitch was no exception. One rehearsal when I was being particularly silly with Mr. Stitch, Jim said to me "More balls, David, more balls!" At which point the hilarious comedienne and fellow cast mate Marcie Stringer yelled, "PROPS!" This got a huge laugh from all of us, but I was particularly delighted one night in Sardi's to hear someone tell that story in the next booth. Proudly I turned around and said, "That was me!"

Aladdin was by far the most fun to play, partially because of the brilliant actor, Will B. Able, who most often played the Genii. This 6' 6" vaudevillian-pro never said the same jokes twice on stage and was screamingly funny. Trying to keep a straight face when playing opposite him in a scene was almost impossible. Also the trips to and from the theaters were non-stop laughing, if you got to travel in Will's car. I don't think I've ever known anyone who was "on" all the time, like he was. My friend Vince Tampio played the Genii sometimes, and he was also a hoot. Plus I got the chance to play the Emperor-of-All-China with my black shoestring mustache, so it was definitely my favorite of the Prince Street musicals.

* * *

The other professional acting job I got was in a production of *The Fantasticks*, which turned out to be the first of ten productions of *The Fantasticks* I would be involved with over the years (so far). I had seen the original production on Sullivan Street in the Village many times and I fell in love with it. Baritone Jerry Orbach played the original El Gallo and I certainly didn't see myself in that role at the time.

It was in June when Reynolds auditioned to play Matt in some out of town production. He was to replace an actor who had to leave in August. They cast Reynolds for August, but also they asked him if he knew of anyone who was free to play El Gallo - right away. He recommended me, believing that I wouldn't be cast or that I wouldn't be able to go. I don't have the low a baritone voice that is needed for El Gallo and I was definitely too young, but they were desperate so they cast me.

The production was in San Juan, Puerto Rico and I had to leave *immediately*. I had just begun a new teaching job and I needed to get permission to leave a week before school was out. Fortunately, this job was to teach drama, so when I told the principal that I was cast in a play in San Juan for the whole summer, he was impress and released me. So off I went, alone, to Puerto Rico to begin rehearsals for my first adult professional industry gig.

The Fantasticks was scheduled to open only two weeks after I arrived, in the Peacock Room of the Caribe Hilton Hotel. It was a basement dining room, which they half-heartedly converted into a theater, that looked out onto a garden with real peacocks strolling around. Our rehearsals were held in a gorgeous house in the suburbs, up on a mountain. We rehearsed in the "music room", a glass enclosed structure that overhung the jungle on tall stilts and looked out at the blue-green ocean. The view was magnificent, particularly at sunset!

It wasn't an easy musical to learn in two weeks, and our director had never seen the production in New York or anywhere else. He was also a radio director, so he listened more that watched, and those of us who knew the show were easily frustrated by many of his choices. He didn't like any pauses, even though we filled them with acting that he didn't see. But, as contracted, we worked hard and all too soon we moved into that beautiful hotel on the Condado, a sandy strip with many luxurious hotels. We were only allowed two dress rehearsals in the theater. All of us extremely nervous, we opened on a Friday night, to a small, but very enthusiastic crowd of American tourists. Everyone seemed to accept my youth and tenor voice, and I got excellent reviews in the local papers. And so my fabulous summer in the tropics began.

The Caribe Hilton Hotel, where I played El Gallo for the first time.

I rented a small bungalow on the beach, a short bus ride from the hotel, but I spent most of my days at the Caribe Hilton in their pool or on their beach. We would do the show at 8:00 PM, go out partying, sometimes until dawn, sleep until noon, go to the pool, do the show and start all over again. *This was a job? What a life!* And this went on all summer. Reynolds joined the cast in August and it was the vacation of a lifetime – and we were paid for it. There was an airplane strike that summer, so many tourists were stranded and looked for more entertainment, so they came to our show. Our poster was up all over town with our picture, so we became sort of celebrities around the pool or when we went out at night. This was the life of a professional actor - sheer heaven.

An amusing thing happened during that run. One night while Louisa was saying in her opening monologue: "One morning a bird woke me up, it was a lark or a peacock...", a peacock outside in the garden gave a loud squawk, and the audience (and cast) got a huge laugh out of that.

At the top of the hotel was the "big room" where real celebrities performed, and we were able to go up and see their late show for free. I loved hearing Jose Feliciano, the blind guitarist/singer, whose "Light My Fire" was a big hit at the time. But my favorite entertainer that summer was Dionne Warwick, who was also one of our passions back in New York. Her show was extraordinary and Reynolds and I watched it every night. She saw us there and after the show one night she asked us where we were going. There were lots of gay clubs and bars in the Old Town section of San Juan where we usually spent our nights. We told her this and she asked if she could come along. *Of course!* Dionne Warwick travelled with us on the city bus into Old Town and bar-hopped with us all night. It was quite a high watching the queens of San Juan react when we brought Dionne into the clubs with us. She was even gracious enough to sing in a couple of them. That was easily the highlight of the entire *Fantasticks* experience.

We became friends with guy who would become quite well known, Danny Apolinar. He and his lover worked in a club in San Juan, singing his original material that was utterly delightful. They went on to write the first "rock musical", called *Your Own Thing*, which was loosely based on *Twelfth Night* and opened Off Broadway in 1968. Danny played in cabarets and piano bars all over the world for the rest of his life. But that summer in Puerto Rico, we all just hung out in his club and had a ball.

*Danny Apolinar, his lover David and a friend
in their apartment in San Juan*

Although I have acted and directed in several professional companies over the years, Prince Street Players and *The Fantasticks* in San Juan are the only long running professional jobs I've ever had.

My Top Ten memories from these experiences are:
11. The reaction of the Bronx children to Gepetto.
12. Learning and singing "I Can See It" for the first time.
13. Attaching my long, black shoestring mustache and twirling it like tassels.
14. Being able to improve *The Fantasticks* after the ignorant director went back to New York.
15. Singing "Stitch and Sew, Sew and Stitch" to the preview audience, and getting a wild applause.
16. Dionne Warwick......
17. Marcy yelling, "Props".
18. Lounging around the pool at the Caribe Hilton, signing autographs.
19. Watching the poor "dwarves" trip over the circular platform.
20. Meeting Danny Apolinar and singing with him in his club.

Nine

The Drama Club

One of the basic philosophies in my life has been, that when a situation is not making me happy – I change it. I've not been afraid to step into the unknown, leaving an unhappy status quo to see if a completely different situation will work better for me. Getting stuck in a rut is not the best policy for me and I've always strived to avoid it. Leaving professional acting and jumping blindly into teaching, for example, is a decision I've never regretted.

While I was teaching music in Waldwick, both high school and middle school, I was also coaching drama, off the record, on Saturdays to some of my favorite students. I was also busy producing, directing and acting in Theater World Four productions. Obviously, my love for the theater was coming to the fore again, and teaching music was getting tiresome and uninteresting. When I realized this, I easily made the decision that I should be officially teaching drama not music.

So with little trepidation, I quit my job in Waldwick that year even though I had no specific job awaiting me. I began looking for drama teaching job during the summer but there weren't any available, so I was out of work when September came. Then in December, much to my relief, the teacher's employment agency found me a position that would begin in January. This brought me to Roselle Park, New Jersey, where a whole new era of my life would begin.

Roselle Park is a suburb south of New York, so my commuting changed from the elegant George Washington Bridge to the seedy Holland Tunnel. Waldwick and Roselle Park were about the same distance from Manhattan, but the commute was much more stressful to Roselle Park. I travelled on the Westside Highway, the Holland Tunnel, Route 1-9, the Pulaski Skyway, Route 22, and the Garden State Parkway, any one of which could be screwed up with traffic jams, going either direction.

I still had my VW bug and it was often a long and harrowing trip coming home or going to the new school from our 76th Street apartment in New York. The one pleasure of these drives was seeing beautiful ocean liners, like *Queen Elizabeth, Queen Mary, France, Normandie,* parked on the Westside piers every day. I became able to recognize them by their smokestacks.

The makeup of the two towns were also very different. Waldwick was primarily made up of middle class, New York commuters, while Roselle Park was predominantly working class families of Italian or Polish decent and was considered more a suburb of Newark, New Jersey. Sports was big in this school particularly football and the wrestling team, which won many championships.

But at least the school had a fairly active theater program, although I was not officially a part of it yet. They produced a Junior and Senior play every year, directed by one of the English teachers. My job was teaching Public Speaking to every kid in the high school, taking groups out of their English class for six weeks during their freshmen, sophomore and junior years. It was also a fairly new program, which I was asked to develop. That first semester I struggled because it was the middle of the year and I didn't really have a plan yet. But by the next year I had a healthy program going and became quickly acquainted with the whole student body.

Although I wasn't able to direct any of the plays right away, I did start a Drama Club, which became a popular hit and grew every year. In my first year, I had about 20 enthusiastic students in the club. We worked on short plays and since most of the Drama Club kids were trying out for the school plays, that got me involved. The director was blond bombshell English teacher, Darlene Mangold, and she had produced successful work thus far. I asked her if I could help out with the play and she was happy to have me do so. The play was *Arsenic and Old Lace* with a large cast comprised of many Drama Club students which made working on it great fun.

When Darlene saw how well I worked with the students, she asked me to direct the musical the next year, which she never really liked to do. So I helmed my first school production, *Bye, Bye, Birdie.* And my career as a high school Drama teacher went into full swing.

My first two plays at R.P.H.S., Arsenic and Old Lace

and Bye, Bye, Birdie

    Although my teaching job was in Roselle Park, Theater World Four was still functioning up in Northern New Jersey, so I continued to have this extracurricular theatrical project to work on as well. I believe we were doing *The Physicists* that year. Since I was teaching in Roselle Park, Reynolds became more involved with the people in the Theater World Four group, which I had originally been directing. Mary Kleban and I saw things the same, but Reynolds and Thelma had other ideas, so it caused awkward tension between us.

    After ten years together, my relationship with Reynolds was beginning to crumble. His neurotic, passionate and sometimes unstable personality was getting harder and harder to stand. That, combined with the hateful commute, gave me reason to move out of our Upper West Side apartment to a place by myself in New Jersey. It was a hard decision for me to leave Manhattan. I hated not being "a New Yorker" but it seemed a good decision for my functionality as a teacher in Roselle Park and a calmer home life. I wasn't "officially" leaving

Reynolds, and we worked together for many years after that, but in reality, the move meant that I had broken up with him as a life partner. We were together ten years.

In my second year working in Roselle Park, I met the next person who would affect my life profoundly, though I certainly didn't realize it at the time. One afternoon this short, energetic Jewish boy (the only Jewish person in the school), came striding into my Drama Club, stuck out his hand to me and announced, "Hi. I'm Gary Cohen – I make movies!" He was a freshman at the time and was avidly using a Super 8mm movie camera to make his movies.

We welcomed him into the club and it was amazing how his forceful personality soon had the club under his spell. He encouraged the drama club kids to spend their afternoons and weekends making "movies". Here were juniors and seniors, asking this little freshman kid, "Where do you want me, Gary? What should I do now, Gary?" He even convinced me to be in one of his movies that first year, recreating El Gallo's death scene on the roof of the high school. He was just amazing his first year, and continued to be a creative powerhouse for all four years at RPHS. Gary was the heart and soul of the Drama Department, acting in many plays, including the lead in *The Music Man* his senior year. In addition, we became friends in his freshman year, a friendship that has lasted to today, with him becoming my director and producer as well.

Some of Gary's high school performances:

Snoopy in *You're a Good Man, Charlie Brown*

Mr. Stitch in
Emperor's New Clothes

The Harp in Prince Street's
Jack and the Beanstalk

Mr. Dussel in
Diary of Anne Franck

Harold Hill in *The Music Man*

A constant help with all the high school productions that I helmed was my good friend Ed Williamson. Ed was a Texan who was a beloved, master English teacher (his friends called him "Massa E'ward") and he was also gay and an ardent theater queen. He took this teaching job in the New York area to be near the Broadway shows. He loved musicals most of all, *Hello, Dolly* being his favorite, and had a great understanding of scenic design and construction. So as I got more and more involved in directing the plays at the school, he became my creative partner, designing the set and organizing the backstage crews with aplomb.

Ed and I were also great theater-loving friends, going to lots of theater together. We discovered Stephen Sondheim one day in New

York because we liked the purple and orange poster of "Company". We chose not to go to *Sugar*, because the ticket price went up to an exorbitant $45.00. We travelled to Boston to see Angela Lansbury in *Mame* for the out of town tryout and almost fell out of the balcony when Bea Arthur sang "The Man in the Moon is a lady…".

Massa E'ward, with his dog "Party", (short for "Participle")   *Ed and I caught in a follow spot, this picture made the yearbook*

Since he didn't know Edward Albee's *Who's Afraid of Virginia Woolf*, I chose to share my favorite play with him. I had obtained the original cast recording of the whole play, which took four 33rpm records. I took them over to his apartment one night and we played the entire play non-stop. Like George and Martha, we drank bourbon (or "bergen" as George tells it) the entire evening, consuming an entire bottle as we listened to the recording. Unfortunately, it was a school night, so we staggered into school the next day still a bit drunk, until the hangovers started. It caused a difficult day – but the night of drinking and Edward Albee was worth it.

Drama Club regulars, Gary with the guitar and Ed Williamson sitting on the right

Massa E'ward really worked miracles on the RPHS stage and was a major part of why our shows were so successful. And successful they were! Over my 11 years in that school, our drama department became famous in the area, packing the houses for our musical and dramatic productions and winning all sorts of awards. Some highlight productions were: *Mame, Skin of Our Teeth, Hello Dolly!, The Music Man, Pajama Game, Up the Down Staircase, Damn Yankees, Bells are Ringing, The Diary of Anne Frank,* and *You're a Good Man, Charlie Brown,* as well as the many children's plays we produced.

Damn Yankees

The Music Man

The Skin of Our Teeth

Hello, Dolly!

Hello, Dolly!

The Drama Club established a Children's Theater program, which performed plays for the elementary schools. It became a tradition that every spring our auditorium was filled with all the grammar school children, who got their first glimpse, and I hope a love, of theater. I introduced the Prince Street Player's musicals, which were extremely popular. I'll never forget Gary as the Golden Harp in *Jack and the Beanstalk*.

During Gary Cohen's senior year he and another student, Paul Kaye, wrote a musical they called *Hello, Dragon!* It was based on "The Reluctant Dragon" and had clever, parody lyrics to Broadway show tunes. The townspeople of Tea-and-Crumpet, upon hearing there is a dragon in the hills, sing, "Oh, oh, we got Trouble, right here in Tea-and-Crumpet" (*Music Man*). And St. George sings, "I'm, the greatest Knight, I love to fight...." (*Funny Girl*). And of course the big Dragon number, with all the "Dragonettes" was "Hello, Dragon!" When we took *Hello,*

Dragon! to Buck's County Playhouse High School Drama Contest, where we had won many prizes over the years, the other schools scoffed because we were competing with a children's play. But it took everyone by storm, taking top place in all categories.

St. George and Dennis the Dragon, in <u>Hello, Dragon!</u>

The year I directed *Mame* at Roselle Park, it was the Senior musical and tradition had it that a senior would play the lead. Many of the senior girls were licking their chops and sharpening their claws over the title role – competition was fierce. Before auditions, a student that was a friend and a very active actor, Peter Adams, told me that his sister was trying out for the musical. I recalled his sister to be a quiet, shy junior in my speech class, Judi Adams, who hid in the back row behind her hair. "Okay", I said, expecting very little.

At auditions while we struggled through short solo songs from every girl auditioning, I was looking down at the table when suddenly my ears perked up. I said jokingly to the music director "Did Barbra Streisand just walk into the room?" There on the stage was Judi belting out some Streisand song with power and superb musicianship. I immediately had her sing one of Mame's songs and it was like hearing a Broadway show right there on our stage. "Wow," I said, "If she can act like she sings it will be phenomenal." But I knew how shy she is in speech class, so I didn't expect much, again. She took the script and suddenly transformed on stage into a mature woman – Mame!

I didn't know what to do. She was obviously, by far the best Mame, but she was a junior. A few years earlier I had insisted that all classes could be in all shows, but the leads were always from the class that sponsored it. Well, much to the anger and disappointment of my senior girls, I cast Judi as Mame. As rehearsals progressed, everyone in the cast started to realize how special Judi was and how powerfully she played the role. I'm happy to report that the seniors got together on opening night and presented Judi with a huge bouquet of flowers, thanking this talented junior for making their play such a wild success.

Judi Adams as <u>Mame</u> in her junior year in high school

Right after she graduated high school, Gary Cohen got out of college and wanted to start a theater company. He asked me to repeat my role of Littlechap in *Stop the World, I Want to Get Off*. I said "Sure!" and told him I knew who would be perfect for the demanding, multiple role of Evie/Anna/Ilse/Ginnie: Judi Adams. Gary was a couple years ahead of Judi and didn't know her, and condescendingly said, "Have her audition".

Well, she not only got cast as Evie, but the leads in three other shows that season. Judi is maybe the most talented actor I've ever known, but after doing a number of shows with Gary's theater for many years, she decided to get out of show business, get married and be a housewife and mother. Fortunately I recently tempted her out of a 15 year retirement with the role of Mrs. Meers, in *Thoroughly Modern Millie* and in classic Judi style, she knocked 'em dead - again.

Judi Adams in <u>Philemon</u> soon after high school

And years later as Mrs. Meers in <u>Thoroughly Modern Millie</u>

Over the 11 years I taught in Roselle Park, I directed many productions that I am still extremely proud of today. Many of those talented students are still my friends, such as Gary Cohen, Peter and Judi Adams, and Paul Kaye, (and many more thanks to Facebook).

As I look back on my 17 years of public school teaching, I realize that overall it was a scintillating and gratifying part of my life. I think that I was a born teacher, and that acting and directing was just part of that package. I intuitively, with no real training, figured out what students needed, and more importantly, wanted. I was a popular teacher not because I was soft, but on the contrary, I demanded that students look in new places in themselves and stretch themselves, striving for their best.

My music students in Waldwick hated music when I arrived, but ended up reveling in singing and even playing the guitar. The children I introduced to theater in Waldwick, who had hated their acting teacher, were excited when I introduced them to authentic acting experiences, albeit not in an official classroom.

The mandatory speech classes in Roselle Park were unpopular at first, but as the students were goaded into expressing themselves in ways they hadn't before, they grew to be proud of their improvements and enjoyed their classes. Putting in a faux radio booth in the classroom and making them give news reports and commercials on a microphone was a clever way to make them use their voices to express themselves. I found that classes which the English teachers found difficult to control, were some of my favorite classes. I insisted that they toe the line, but with humor, so they respected me and were able to perform. I always believed that respect was the best way to gain discipline and it proved true again and again.

The plays I directed were successful, and so many of the students loved their experience in them, because I strove for Broadway quality and demanded students work at their personal best. And, consequently, we achieved high quality high school theater, which can be very good indeed.

The crowning academic class that I am most proud of creating was called Communication. It was a senior elective, in which I taught the many ways to communicate beyond simply writing. In every English class since grammar school, students only read literature or wrote papers, but in my class we would study visual art, music and musical lyrics (not just poetry) and film most particularly. They devised drawings and collages that had a message, they played records they felt spoke a message and they often performed original songs. A large component of the class concerned the concepts of film making, which led to students to watching, analyzing and even creating their own movies.

One day in that class, I taught a lesson that was completely extemporaneous, but it demonstrated the art of communication better than any other lesson I'd ever taught. It was a lovely spring day, a few weeks before graduation. Nobody, including me, wanted to be in a classroom. So I got an idea how to use the concepts from my acting classes and I made the spontaneous decision to take the class outdoors into the sunlight.

"What are we going to do?" the students asked me.

"We're going to have a game of baseball", I said.

"What?" they cried. This being the "intellectuals" of the senior class they had little love of sports.

"We don't have any bats or balls", they exclaimed.

"Precisely", I told them, as I led them out on to an unused baseball field.

I divided the class up into two teams, giving each team their positions on the field. I said that they would play a complete game of baseball, but without any ball, gloves or bats, that these had to be in their imagination. One of the boys was on the baseball team, so I told him that he was the umpire. It would be his job to be sort of God, deciding everything about the game, determining whether a pitch was a strike, ball or a hit, and where the ball went if it was a hit. He would determine if the ball reached the player's hands in time for an "out", or if the running player was "safe". He would control the whole game, but the players had to follow and react to whatever he determined. I called it "Invisible Baseball" and it was a perfect lesson in communication.

Dubiously, they began an inning, but as they saw how the game worked, and how they had to imagine where the ball was at any given time, they started getting into the game. By the second inning, they were cheering on their teammates and groaning when a player would swing at the "ball" and the "umpire" would call "Strike". And they would cheer on a player to run, when the ball was "a long fly ball into left field", then groan if the Ump would say that the ball was caught, causing an out. They would scream and holler when a run was made for their team, and I knew that most of these kids had rarely attended any of the real baseball games, let alone cheered for their team.

The key to this typical improvisational acting exercise was that the students had to watch the imaginary ball at all times. They had to listen carefully to the umpire and follow his every call. I had never seen a group of students work so closely and with such determination in such a short period of time. It was the epitome of teamwork.

The exuberance of our class was so noisy, classes in the school began coming to the windows of the their classrooms and watching the game. Cars stopped along the road to watch our game, marveling at the Invisible Ballgame. It was a highlight for everyone involved and I'll never forget it.

Recently, I attended the 1972 Roselle Park High School class reunion and a man came up to me who was obviously a jock, that I didn't remember at all. He said, "I was in your Communication class. I bet you didn't think I was listening, but that class changed my life. I made a collage in your class (like this was a big deal). I'm a union organizer now and I use what you taught me every day. I'm glad that I got to see you because I always wanted to thank you."

Thanks to Google and Facebook, I hear from students from the past all the time now. Years ago, in early email days, I received a message from a Waldwick student who found my address somehow and wanted to tell me that she still sings *Ragtime Cowboy Joe* to her kids and remembers her music classes with me all the time. It has been extremely gratifying to often hear this kind of testament from students who appreciated the learning as much as I appreciated the teaching.

Ten

The Swingin' Sixties

The hippie teacher.

Education was changing in the Sixties, and there was a polarization between the older and younger generations. This occurred in the faculty as well. The younger teachers were trying new methods of reaching the students, but the old guard stuck to traditional methods and that did not always lead to pleasant teacher's meetings. Being the first teacher to not wear a tie, to grow facial hair, and to let my hair and sideburns grow, I became quite popular with the students, but not well liked by all the teachers, particularly not with the longstanding, head of the athletic department, "Puggie" Williams. Puggie was a bigoted, bloated, far right-wing, squat, little tyrant, and he literally hated me.

He hated that I got his athletes to be in the musicals, he hated my long hair and attire, he hated that I was friends with the "hippie" students, he hated all the standards I upheld. On the day that Martin Luther King was assassinated, a number of teachers sat around the lunch room and Puggie actually congratulated the assassin, making light of the situation. Most of the teachers were too intimidated by him to respond, but I immediately protested, proclaiming that it was a major tragedy, that Dr. King strived for peace and harmony, gaining freedom for the black people through non-violence.

Puggie turned red, steam coming out of his ears, he stood up and stormed toward me, fists clenched. He stood over me, glaring down, because even though he was short, I was sitting down. Bringing back memories of the bullies in my life, I was honestly scared. He hesitated for a moment, shaking with rage, then he turned and walked out of the room. One of his young coaches was sitting next to me and he quietly said, "I wish he'd grabbed you, then I could have decked him." Puggie, once a popular coach, was not loved by many anymore. His time was over and it was rather sad.

During those years in Waldwick and even more in Roselle Park, my teacher/student relationships became rather fluid, frequently blurring the line between teacher and friend. I was the first "hippie" teacher so all the "hip" kids wanted to get into my classes, many of them working on the school plays with me as well. When the generational gap was created by the era, I was on the side of the kids, not the parents, protesting the Vietnam war, loving rock music, dressing in "mod" clothes and flashing the peace sign.

My bachelor apartment became a hangout for many of the students. They enjoyed my day-glow bedroom with posters of Jimmy Morrison and Jimi Hendrix lighting up the room with the black light. This bedroom was even being used for teen-sex assignations at times, with Gary bringing over his various girlfriends. In my red-white-blue kitchen, where everything in the room had to be of those colors, I often gave hair-cuts to the boys. They wanted to keep their long hair, so by giving them just a trim, they could tell their parents they got a hair-cut. Pot was smoked in my living room on countless occasions. The musical "Hair" was our favorite show and we all considered it the wave of the future. I was just "one of the guys" and it seemed perfectly natural to all of us.

I had traded in my VW bug for a flashy, yellow, Firebird convertible as soon as I moved to New Jersey. One weekend, Gary and a bunch of boys (all straight, by the way) came over to my apartment. We all got wasted, climbed into my car to drive down-the-shore for some amusement park fun. The effects of the grass made it seem like we drove and drove and drove until we finally reached the end of my apartment complex to see the diner across the street. "That's the BETTY LYNN", we yelled, "we're <u>only</u> at the Betty Lynn!"

Laughing all the way to Seaside Amusement Park, we got onto our favorite the ride that spun around, sticking it's patrons to the sides by centrifugal force. As we rose higher and higher, we sang the opening theme "2001 Space Odyssey", *Also Sprach Zarathustra*, at the top of our lungs. This was a teacher and his high school students! But hell, it was the 60s!

Stoned with Gary and his friend Bobby

Gary Cohen and I developed a close friendship which started even when he was a freshman. I was having a minor affair with one of his buddies at another school, and the boy and I felt bad about lying to Gary about our whereabouts when Gary wanted to do something with one of us. I was terrified to tell him what was really going on, and possibly spoil our budding friendship, but I felt it was necessary to do so. Therefore, one day I took him up to his bedroom, sat him down on his bed and enlightened him about my being gay and the relationship I was having with his friend. Being a nice Jewish boy in a nice Jewish home, he had never suspected this and was shocked when I told him. But he was quick to accept it, and it became an simple understanding in our friendship from then on. This talk and the change in our relationship showed how much I trusted him and how much he liked and respected me.

On my 33rd Birthday, my students threw a surprise birthday party for me in my apartment. Half of the Drama Club was there (the pot smoking half), and I was surprised and touched. The elaborate decorations included potato chips hidden EVERYwhere around the apartment, because I had a penchant for them as munchies. Days later I found chips in coffee mugs, under the sofa, and one taped over the shower-head. There was no alcohol at these parties, just a lot of pot smoking. For such an unforgettable birthday, I don't remember a thing.

The Olympus of our inspiration for life was the revolutionary musical *Hair*. Many of us had gone to see it's original production at the Public Theater, and felt that this was "where it was at!" Then it moved to Broadway, under Tom O'Horgan's direction, and I even took my Drama Club, a secret kept from many a parent. The play became the controversial loadstone between the generation gap.

Right after it opened on Broadway, the summer following Gary's junior year, he and several friends organized a production of *Hair* with high school and college students, along with a couple adults - me - enthusiastically included. They didn't have a script, but knew all the music and had seen it enough times to write their own script. Gary played Berger and directed, his friend Mark (the boy I'd had the fling with) was Claude. I played some small roles, including the Statue of Liberty on roller skates with a Playboy Magazine and a flashlight singing the "Star Spangled Banner", in falsetto. I also played a looter of war corpses singing the poignant duet "What a Piece of Work is Man" as we picked the pockets of the dead soldiers. The irony was so powerful that I had a difficult time not crying as I sang this beautiful song.

The cast was so excited by our rehearsals that we all wanted to actually perform the play for an audience. So Gary went to the office of the Broadway producer, Michael Butler, and pleaded with him to give us the rights. Wearing the guy down with his persistence, Butler finally consented, provided we didn't charge or publicize, a gesture that would absolutely in no way be granted today by any producer. But this was *Hair*, in the 70s.

We had been doing our rehearsing at Upsala College, a conservative, Lutheran school. When the powers-that-be looked in on a rehearsal they were horrified and virtually booted us out for "indecent material". Now we had no venue to do our show and we all were crushed. Fortunately, someone had a connection at Rutgers University, and they, being a more liberal organization, let us use their student recreation room. So that is where we put on our production of *Hair*, and it was an instant smash.

For both scheduled shows, we had so many people lined up around the campus, that I had to go out and tell half of them that the show was full up. They shouted in "protest" so we told them, "What the Hell – we'll do a third show!!" The audiences were so moved by this production that they stood and cheered all the numbers.

And at the end of the show, the cast walked through the audience on their arms of the chairs, while holding their hands and singing "Let the Sunshine In". There wasn't a dry eye in the house, including the cast's. I was bawling like a baby at every performance, as I grasped weeping audience member's hands. I've never had another theatrical experience like it.

I think this production captured and combined the best of the original Off Broadway and Broadway productions. For many years people would come up to me and enthuse that they had seen our *Hair* and it had changed their lives.

<u>Hair</u> directed by Gary Cohen, also center as Berger

"What a piece of work is man....."   "Hair, hair, hair-hair-hair.."

*   *   *

My own creative juices were inspired by Gary when we made a collaborative Super 8 movie together called *The Peace Trilogy*. The three parts were divided by my making part one, Gary making part two, and both of us working together on part three. Since the Vietnam war protest was a part of our "revolutionary" mentality at the time, each part was our depiction of this idea.

I have always been a lover of animation, starting with *Pinocchio* at age four, so for my section I chose to do a stop-action animation movie. Photographing one frame at a time, I made a cartoon drama about the word "Peace". On my white, sheepskin rug, a pack of colorful construction paper appeared to have each piece of paper slide out and "cut itself" into a P, E, A, C and E. Then they arranged themselves into the word, followed by a cutout of a peace sign and a rose adjusted itself on top of the frame. Then an ominous kitchen knife appeared and slithered it's way to the paper letters, slicing them in half. At the devastation of word "PEACE", the rose shed a single tear.

For Gary's part, he made a still-photo collage with Life Magazine pictures of the horrors of war, political leaders, hippies, rock stars, and most important, symbols from the musical *Hair*. Most shots went from 18 frames to 6 frames, but as a joke, Gary put in a 2 frame shot of Dougie Goger's penis (shot in my living room, by the way). We wanted it to be a subliminal shot, knowing that no one would really register seeing that quick a shot in a movie.

Then for our joint venture, Gary and I took the camera into Manhattan. We spent a cold wintery day filming people holding up the two finger peace sign. Some people were cooperative, but some gave us the middle finger or angrily refused. But we managed to get all sorts of people: soldiers, nuns, business men, school groups of children and Eastside matrons to make the peace sign for us. Then we spent hours selecting and editing the footage, cut and glue style, into a movie.

When we were done with all three parts, we were very proud of the finished product. Since the project came out of the Drama Club, I showed it to the principal of the high school, Dale Springer, and he was quite pleased. He decided to show the movie to the whole school at an assembly. Through our excitement, we completely forgot about Dougie Goger's penis! After the showing, we got enthusiastic congratulations from everyone.

But Miss Wood, an old spinster, who had been head of the English Department for many years and my immediate boss, took the principal aside and said, "I believe I saw a naked penis included in that movie collage!" The principal called me into his office and asked if that was true. I blushed and admitted that the boys had done that short shot as a mini-protest of their own. Dale, a good guy (who I found out later got my ass out of many sticky situations) sat a minute and then let out a huge guffaw. "Why" he said "was Miss Wood, of all people, the only one who noticed it?" After we laughed awhile, he told me that if we were to exhibit this film later, under the name of Roselle Park High School, we had to take the offending frames out of the movie. I sadly agreed and told Gary. I think he held on to those two frames and re-inserted them at some later point, but I don't have that copy. Too bad.

THE PEACE TRILOGY

Part One,
    by David Umbach

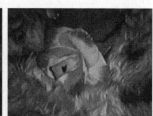

Part Two,
    by Gary Cohen

Part Three,

by Gary & David

I went on to make two other films on my own after Gary graduated and went off to college. My favorite consists of cleverly shot scenes, some with stop action, that were edited to fit exactly to the lyrics of Carole King's *You've Got a Friend*, as sung by James Taylor. I used my student/friend Peter Adams and my current boyfriend, Alan Tulin as the "friends". I took them all over the place; from Greenwich Village, to "down-the-shore", to a baseball diamond, and to a cemetery. They acted out each line from the song, in an amusingly, literal way.

For example, when it says, "They'll hurt you, desert you, they'll take you soul if you let them." We showed one boy on the beach being beaten with a towel by the other, then he magically disappeared, then come back and steal the boy's sandal.   And their clothes instantly changed on "Winter, Spring, Summer and Fall". We had such fun making that film and I still love watching it. Later I over-dubbed James Taylor's singing with my own, with Gary playing guitar, which made it even more personal.

YOU'VE GOT
A FRIEND

a film by
David Umbach
song by
Carole King

The Diner was the last movie I ever made. It was a serious, dramatic story, with Peter Adams as a nasty biker, who robs and terrorizes the proprietor of a small diner. We find out at the end that the boy is the man's son. We used a lovely little diner in Roselle Park as the location, and I got a excellent New York actor to play the father. It's well acted, and for a Super 8 movie, I think it tells the story quite well, even if the camera work is a bit artsy-fartsy.

THE DINER, a film by David Umbach

I've always felt so lucky that I spent my thirties in that '60's environment, because I was able to be an adult, but experience the "youth revolution". The Sixties and Seventies were lots of fun, but they fucked up lots of kids. I hope I helped some of my students wend their way through that tricky era without it harming them.

*   *   *

Of all the "highs" (in every sense of the word) during my high school teacher years, the highest was the cross-country trip that Gary and I took together the summer after he graduated. The two of us, with long hair and "hippie" attire, set off in my yellow Firebird convertible for the West Coast taking the whole summer for the trip, there and back. Gary had never been west of Pennsylvania and I'd never been west of Illinois, so it was an adventure for both of us.

In Chicago we stayed with my parents in Highland Park, but not for long since they didn't have a lot of room in their house and I didn't feel that they really approved of our hippiedom, either. We did tour a little of Chicago and one day, as we cruised down the Outer Drive after finishing a joint, we spotted a billboard with a huge, three dimensional cow sticking out of it. I howled from the open, yellow convertible, "I'm a Yellow Moo-Moo", which caused stoned hilarity for hours. This became a catch phrase for the rest of the trip.

Then at the Chicago Theater we saw the new movie *Start the Revolution Without Me,* with Gene Wilder and Donald Sutherland, in which Hugh Griffin, as King Louis XIV, wandered around a dress ball in a chicken costume, apologizing heartily to everyone through his beak, "I thought it was a costume ball. I thought it was a costume ball." We thought it was the most hilarious movie ever made.

Leaving Chicago we had to drive through the Great Plains of Illinois, Iowa and Nebraska which seemed endless and we weren't even high through most of it. Just miles and miles of straight, flat highways with corn or wheat on either side. It was so boring. Even though Gary had never seen this type of landscape before, it still became tiresome in a short time.

When we got to Omaha, which was at least a city, we got a motel and decided just to take pizza and some beers into the room, crash and watch TV. There was a bar nearby that sold pizza so we went in and sauntered up to the bar to order. Suddenly we realized that the noisy room had gone deathly quiet and everyone was staring at us. We stood there with our long hair and colorful attire (I may even have been wearing my American flag shirt) and we were in the middle of a redneck, trucker bar, at a time before even bikers had long hair.

Although I was scared to death, I croaked out, "We'd like a pepperoni pizza, please and a six-pack." The bartender just stared at us and there wasn't a sound in the room. Fearlessly, Gary plopped down on a bar stool, leaned over to the bartender and proclaimed, "I thought it was a costume ball." I am sure the bartender had not seen the movie, but it seemed to break the tension, and he nodded and called our order into the kitchen. We waited nervously at the bar for our pizza, while the patrons eyed us hostilely. Finally we hastily made our exits and were very glad to have gotten out alive. But in the car we burst into hysterical laughter. I still think that was the funniest quip Gary has ever made, in a lifetime of funny quips.

One of my favorite stories, that defines me, as well as Gary, happened at the Grand Canyon. We were so happy to get out of the plains, going through Denver and being awed by the Rocky Mountains, we decided to visit this great national monument on our way to California. Yes, there is some breathtaking scenery in Colorado and Utah, but as we got into the deserts of Arizona, it got a bit barren for us, so we were looking forward to the spectacle of the Grand Canyon.

When we arrived, in the late afternoon, the parking lot was full, so our walk to the canyon was hot and long. We finally reached the viewing area (predating the see-through Sky Walk), peered out over the vast expanse, looking left, looking right, then looking at each other, I said, "Let's go to Vegas!" Gary nodded in agreement, and we headed back to the car. I fear that is my taste in touring, even today: glitz and show-biz over scenery, any day. As a boy, when my parents would take a Sunday drive with the family just to look at the scenery, I uttered a similar sentiment: "You seen one tree, you seen 'em all."

But Vegas was magic! Gary's father, who worked in the entertainment concession trade, had friends in Vegas so he arranged for us to get free tickets to several big shows. And although neither of us were gamblers, the atmosphere of the casinos, seedy though it was, just thrilled us. We were able to see headliners like Dean Martin, Todie Fields and Tom Jones, but our favorite show was Don Rickles. OMG he was so funny! And to think that he's still insulting audiences for laughs, well into his 80's.

Gary and I were aware of the each other's sexual tastes – blonds (girls for him, boys for me). So we would each keep an eye out for someone that the other might enjoy "cruising". I would nudge him when a cute girl would be coming, and he'd elbow me for a cute guy. We loved it when a pair of cuties came towards us and we'd shout, "Both Great!"

We didn't "hook up" much during our summer together, but Gary befriended a chorus girl from the production of *Hair* in Vegas at our hotel. He waited for her in his room for what he hoped was a "night of love", but she never showed. Depressed by this, he consoled himself with playing a slot machine, and ended up hitting a pretty good jackpot as a consolation prize. I, however, did get lucky in Vegas. I met up with a guy there that I had known on the Jersey shore and he invited me up to his apartment for the evening. I turned out to be less than a good idea, since when I got back to New Jersey, I found out had given me the clap.

After this eventful time in Las Vegas, it was then on to Hollywood, our primary goal. I had written to my Uncle Chuck that we were coming and he said that we could stay at his place in Beverly Hills. We zipped through the roasting desert and arrive at my Uncle's home in "lower" Beverly Hills. By lower, I mean that it was not the "Home of the Stars", by any means. He just had a bungalow in a fairly seedy part of Los Angeles which was officially in Beverly Hills, but way at the bottom of the hill. We got there in the evening, hot and tired from long drive through the desert, and my uncle was nowhere to be found. We ended up breaking and entering through a window, found a room with a carpet, and fell asleep. My uncle came home to find two hippies sound asleep in his den.

Luckily, my Uncle Chuck was a fun, liberal guy, who greeted us in the morning with pancakes and a big smile. He couldn't wait to take us for a tour up into upper Beverly Hills, so after breakfast we crammed into his VW Bug and took off for his tour of the Homes of the Stars. It turned out to be one of the most terrifying rides I have ever taken outside an amusement park.

Uncle Chuck was tall and had to scrunch himself into the driver's seat, while I was in the front seat, desperately holding the dashboard, with Gary in the back clinging for dear life to the back of my seat, because in those days there were no seat belts. My uncle was a brake-clutch-shift-accelerator-brake-again kind of driver, speeding around those curves up and down the hills while he pointed out the sights, never seeming to look at the road. But he was so proud to be able to show us the famed Beverly Hills that we couldn't complain. We just held on tight, trying to keep our pancakes down.

I was excited to see my cousin Marianne, Chuck's daughter, whom I hadn't seen in many years. She was then married and lived in Orange County with a man I didn't know. We spent an awkward afternoon in her home and it was upsetting to see a different woman than I remembered, the Married Marianne. It was a strained visit, and I didn't know if it was because of my "hippie" attire and Gary, or that Marianne was not comfortable in her new life. She just wasn't the same as my dear childhood friend.

Years later, I was happy to see that she was her old self again, the liberated woman, after divorcing her husband, moving back to Illinois and marrying an old flame from high school.

Fortunately, I had a connection into the real Hollywood, because I reunited with an old acting buddy from New York that had moved to the West Coast and made a successful career as a set designer for television. Vince Tampio, who had been an alternative Genie in *Aladdin*, was one of the warmest and funniest people I've ever known. He welcomed us into his apartment for several nights and escorted us around town in style.

The most exciting part of his tour was taking us to the home of famed producer Joseph Pasternak, most famous for introducing Mario Lanza in *The Great Caruso*. His house in Beverly Hills was the kind you dream about, with hundreds of photos and paintings of movie stars, a gilded grand piano and a huge swimming pool. Mr. Pasternak was very old by then and we didn't even meet him, but Vince had the run of his house and pool, so we spent several afternoons with beautiful young actors lounging poolside, drinking exotic drinks brought by a servant. We were told that Mr. Pasternak observed the youthful parade in his back yard from his bedroom window upstairs.

While in Hollywood, Gary and I went dancing in gay clubs on several occasions, heard an excessively loud rock concert at the Filmore West, saw Burt Bachrach at the Greek Theater (with the opening act by The Carpenters), and spent a riotous day at Disneyland on mescaline.

After enjoying the Hollywood sights, Gary and I had a reason to go to San Diego, because a classmate of Gary's, Lisa Flammia, was visiting her family there and we wanted to meet up with her. Lisa was a major force in our high school theater department and I enjoyed her company enormously, so we headed south. After we got to her place, we all thought it would be fun to go across the border to Tijuana. So the three of us hopped into the Yellow Moo Moo and headed for Mexico.

We were told not to bring our car into Tijuana, that parking it there was likely to have it vandalized or stolen. So we parked in a huge lot on the U.S. side, and walked to the border crossing.

Our first obstacle was the United States Customs. None of us had passports, because they weren't needed in those days to visit Tijuana, but you did have to check in with the authorities. Their obvious question was "Who is this under-aged girl you are taking across the border?" "A student, I'm her drama teacher in New Jersey", I said proudly with my long hair and '60's clothes. Needless to say, they would have none of that and we were denied exit from the States.

So, disappointed, we got our car out of the lot and had to drop Lisa back to San Diego. But Gary and I didn't want to give up our excursion into Mexico, so back to the parking lot we went and easily got through U.S. customs. But now we hit the office of Mexican Customs. They took one look at us and firmly, if not viciously, said "No Heepie!"

"What?" I cried, "I'm a teacher from New Jersey!"

"No Heepie! No long hair!"

Then Gary actually said to this humorless border guard, "I eat tacos....?".

The response was the same, "No Heepie!" So back to the car we went.

Undaunted, we went into a gift shop and bought some leather hats. We stuffed our hair into the hats, changed into less colorful shirts, put the top down on the Firebird convertible, and drove to the border cross-point. We sailed through both customs stops, the Mexicans being more than happy to have rich American tourists come to spend money in their country.

Tijuana was a pretty crappy town after all the trouble getting there. The most amusing thing was how often we were approached by the people with "Hey, Hippie, wanna buy a watch? (or grass? or girls?)" We did buy some stuff, including a red, white and blue, stained-glass ceiling lamp, which went into my red, white and blue kitchen, and even now hangs in my den. Our car was unmolested and we exited Mexico with no problems at all.

Of course Gary and I were always looking for theatrical events and the two that stand out in our trip were both in San Francisco. In a small, Off Broadway-like theater we saw a production of *One Flew Over the Cuckoo's Nest*. I'd seen the play in New York with Kirk Douglas and had not been too impressed with it, although I had loved the book. Unlike Broadway, this production was brilliantly done and was performed intimately, in-the-round. William Duvane gave a stunning performance as McMurphy, but most memorable was a dwarfish, little guy who ran around with hilarious hyper-energy as Martini. He was wonderful, but I thought it was a shame that such a good actor should be so short and therefore probably never make it in the real world – his name, I later realized, was Danny DeVito.

The other great theater experience was Paul Sills' *Story Theater*. Using his now-famous improvisational style, this Chicago-based ensemble troupe told Grimm's stories with actors narrating the story while acting out all the roles. This was all revolutionary to us at the time and made for extremely exciting theater. Among the ensemble members were: Valerie Harper, Linda Lavin, Paul Sand, Peter Boyle and Melinda Dillon, who were all unknowns at the time. In years to come I would direct or act in several productions of "Story Theater" and teach Paul Sills' use of Theater Games in my classes.

The drive back to the East Coast was mind-numbingly boring. We made no interesting stops, just driving long days to get as far as we could. The summer of fun was definitely over and we were anxious to get back to New Jersey, but it left us both with one of the best summers we'd ever know. And it bonded Gary and me for a lifetime of friendship.

* * *

Before he went off to college, Gary and I attended several 70s theatrical experiences in New York. Inspired by *Hair* and the new freedom for sexuality in theater, many Off Broadway plays featured nudity. Gary and my more progressive high school students were excited by this and sought it out whenever possible. So when we spotted the ad in the New York Times for the play *An Artist's Life,* which featured "Frequent and Prolonged Nudity", it sparked our interest.

One Saturday afternoon, lured by the ad, Gary, Paul Kaye and I trekked into lower Manhattan in search of this play. We found the address on 14th Street, with no marquee, just a small sign pointing to a long flight of stairs leading to a seedy lobby. Behind the box office window was a middle aged woman, with a Tallulah Bankhead voice, who eagerly sold us tickets. Tacked up in the lobby were photographs from the play, showing an artist painting a very beautiful model, who was obviously naked. Tallulah-Voice told us to come back at 7:30, when the theater would be open. The boys were excited by the photos and we all went out for a bite anticipating a titillating theatrical experience.

When we returned, we were greeted again by Tallulah-Voice who took our tickets and told us to take any seats we wanted. The intimate stage was surrounded by two rows of chairs and we eagerly took our seats in the front row. On the stage was an easel and a rolling, fold up bed. After about 20 other theater goers joined us, Tallulah-Voice came on stage to make an announcement. She welcomed us and introduced herself as the playwright, Amy P. Bell. She proudly announced that there would be a replacement in the cast, and the part of the model was now being played by herself. Gary and Paul were not happy about this, as the actress in the photos was much younger and prettier.

When the play began, the "artist" discussed with a friend how he was besotted with his new model, describing her as the most beautiful woman he'd ever known. When this exposition finished, in walks Amy Bell, who was definitely over-the-hill and perhaps the worst actress I'd ever seen. Mincing and indicating around the stage, she then proceeded to remove her clothes and drape herself on or around the bed, "posing" for the artist's painting. After some more pretentious dialogue, where the artist professes his love for her, there was an act break.

The three of us went out into the lobby to hear the reactions of the rest of the audience. Even though Amy Bell was now selling refreshments, the comments were as scathing as we were feeling. Being aware that the whole audience felt the same way about the play, and the leading lady, made it easier to go back into the auditorium, because we needed to see what the rest of the play had in store. We all wished that Miss Bell would keep her clothes on for this act, but we didn't have much hope.

The second act continued where the first had left off, and now it came time for the seduction. This of course led to the artist removing his clothes and he was no Adonis either, much to my disappointment. After Miss Bell removed the sheet she was wearing, she sat on the bed, this time in profile for us, and her stomach pouched out in a most unattractive way. The two actors badly simulated sex on the creaky bed. It was excruciatingly embarrassing. But it was also hilarious, and Gary, Paul and I were beginning to loose control of our giggles.

Since we were just a few feet from the actors, I didn't want to hurt their feelings, so I held my pea coat in front of my mouth, biting into it to cover the laughter. I almost bit a hole through the thick fabric. The three of us were silently laughing and shaking the chairs that we were sitting on, trying to hold it in. When the play ended, we applauded loudly and then rushed down the long flight of stairs. When we reached the sidewalk, we collapse on it with hilarity. On our drive home, we had to pull over to the side of the road because we were laughing so hard, as we recalled the most outrageous moments of this ghastly play.

The experience was so special that immediately after I got home, I wrote a letter Miss Amy Bell, complimenting her on her performance and asking her to send an autographed photograph of herself – signing the letter, Gary Cohen, with his address. I wish I'd been there when the picture arrived.

The term "Frequent and Prolonged Nudity" has stayed with me as a catch phrase for truly tacky theater.

But by no means was *An Artist's Life* typical of the theater that we saw in Lower Manhattan during that period. Some of it was absolutely brilliant, like Performance Group's *Dionysis '69*, where innovative and powerful story telling, along with excellent acting (as well as nudity) told the tale of Dionysis' life and death. Or Julie Bovossa's hilarious *Moondreamers*, a bizarre comedy at Café La MaMa, that featured "Dr. Ababa - the first doctor in the phone book" and "a Truly Rotten Chorus".

The "birth" and "death" of Dionysis, in Performance Group's <u>Dionysis '69</u>

The 1970s was an inspirational era for the theater and for the joy of life. I was of an age that I might not have been able to take part in it, being an adult and a teacher. But because I embraced the 70s culture, for good or bad, and joined the students instead of the parents in this generational war, I was able to experience it to the full.

Eleven

First Hippie on LBI

I had two interesting summer jobs during this period. The first was working at the Cape Cod Melody Tent in Hyannis as manager of the concessions stand, a job that Gary's father, Elliot Cohen, arranged for me. I took a boy I'd been dating with me to help with the concession job. We rented an apartment that we were told Elaine Stritch had rented the previous year, and we ensconced ourselves into the world of summer stock.

It was a wild and wacky summer. The job of preparing and selling concessions wasn't exciting, but the fascinating part was being able to observe the goings on at this professional, summer stock theater. One well known star was cast in each show, like Donald O'Conner in *Promises, Promises*, Jean-Pierre Aumont in *Fanny*, and Mitzi Gaynor in her own show, *The Mitzi Gaynor Show*.

Sad to say, at that time of his life, Donald O'Conner had a terrible drinking problem. It showed every night in his erratic performance. Everyone was excited to see Mitzi's show and we wanted to impress her at how professional our theater was. Therefore, the hard working apprentices stayed up all night painting the round stage to look like a tufted, pink cushion. Being theater-in-the-round, the painted pink cushion would be the primary scenery for this one-woman show.

The next morning Miss Gaynor arrived with her entourage, including a husband who's job it turned out to be to follow her around apologizing to the people she screamed at and offended. The scenic designer and the kids who had arduously painted her stage waited to hear her reaction, expecting her to be ecstatic. She shouted, "Who put all that pink shit on my stage? I want it painted over in black!"

After much ranting and raving, her show opened and although nobody could stand her, we had to admire how beautiful she looked and what an entertaining show she performed. I remember her interrupting some song or intro she was making with a spontaneous cry, "I quite smoking!" The audience would cheer her bravery and candidness. Of course, this was part of the act and she made the same "spontaneous cry" every night in the same place.

Every night just before her show her dresser would come to my concession stand with an empty pitcher and coffee pot. She'd ask me to fill each one with ice and then she took them back to Mitzi's dressing room. On closing night I just had to ask, "What does she want the ice for?"

The dresser, who was not any more fond of Mitzi than anybody else, said, "She rubs ice on her tits just before she goes on stage, to make them stand up and out."

Well, I couldn't leave this alone, so I got some masking tape and put a label on each container saying, "For the Right One" and "For the Left One". Forevermore she will be referred to by me as "Titsy Mitzi".

Jean-Pierre Aumont was known in Hollywood as a famous ladies man having had romances with the likes of Maria Montez, Paulette Goddard and Grace Kelly, including several marriages. Now in his late sixties, he was still a handsome man. He was cheerful and charming, and was always friendly with me and my boyfriend in the concessions stand. He would stop and chat every time he passed the stand. Hearing all this Hollywood gossip, I was thrilled, but the boy was shy around any of the famous people. Nearing the end of the run of *Fanny*, Jean-Pierre asked me if I'd like to have dinner with him after his closing show. Surprised, I told him that I would love to and could I bring my friend, to which he said, "Of course". I told the boy about our dinner invitation, but he was too nervous to go, so I went alone.

I took a taxi to the hotel where he stayed and went up to his room where he told me to meet him before dinner. When I came into the room, he was standing by the fireplace, in a smoking jacket, leaning on the mantel and holding a glass of champagne and a cigarette in a long holder. He appeared to have stepped right out of a 1940s romance movie. Then with his charming, but smarmiest, French accent he proceeded to woo and ultimately try to seduce me. I was shocked. I had never imagined that he had any interest in me sexually, just as someone to talk movies with. He was such a famous heterosexual!

I wasn't the least bit attracted to him and I felt very embarrassed for him: *did this corny routine still work on anybody?* After several clumsy attempts, I warded him off with the excuse that I never cheated on my boyfriend. He accepted this with grace. He dressed, and we had a lovely dinner in the hotel dining room, chatting about Hollywood again, without any reference to what had happened upstairs.

* * *

The second summer job was with my two friends from Theater World Four, Mary and Thelma, who decided they wanted to open a hippie/head shop on Long Beach Island, New Jersey. It would be based on the many shops in Greenwich Village that sold rock and movie star personality posters, wildly colored day-glow posters, anti-Vietnam War banners, pro-pot tee-shirts, anti-establishment buttons and bumper stickers, and marijuana paraphernalia. Being that LBI was a rather conservative place, Mary and Thelma knew that the marijuana items would have to be kept to a minimum, but they hoped all the youth-oriented stuff of the era would be popular with the kids on this family vacation spot.

They asked me if I would come down for the summer and handle the poster section of the store. I thought it would be a hoot, and a paid summer down-the-shore seemed like an excellent idea, so I accepted.

Long Beach Island is indeed a long, sandbar island off the coast of New Jersey, with beaches along the entire ocean side of the island. There is only one entry by automobile via a causeway at the middle of the island that connects to the mainland. The bay side is covered with homes and boating docks, where hundreds of sailboats and motorboats are stored. The island has one road that goes from one end to the other, the Boulevard, and the island varies from two blocks to five blocks wide at different points. Thousands of primary and summer homes fill the island, from Barnegat Lighthouse on the north to the town of Beach Haven on the south.

Mary and Thelma picked a prominent location in a new mini-mall right off the causeway and rented a two-story unit, that had a wooden staircase in front leading up to the second floor. The downstairs room would be for Mary and Thelma to sell all the buttons, tee-shirts and fun hippie stuff. The upstairs would be my domain, exclusively devoted to the posters that were so popular at the time. They named the store after our first Theater World Four success, STOP THE WORLD.

We spent time before the season, setting up the place. On the second floor I constructed a raised platform that held the cash register, and was decorated with day-glow paint and posters making it a sort of go-go box for me to overlook everybody and take the money from the customers. A black light and a strobe light was installed to give the room a disco feel, with the controls for the lights and music up in my booth, so that I could change the atmosphere as I wished. The walls were completely covered with all the posters that were on sale. Everything from Paul Newman and Robert Redford in "Butch Cassidy and the Sundance Kid" to bikinied Ursula Andress in "Dr. No"; from Jimmy Morrison to Jimi Hendrix to Mary Poppins to Janis Joplin; and brightly colored day-glo Andy Warhol or Peter Max posters. When it was done, the place had an exciting mod-60's feel that we knew was totally new to Long Beach Island.

This was my long-haired period, so I thought that while selling in this store I should emphasize the hippie look with my clothes and accoutrements. Mary gave me a batik mu-mu that I wore on the cooler days and evenings, or short shorts and beads in the hotter days. So, complete with headband and bracelets, I would fit beautifully into any cast of *Hair*.

Since LBI is more a Philadelphia and South Jersey based resort than New York, the vacationers were less sophisticated and not really familiar with the "hippie" thing. Therefore, Stop the World was a real novelty for most of the vacationers. I'm sure most of the people had never been to Greenwich Village and never seen a "head shop", so they came into our place with fascination and awe.

My upper room in particular was a magnet, especially for all the teenagers. I had rock music playing constantly and I would stand up on my go-go pedestal, turn on the strobe light and dance the frug and mash potato, and the kids ate it up. Sometimes my room was so crowded, people had trouble moving around, but we sold lots of posters. Summer homes need cheering up and the adults liked the personality posters with movie stars, while the teenagers liked the rock stars and day-glow posters. And every evening, when people got off the beach and needed something to do, my poster room was a popular place to come and hang out.

I made two friends that summer that made my work-vacation even more enjoyable. My daytime friend, Timmy, was an 8 year old urchin from a very poor family nearby the shop. He and his family lived on the island year-round and Timmy had to care for his younger, mentally challenged brother while his mother was at work. Having grown up on the island, the beach held no pleasures for Timmy, and his brother wasn't allowed to go there anyway, for fear he would wander into the water. Therefore Timmy, having nothing to do all day but hang around the store, attached himself to me all summer and I thoroughly enjoyed his company.

On the "beach days" when business was slow, we played games or we just talked and joked. He had a sharp sense of humor for a little kid and he kept me laughing all summer. I would also buy his brother and him lunch most days, because it was obvious Timmy didn't have the resource to get it on his own.

My nighttime friend, Scott, was different matter entirely. Long Beach Island is not known for having much of a gay life, at least an obvious one, so I never saw many gay men in the store (at least attractive ones) and very few on the rest of the island either. My shop was often crowded with shirtless teenagers in shorts, so there was lots of eye-candy, but that's all.

One evening I noticed a beautiful blond boy hanging around much longer than the usual customer and he seemed to be looking at me more than the posters. Then he was back the next night and stayed even longer. I didn't want to be the aggressor, as it could cause major legal problems for the store and for me if I was wrong about him, so I contented myself with just watching him when he came in the store.

On the fourth night that he came in, he approached me and asked what I did after the store closed and would I like to go out for a drink or something. *Would I ever!* So we went out that night and found we were quite compatible, and became friends for the rest of the summer.

Scott turned out to be a sophomore in college and was staying with his family for the summer. He basically hated coming to LBI because it had been the family summer vacation place every year since he was young. He was completely out of the closet to himself and his college friends, and was lonely on LBI because it was so straight. He had hoped that I was gay and wondered if we could spend time together. And we did -- almost every night, in fact, we managed to at least take long walks along the beach, if not go back to my rented room to be more intimate. We also had some hot encounters in the dunes, late at night. Our time together in this delightful summer romance, made my stay on LBI much more enjoyable than it could have been.

The front of Stop The World, with
Scott on my daisy-covered VW bug

Mary, Thelma and I
in the downstairs store

Scott upstairs in my poster room

With my young friend Timmy

    The following year Mary and Thelma moved Stop the World to a larger mall in Beach Haven and I chose not to work there. I had done my summer at the shore. Along with a strobe-lit disco, LBI now had several "hippie" shops, following our influence. The new Stop the World primarily specialized in custom-made Hoppi coats, that Thelma created, and it was not the same exciting place that it was that initial year.

When I visited that summer, I felt badly that I couldn't hang out with Timmy, though I did see him a couple of times. Scott chose not to come to his parents summer house that year, but stayed in Las Vegas where he attended cooking school. I saw him when Gary and I passed through Vegas on our cross-country road trip.

Though I am not a "beach" person, and thus don't go there often anymore, I will always treasure my time on LBI. The thrills, the affairs, the friendships. And although the island has changed over the years with new families, new stores, and new homes, the spirit of the island still remains. Even the tragedy of Hurricane Sandy, which caused immense devastation and destruction for many on Long Beach Island, could never strip it of its spirit and sense of "summer vacation down-the-shore". I will never forget that summer when I was the first hippie on Long Beach Island.

Twelve

Make A Celebration

During the time Gary Cohen was in high school we were involved in several productions at Actor's Café Theater in West Orange. It resided under a liquor store, in a neighborhood that was rather frightening, especially at night. But some quality theater was created down there in that basement, under the auspices of David Kennedy, a megalomaniac actor/director. He preferred heavier plays featuring deep, conflicted characters and rich, meaningful themes, like those of Samuel Beckett, Eugene O'Neil, and Eugene Ionesco; and often directed himself in the lead role. One of his most powerful performances was Beckett's *Krapp's Last Tape*, a one-man play about an old man who rambles on and on about his past life into a tape recorder.

David Kennedy, however, didn't like musicals, or anything that he found, in his opinion, "frivolous". So other people put them on in his theater (or "temple", as he called it). Our introduction to this theater (or temple) was a production of *The Fantasticks* where Gary played the Old Actor and I reprised El Gallo. It was the first time Gary and I had performed together and we had an absolute ball, even though we weren't nuts about the director, particularly since we knew the musical better than he did. This began our relationship with Actor's Café and we produced and performed there as often as we could.

At that time, Gary and some other high school friends had become familiar with my ex-lover, Reynolds Callendar, who still lived in what was our apartment together on 76th Street, and wanted to involve him in some theatrical endeavors. So they planned a production at Actor's Café of *Stop the World, I Want to Get Off,* and they wanted me to reprise the role of "Littlechap". Gary and his friend Mark Gerstein (who was the boy I was carrying on with when Gary was a freshman) would be in the chorus and Reynolds would direct.

Lisa Minogue, the girl I had cast as Louisa in Theater World Four's *The Fantasticks,* was now living part-time with Reynolds, even though she was still in high school, because she was madly in love with him. She was cast as the four-character leading lady, to play my character's English wife, and 3 mistresses (German, American and Russian). It's a tough role and a stretch for a high school kid, so she had her work cut out for her. Due to her current relationship with Reynolds, I never felt that she was completely comfortable with me, though I still enjoyed working with her again.

The play was a success, until closing weekend. Reynolds and I remained friendly with each other, but there still existed an undercurrent of resentment in him, for my leaving him. The Friday night before closing, we got into an argument and at some point I snidely referred to him and the two actors who came in with him from Manhattan, Mark and Lisa, as "The New York contingency". I'm sure it had something to do with their superior attitudes, but it was really just Reynolds' attitude that set me off. This resulted in his screaming something at me and storming out of the dressing room, assuring that he had the last word. He spoiled his dramatic exit, however, by barreling his VW out of the lot and bashing into David Kennedy's car. This was not how he had hoped to end the altercation, but he devised a plan to get back at me.

The next morning I received a phone call from Reynolds curtly telling me that "the New York contingency would not be returning to New Jersey". This meant him, Mark, and Lisa, our leading lady. Though I didn't care about Reynolds not returning, and I knew we could make do with one less member of the ensemble, I panicked because how could we go on without Lisa? I called back and asked to talk to Lisa personally. I entreated her, saying that it would mar her theatrical career and that this incident would never be erased. I told her that the whole cast would be broken-hearted, that we had only two more performances and she must not make this tragic mistake. She broke down in tears, understanding what I was saying, but was completely under Reynolds' charismatic spell. She knew he would be unforgiving if his plan to shut down our show didn't work. She made her decision and told me she would not be performing in the remainder of the run.

I called David Kennedy and told him to cancel the Saturday and Sunday shows, telling him the reason. He exploded and fumed for awhile, then said that his girlfriend, Barbara, had played the role only a year ago, and could probably pick it up again quickly. I considered Barbara a pretty solid actress, though with a cold-fish personality. But, at this point, I thought "I'll go on with a chimpanzee before I let Reynolds close down this play". So we spent the afternoon running

Barbara though the blocking, which was quite different from her previous production, and went on Saturday night hoping for the best.

Amazingly, for the first time the play actually worked. There was a marvelous give and take chemistry with me and Barbara that I never had with Lisa. Barbara may have had no personality off stage, but she was terrific on stage. I eventually realized that it was most likely Lisa's infatuation with Reynolds that had prevented her from opening up and connecting with me on stage. Years later I worked with Lisa again and saw her in many productions and knew what a fine actress she really was; we became dear friends, sharing our history with Reynolds.

The actress who played Evie at Theater World Four was decent, but not terribly strong, therefore performing opposite Barbara, where there was a true connection, was a revelation. This would happen even more so in a few years when I did the part one more time, with my ex-student Judi Adams.

Littlechap with his second Evie, Lisa Minogue

One summer while Gary was still studying at Hofstra University, he wanted to work on a theater project outside of school and asked me if I would perform in a play that he would direct. This felt like an odd request, being that I had been his teacher/director for so many years, but I thought, "What the hell," and agreed to do the play.

We arranged to mount *A Funny Thing Happened on the Way to the Forum* at Actor's Café with me playing Pseudolus. Mark Gerstein played Hysterium, with another high school friend of Gary's, Neil Cerbone, as one of the Proteans. It turned out to be another great success. Mark was a brilliant comedian and singer, and Neil was trained as a dancer but a wonderful comedian, as well. The other Proteans were John Richkus, a student/friend of mine, and Mary Lynn Picyk, who was Gary's girlfriend at the time, and all three were hilarious.

Pseudolus plays with the Proteans

It was evident in rehearsals that the cast was full of funny people who created wildly funny characters -- except me. Using my "method" training, I worked on creating an authentic and believable Roman slave, being present in all my moments, but inevitably not funny. Gary took me aside after a rehearsal one night and gave me one simple note, "Pseudolus is a con artist and everything he does is to get his way. You are a manipulator and you have to care desperately to be free, and go to any means to get it. You have to try harder." He didn't ask me to be funnier, he just gave me a valid character note. After incorporating this note, my performance reached a new level, a funnier level, that complimented and enhanced the performances of the rest of the ensemble. I have trusted his direction ever since.

After four years at Hofstra, Gary Cohen returned to his home town and wanted to channel his creative energy into a new project by starting a theater company with is friends, Mark and Neil. They rented the basement of a catering hall in Roselle Park called Roland's, rounded up some talented folks, and set up a season of plays. One of their favorite musicals was *Celebration,* by the authors of *The Fantasticks*, thus they named the theater Celebration Playhouse. The lucky people who became involved with this theater, myself included, still consider the six years that Celebration produced plays under the original team, the Golden Years of their theatrical lives.

During those Golden Years, Celebration Playhouse gathered some phenomenally talented actors. Besides Gary, Mark and Neil, it featured (in no particular order) Linda Herman, Carol Vucoulo, Paul Kaye, Oscar Stokes, Angela Intili, Lisa Minogue, Judi Adams, Amy Epstein, Jim

McClain, John Richkus, Kate Brown, Trish Parfitt, Bobby Phillips and more. Many of us are still friends today.

The group was fortunate to include the high school musical prodigy, Ted Kociolek, who played piano brilliantly and eventually lead the orchestras. He was a fascinating kid and a musical genius, who stayed with the theater for many years. Since then he has worked professionally all over the country and has written several musicals that went on to be produced. Also, one of my high school students, Carolyn Kostopolis, who had a natural talent for designing and creating costumes, costumed many of our shows, including the beautiful *A Little Night Music* and *Two Gentlemen of Verona*. She made every costume and they were gorgeous. She now has her own company that builds costumes for Broadway, Radio City Music Hall and touring companies. We gathered some amazing talent at Celebration, and not just in the acting department.

The design of the theater followed Actor's Café with café tables and chairs, but each table was topped with a Broadway show poster. When tickets were issued, patrons would be assigned to specific tables after the particular show featured on the table top. Thus a ticket could read, "seats 1 & 2 at *My Fair Lady*", or "seats 3 & 4 at *Oliver*". The stage was one side of this basement room, with virtually no back stage area, just some tiny wings created by black curtains.

Celebration Playhouse's inaugural season, mounted some amazing productions. It began with *You're a Good Man Charlie Brown* and continued with *The Fantasticks* (where I reprised El Gallo), *Butterflies Are Free*, *Stop the World* (where I played Littlechap, yet again) and *Dames at Sea* (where I played Hennessy/Admiral).

In *Dames at Sea* I had to at least simulate tap dancing so I bought these huge, very 70's, shiny white shoes, that looked like King Kong's tap shoes. In the number "Raining in My Heart", while feigning tap choreography with the five other cast members (who were excellent tappers), we posed in a pyramid holding and twirling umbrellas. As the tallest, I was the top of the pyramid.

One night as we sang the finale of the number, Carol who played the "tough cookie", was crouching at the bottom of the pyramid and she lost her balance causing her to fall over with her umbrella. At the top of the pyramid I was oblivious of this fact, but the rest of the cast were thrown into a fit of laughter and could barely sing. Carol sat on the floor, the others tried to sing "Oh yes, it's raining, raining, raining in my heart", while twirling their umbrellas, but few of their words came out. I, on the other hand, clumped the dance in my monster boots and lustily sang my harmony part up at the top, all by myself. I didn't know this had happened until I was back stage and everyone was hysterically laughing.

The first Celebration Playhouse production "You're a Good Man, Charlie Brown"

"Dames at Sea" with Neil and Mark with Ted on the piano

"The Fantasticks"

"Stop the World..." with Judi

The season was a huge success and the team looked forward to another season, which would include the musical namesake *Celebration*. I was only in one play in the second season, but it was the ground-breaking, blatantly gay play *Boys in the Band*. Gary played the tortured lead, Mark the "pock-marked, Jew fairy" (he also directed), Neil the flamboyant, nellie-queen, and I played the straight-acting, gay teacher. Talk about gutsy. I was a high school teacher in the early 70's playing a gay teacher in the town where I taught.

The set was a realistic looking New York apartment, with a small dining table down front. One night some audience members sat at the dining table on the set, instead of their assigned café table, and no one noticed until the play began. Gary came on stage, into "his apartment" and there sitting at his dining table were a strange family. I believe he was so surprised and flummoxed that let out a shriek (in character of course), left the stage, stopped the show, and had the family reseated to begin the play again.

"Boys in the Band"
Gary Cohen,
Bill Biach, Mark Gerstein, David Christopher
John Richkus, Neil Cerbone, Marc Slavin, Billy Beckman

Roland's Restaurant was not the best landlord, however. It wasn't easy trying to make a quiet, dramatic moment in a play with the Bunny-Hop is being stomped on the floor above. After four productions that second season, they decided to move the Playhouse to another location. Enter Bill Biach. He was primarily a back stage person, but he ventured onstage to play the straight guy in *Boys in the Band* (upper left in the photo). His family owned some property in Cranford, which had been Trubenbach's Feed and Grain Store for many years, but had recently closed. Bill's mother was willing to rent the building to Celebration Playhouse for a minimal fee. So Bill became a partner in the playhouse and we all set out to make this new location into a prime theater.

However, this was not an easy task. The building was old and had been a feed and grain store for decades and a farm house before that. There were bins constructed on the first and second floors to hold the grain that first had to be dismantled and removed. Then the whole building was full of left over seed, grain and mouse turds. It took weeks to clean it out.

Once it was cleaned, we were faced with the challenge of how to transform this space into a viable theater. A staircase stretched across the back wall and led up to the second floor where we put the dressing rooms. Below that was a door that led to the basement, which would be an "off stage" space. These staircases became the back wall of the stage area. We put in about 100 seats on the other three walls, leaving the center of the room for the stage. On one side, were the double doors that led onto the street, and on the other side was a small lobby area, so the street, second floor, lobby and basement were the "wings".

On either side of the room there were two steel pillars (one with a brick chimney next to it) going right up through where the stage was. It took several years to remove the chimney, but the two pillars remained. They always caused audience sight line problems, thus any seat in the house had some area blocked behind one of these pillars. It was a low ceiling, but lights had to be hung, and many a head bonked into a lighting fixture at one time or another. But with several coats of paint, some used theater seats and lots of ingenuity, this bizarre, completely unsuitable building, became Celebration Playhouse, where some of the best theater I've ever seen and participated in would take place.

The opening show for the Cranford theater would be *The Man of La Mancha* and Gary wanted me to play Cervantes/Don Quixote. This would be the first new major role I would have to prepare for in several years and it seemed a daunting task. The few musical leads I'd handled before required more acting than beautiful singing, but Quixote had to sing "The Impossible Dream", one of the most famous songs in the entire musical canon, and sound terrific. Like Littlechap, Cervantes is on stage most of the play, transforming from an author to the farmer, Alonso Quijana, to the mad knight, putting the make-up on to become Don Quixote in a dingy prison in front of the other, hostile prisoners.

The other two featured actors were the powerhouse Carol Vicolo as Aldonza and director Gary as Quixote's sidekick, Sancho. So, backed up by an excellent cast, I plowed my way through this role and the outcome was immensely satisfying. We opened the new Celebration Playhouse to rave reviews and were thrilled to have such a grand beginning to our new theater.

The front of our new playhouse, with many of the core company.

The oft repeated story of one of my classic goofs is that one night as Alonso Quijana goes mad and turns himself into Don Quixote, I said the line, proudly and loudly, "No longer the humble farmer, Alonso Quijana, but the noble knight, ALONSO QUIJANA!" This would not be my last "re-written" line during my career.

*As Don Quixote singing
"The Impossible Dream"*

There is no way I can list all the amazingly memorable theatrical events that went on in that building over the five more years that Gary, Neil, Mark and Bill ran the theater. For one thing, unlike most amateur theaters, it featured productions 52 weeks a year. A play would run 5 or 6 weekends. During that time the next play would rehearse on the stage with the current set. Then on a Saturday night the play would close, they would strike the set, and on Sunday would build the set for the new show, sometimes with a rehearsal that night. Then Monday through Thursday the new play would work on their now built set and open on Friday. With not one dark weekend the entire year. Plus, there were often midnight shows of more outlandish plays, like *Women Behind Bars* and *The Rocky Horror Show.*

Another amazing component of the Celebration Playhouse was that they produced every genre of play and musical: drama, comedy, avant-guard, absurd, etc. They would produce courageous plays that no other theaters in the area would attempt at that time. A prime example was *The Persecution and Assassination of Jean-Paul Marat as Performed by the Inmates of the Asylum of Charenton Under the Direction of the Marquis de Sade* – with the nude bathtub scene.

Marat/Sade, takes place in an insane asylum where the Marquis de Sade stages a play for prominent townspeople, with the inmates as the actors. They present a play about the assassination of Jean-Paul Marat, which ultimately arouses the inmates to riot and attack the "bourgeois playgoers ". Although the dialogue is the "play within the play" the action that moves the story for the audience is watching the inmates during the enactment. Gary cleverly put "bars" between the real audience and the performers, with "locked gates" that were "unlocked", to let the audience get to their seats then "locked" before the inmates were led onstage and the "play" began.

I played Count DuPere, an aristocrat with an insatiable sexual psychosis, and my costume included a "permanent erection", created by a large, realistic dildo under my tight, soiled trousers. DuPere was assigned a nun/nurse to look after him attempting to keep him under control, but throughout the play I, in character, would look for female audience members with whom I could interact. My "nun" and I had a code for how far she would let me go when I went up to the bars making lewd gestures to some unsuspecting audience member. I could put one hand on the bars while teasing her, but as soon as I grabbed with both hands, my nun would come over and beat me back to my seat.

My big scripted scene in the play involved DuPere proposing to Charlotte Corday, who ultimately is the one who murders Marat in his bathtub. In the scene, I was supposed to be speaking the dialogue with her, but be so overcome with my sexual urges for the actress that I couldn't control myself and would ravish her, requiring my nun and guards to pull me off the actress, ruining the scene.

In the early rehearsals I assumed that DuPere's "objective" was to seduce every woman he could, being this obsessively horny guy, and his "obstacle" would be those who stopped him. But, this became a one-note exercise and boring to play. Upon studying my role, I decided to try a different direction. Given that Dupere was so vain, his objective would be to impress Marquis de Sade by being the best actor in the "play" and his obstacle would be his illness, which he hated. This approach worked wonders. When I had my scene with Charlotte, I tried so hard to do the lines brilliantly, but I couldn't control my urges, thus attacking her and ruining the scene. When the guards pulled me off her I burst into violent tears and wept on my nun's lap. This worked for me every night of the production.

At the end of the play, when the inmates revolt, DuPere gets carried away in the frenzy of the riot and rapes his nun. Just as the chaos rose to a fevered pitch, an inmate grabbed the keys from a guard and went for the "locked" gates opening them so the inmates could attack the audience. But there was an instant blackout, followed by a strobe flash with all of the actors in a freeze of the horrific scene. It was chilling and one of the best moments in Celebration Playhouse's history.

The inmates of Charenton, in *Marat/Sade*

DuPere making love to Charlotte Corday

* * *

Here is a list of some the plays in which I was fortunate to perform during that period: *A Lion in Winter, Company, One Flew Over the Cuckoo's Nest, The Rocky Horror Show, Marat/Sade, Jesus Christ, Superstar, Private Lives, Arsenic and Old Lace, El Grande de Coca Cola, Funny Thing Happened on the Way to the Forum,* and my two all time favorites, *A Little Night Music* and *Who's Afraid of Virginia Woolf.*

Funny Thing....Forum, with Paul Kaye, Gary Cohen and Tommy Phillips

If you speak to any actor for long enough, he is bound to bring up some story of a goof or mishap that happened during a performance. Here is one of my favorites:

In *A Little Night Music*, there is a elegant dining room scene with a huge, elaborately set table where all the leading characters sit and speak witty Sondheim banter. On the tiny Celebration stage this was difficult, so the scenic designer (Gary, of course) devised a pre-set table on four ropes strung through holes in the ceiling to the second floor, into pulleys in the dressing room. The table stayed as flat as possible to the ceiling throughout the play, until that scene came, and then a stagehand upstairs lowered the table down to about 2 ½ feet from the stage. The actors moved chairs around the table, set the candelabras and wine glasses up-right, and proceeded to play this fairly long, important scene. This setup worked well for all but one night.

During one particular performance the crew person upstairs lowered the table all the way to the stage floor and was unaware of his mistake. We actors had brought our chairs into place, and sat watching the table get lower and lower, past our knees, past our ankles and landing solidly on the floor. We waited a few moments hoping that the crew member would realize what he had done and raise the table up again, but it just sat there on the floor. The audience knew something was drastically wrong, but kept their giggles to a minimum. We actors, however, while reaching down to fetch our wine glasses from the floor for a toast, had a quite the hard time keeping a straight face while delivering Mr. Sondheim's brilliant dialogue.

A Little Night Music and the infamous floating banquet table.

Murder Among Friends, with Oscar Stokes

    The above photo shows the staircase at the back of the stage that led to the dressing rooms, which was used in so many plays as an exit/entrance. It also reminds me of an extraordinary mishap that I used to teach a valuable lesson to all my acting classes.
    Murder Among Friends was not a particularly brilliant piece of theater, but it was great fun because I worked with some of the best actors in the business: Linda Herman, Oscar Stokes, Angela Intili and Stephen Newport. The plot involved a triangle between a married

theatrical couple, myself and Linda, and our agent, played by Stephen. At one point Linda and Steven, who are assumed lovers, are plotting my murder. Steve is supposed to be opening a bottle of champagne as they discuss the plans for my demise.

One performance as Stephen struggled with the bottle, it slipped from his hands and smashed on the stage, spreading ginger ale and splinters of glass all over the "living room" area. The two actors continued without loosing a beat, with dialogue about cleaning up the mess before the party guests arrived. This was right at the time of my entrance, and I walked in on this improvisation. Linda told me to make the martinis (which Stephen was supposed to make) while he picked up some of the shards, then she exited (as she was supposed to do – leaving the men alone).

The major plot twist was then revealed, which was that Stephen and I were lovers and were plotting to murder my wife. We didn't want to muddy the waters, so we moved into the "dining room" to do the scene, which led up to a big kiss between us. After that scene, Linda returns carrying an empty Kleenex box and some towels, instructing us to pick up the rest of the glass and wipe up the floor with the towels, because our party guests were about to arrive. We did so, as we continued the written dialogue, just as Oscar and Angela arrive. Linda tells them "Watch your step, darlings, as Stephen has broken a bottle of champagne, so the floor is terribly slippery". By this time we've cleaned up as much as necessary and the play continues to the end.

I had theater friends in from New York to see that performance and one of them said to me afterwards, "It's really a silly play, isn't it? And what was the playwright thinking having them break a bottle of champagne?" They had no clue that it wasn't part of the play.

Another favorite goof happened in *Who's Afraid of Virginia Woolf.* In the opening scene George and Martha enter from their front door into the set of their living room. Martha admonishes George for being slow with the keys, he finally gets it open and they come in. She then has the famous line, "What a dump!" The play was directed so that Linda (Martha) and I (George) entered from the street through the exit doors. Well, it happened to be a frigid night and some audience member evidently had felt a draft before the play began and pulled the door close with the panic bar, locking it. So when we did our scene outside the door, and tried to open it to enter, it wouldn't budge. We adlibbed loudly about some problem with the key, with Linda screaming that George was an idiot. Then I said that we should go around and use the back door. So we ran around the theater (in the snow and ice) into the lobby and huffing and puffing made our first entrance from the other side of the stage.

The lighting technician, Mike Driscoll (who, many years later, would direct me in several plays) couldn't see the stage, and was working strictly from sound cues. So when Martha says: "What a dump!", which is the cue for the lighting to come up on the front door hall, he put those lights up. This left Martha and George in the dark for the beginning of the scene, but revealed our stage manager, who had crept across the stage in the dark to open the front door. Awkward. Later in the scene when we said the lines that lit up the living room set, the lighting came back to normal, although the stage manager was stuck in a seat on that side of the stage until intermission.

In this production, Nick and Honey were played quite wonderfully by Ted Kociolek and Lisa Minogue, who were our musical director prodigy and Reynold's then ex-wife. At the time, I was actually too young to play George (just 40), but Gary had faith that I could do it and I'll always thank him for this and the many other opportunities that he gave me.

It remains one of my favorite roles, and plays. I only wish that I had gotten the chance to play George again when I was more age appropriate. I think I could have been even better. Even so, over the years I have seen many George and Marthas and I still feel that Linda and I were right up there with the best.

The other role I tackled with Gary's courageous casting and guidance was King Henry II in *A Lion in Winter*, and again with the wonderful Linda Herman playing the powerful, Eleanor of Aquitaine. Here I had to be a warrior king, a bombastic, crude, non-intellectual boor. This was the opposite of cerebral George, and I can't say it was easy to become Henry.

Linda had been in my acting classes and one of the techniques I often taught in my school was the use of animals to help create a character. I had used this exercise effectively in Irene Dailey's class, by doing a crocodile to help me with the slow, deliberate movement of Brick, in *Cat on a Hot Tin Roof*, since my natural tendency is to be quick and hyper-active.

So I took Linda to the zoo. The closest one to us was on Staten Island, and I'd never been to that zoo. We traveled across the Verrazano bridge into the bowels of Staten Island to find the most depressing, old fashioned, decrepit, pathetic zoo imaginable. All the poor animals were in small cages, and not happy about it. It had none of the open spaces that one would see at the Bronx Zoo or any other modern zoo.

The idea was to find an animal that had some physical characteristics of the character you wanted to create, study it, then recreate the animal back in the studio. Linda, none too happy about the exercise to begin with, was the first to find a suitable animal. It was a majestic bald eagle, which just stood on his perch and glared at everyone, not moving much more than his head. I think Linda liked this because it was easy to copy for the exercise but in reality it was quite a good choice for Eleanor.

I was determined to find some animal that would help me be the powerful, butch leader that Henry was and I wasn't. I thought about a bear, but this zoo had only playful, young bears. However, after watching these bears, and imagining them more mature and angry, I was able come up with some semblance of bear-like movement.

Back in the Studio by ourselves, we began "becoming" our animals (Linda tentatively, me energetically). We imagined them in separate, but adjoining, cages. At first not aware of each other, while we got "into our animal", then becoming aware of each other. An animal "relationship" occurred, with the eagle haughtily observing the boisterous bear below, showing off with macho threats.

We both started feeling that the intelligent strength of the eagle could over-power the posturing of the bear. As we slowly evolved these animals into humans and began our improvisation, Henry and Eleanor's relationship was beautifully clarified. I felt that the animal exercise was a great help in developing our characters, and Linda begrudgingly agreed.

I also grew a full beard, to give me the "bear-like" feeling. Though I couldn't wait to get it off and shaved right before the closing night party.

Henry II and Eleanor of Aquitaine, with Neil Cerbone as Prince Phillip

Linda and I had used private improvisation for George and Martha, as well. Not with animals, but by recreating and improvising their past lives and relationships, it filled in the blanks for us that Albee intentionally does not make clear in the script. So we acted out how George and Martha met, why they got married, finding out that they really were in love, despite all the vitriol in the play.

We discovered and made the choice that George didn't get chairman of the department because Martha's father didn't like him, and most importantly, we discovered and decided which of the characters was the one who couldn't have children. George and Martha do not have children in the play, but rather, as a game between themselves, invent a child that they speak about as though he were real. So, through improvisation, we acted out our invention of the child and how we "played" with it as the years went by and he "grew up". Although the audience needn't know any of this information, we as actors had to know, and this improvisational work was invaluable to both of us.

I found it fascinating that Linda and I flipped our relationships in those two plays. Martha was the loud-mouthed vulgarian and George was the quiet intellectual, while Henry bombasted and Eleanor calculated. I learned an interesting lesson after doing both roles. After *Lion,* I never felt like going out and partying after the play, but after *Woolf,* I could party all night. This seems incongruous since George is the longer and harder role. But later I figured out that the reason for this was because George had a conflict with his overbearing wife but he manages to overpower her by his intellect. Whereas Henry is not only foiled by his wife's cleverness, his sons imprison both of them and take over the castle. In other words: George "wins" at the end of the play, and Henry "loses". So George felt like partying and Henry absolutely didn't. This is how involved I get in a role, even if I don't realize it.

One Flew Over the Cuckoo's Nest was one of the many highlight experiences at Celebration Playhouse, even though I had the smaller role of Dale Harding, the bull-goose loony. Gary had the daunting task of directing this play and playing the tough, leading role of McMurphy. The way he handled all the actors and the staging of that piece on the tiny stage, then jumping in and becoming McMurphy, was astounding. Looking back, since transitioning to director, I'm so awe-struck at this accomplishment, but back then we all just took this achievement for granted.

Dale Harding spends much of the time sitting being intimidated by Nurse Ratchet (powerfully played by Judi Adams). Thus, I gave myself a task – I took a note pad, presumably to keep pinochle scores on, and whenever Nurse Ratchet was there I would draw a picture to keep from her noticing me. I am definitely not an artist, let alone a cartoonist. I worked it out that I would finish one drawing during the course of each performance.

In rehearsals my drawings were crude and primitive works, sort of grade school quality. But as I became Dale, for some unconscious acting reason, my artwork got better and better. And each drawing began to reflect Dale's disturbed mind, and they became increasingly bizarre. One day it would be a ballerina dancing on the bald head of a man, the next a huge snake who had obviously swallowed some guy, as his silhouette was clearly showing. And Dale's drawings got amazingly like a professional cartoonist – way better than David Christopher could ever do. I honestly wasn't aware of them as I did them, they just happened.

One Sunday when we had an evening performance, a large group of us loonies went into New York to the Public Theater to see a matinee of a new musical in previews that we'd heard might be good – called *A Chorus Line*. We knew nothing about it. One of the group couldn't go, so we gave a ticket to a dancer in the lobby and I sat next to him.

Well, being completely blown away by this piece, one can imagine this dancer's reaction. We were all weeping openly during the whole thing, especially the dancer. Our entire group left the theater in complete silence, then walked into Greenwich Village to a pre-arranged restaurant, without saying a word. Once we were seated, someone broke the silence and from that moment on, we talked of nothing else but the brilliance of the show we had just seen.

However, we had to come back and do *Cuckoo's Nest* that night and none of us were in the mood to do anything but talk about *Chorus Line*. But we did it and I'm sure it was a fine performance. Later when I was looking at all the cartoon's that Dale made, I noticed that on that Sunday evening, Dale wasn't really "there", because the drawing reflected David's childish style.

After about three years of cranking out plays and musicals for every weekend of the year, the producers wanted to push the theater forward to a new level and maybe even make some money for all their efforts, so they created a board of directors and applied for "non-profit" qualification. In doing so, they made what I consider was a very poor decision, they changed the name to New Jersey Public Theater.

I think they wanted it to sound more professional, but what it did was take the "joy" out of the name, and to some degree, out of the whole endeavor. But the New Jersey Public Theater under the original creators, Gary, Neil, and Bill (Mark had moved to New York), continued to produce some superb work for a couple more years.

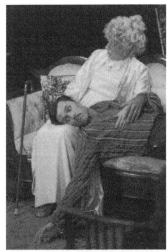

As the "John Barrymore" character, with Linda playing my mother
(which didn't thrill her)

<u>*Two Gentlemen of Verona*</u>, *with Carolyn Kostopolis' fabulous costumes.*
Kate Brown, John Richkus, Carol Vucolo, Neil Cerbone, Trish Parfitt,
Doug Fogel, Angela Intili and Gary Cohen

    Finally the originators were burned out and decided to sell the operation to new-comer, Richard Dominick. This made many changes in the theater and to be honest the quality for the most part deteriorated. I continued to be involved, however, particularly in directing plays much more than I had before. Most of us who were involved in Celebration Playhouse and New Jersey Public Theater will discuss those "Golden Years" and ask, "Was it really that good?"

And we invariably answer, "Yes."

A collage from the Golden Years at Celebration Playhouse.

Thirteen

Inside The Acting Studio

About the time Celebration Playhouse became NJ Public Theater, I was becoming disenchanted with teaching in public school. The last straw was what I still call "That Fourth Period Class".

In the senior English curriculum there was a class that I had developed called "Communications", where we studied films, music, TV and anything other than "literature" or the written word, that English classes had been about for 12 grades. It was a popular class with all the seniors and I was fortunate to be a popular teacher, so I loved teaching that class. But this particular year, I had a fourth period class made up of bright, motivated, hostile, vicious, sadistic students, who made it their mission to make teachers miserable. They were an infamous pack of monsters and all the teachers warned me that they had been that way since grade school and it was a reputation that they felt they had to sustain.

I found myself waking up in the morning and thinking "Oh god, I have to meet my Fourth Period Class again today – I think I'll call in sick." They actually made me physically ill. Whatever we did in class, whatever lesson I'd prepared that was loved by the students in the past, they would, in their subtle way, condemn, ridicule, and generally make me feel like shit.

They were smart so they never did anything that merited sending them to the principal or even giving them poor grades, they just made the teacher feel lousy and uncomfortable. And this was every day for the entire school year. So, this class, as well as generally getting bored with public school, motivated me to move on to a new period of my life.

I had begun teaching adult acting classes with NJ Public Theater during the summer that had been and fairly successful. So I thought, *Hmmm? Maybe I should start my own acting school for adults!* I mentioned to several of my colleagues at Roselle Park High School, that I'd thought of quitting the public school to start an acting studio, and they thought I was completely out of my mind.

"Are you insane?"

"You've been teaching 17 years. You only have eight more years before you can retire."

"You have tenure and a pension that you'd have to give up, for god's sake!"

But the idea still intrigued me.

I had recently purchased a house in Cranford, New Jersey. Bill Biach and I had been living in two apartments in a house in Roselle when the owner of the house kicked us out because he wanted to move in his family from Italy. We thought of renting again, but Bill suggested that we go into the purchasing of a house together. I had no idea what that entailed, but he arranged a loan for a down-payment from his mother, and we started house hunting.

We found one that we thought would work for the two of us living separate lives, right on the main street in Cranford, and we bought it. And I've been living in that house ever since.

It so happened that, in the back yard of the house, there was a second building. It had been the original 1920s garage, but a previous owner had expanded it with another large, two story room to make an artist's studio with a skylight high on the roof, however, he died soon after and never used it.

When we bought the house that building was just being used for storage. After we moved in, we had no use for the separate building, and it just sat there. Then Bill suggested that we make it into an apartment and rent it out. We quickly had a potential renter, Gary and his current girlfriend Carol Vuocolo. So we put in a bathroom, sheet-rocked the walls of the old garage, and planned for the balcony of the studio to be the bedroom. It was going to be the coolest apartment, ever

Then we found out that the property was not zoned for 2 family units, so the township would not permit it to be rented out. But the light bulb lit up in my head. *It could be the acting studio!* So I gave my notice at the high school, and spent the rest of the school year adapting the building in my spare time, in hopes to begin acting lessons in the summer.

I put in a wooden floor in the studio room, a mirror on one wall for dance classes, and a special linoleum flooring so tap dancing classes could be taught. I fixed the many shelves on the balcony to be used for props, and made the back room, which was once the garage, into a lounge with carpeting and couches and a desk for registering students.

At the time I had a huge (unreciprocated) crush on a student, the multi-talented pianist-singer-actor, Randy Hertzog. He had played piano for my classes since he was in junior high, and was now a senior and he either accompanied the high school musicals or was in the plays. Randy was gay, so we'd had many heart-to-heart talks, because he came from a completely fucked up family. He was quite handsome, but unfortunately for me, not "into older men". We were good friends, and that was all. However, I spent my toiling hours building the studio pining away, listening to the radio and hearing pop love songs with new ears – totally sappy – but it passed the hours.

The acting school needed a name. It began in conjunction NJ Public Theater so at first it was long-windedly called, The New Jersey Public Theater Acting School. That obviously needed shortening, so I came up with THE ACTING STUDIO. This sounded enough like "The Actor's Studio" in New York that I thought it would give it a certain panache, without being outright plagiarism.

Both titles worked, because within a couple of years, I had a self-supporting theater arts school, with a dance teacher (Neil), vocal singing teacher (Angela), a Shakespeare teacher (Ed), a movement teacher (Trisha), and myself as the only acting teacher, while also giving private speech classes. THE ACTING STUDIO was fully functional with a dynamic curriculum and ran successfully for twenty years.

THINGS TO KNOW ABOUT THE ACTING STUDIO

Director & Head of Faculty DAVID CHRISTOPHER

WHO ARE THE CLASSES FOR?

The Studio gives Professional training for STAGE and TELEVISION acting to ADULTS, TEENS and CHILDREN (7 to 12).

Also, many students, who are not interested in performing, find that the training helps them with CONFIDENCE and COMMUNICATION, in their personal and professional lives.

WHO TEACHES AT THE STUDIO?

The TEACHERS are highly trained PROFESSIONALS, who have performed extensively in their field. But they are also skilled in the sensitive ART of TEACHING. They want to give their skills to YOU!

ALL ACTING classes are taught by **DAVID CHRISTOPHER**.

Mr. Christopher is a professional director and actor as well as a teacher. He has directed over 25 plays, including: "Brighton Beach Memoirs" and "The Fantasticks"; played leading roles in 30 plays in regional theatre, including "Sweeney Todd," "Captain Hook," "Lion in Winter," "Private Lives" and "Man of La Mancha." He has been Director and Head of Faculty of The Acting Studio for over 14 years.

WHEN ARE CLASSES HELD?

There are FOUR terms a year:
- FALL   Oct. to Dec. (10 weeks)
- WINTER Jan. to Mar. (10 weeks)
- SPRING Apr. to Jun. (10 weeks)
- SUMMER July to Aug. (5 weeks)
(10 classes in each term)

Classes are held once a week, both DAYS and NIGHTS, depending on the students' needs.

WHERE IS THE STUDIO?

SEQUENTIAL COURSES IN ACTING TECHNIQUES

THE ACTOR PREPARES 1.

THEATRE GAMES to free you of inhibitions; IMPROVISATION to develop communication and quick thinking; OBJECT WORK to make you more at ease on stage; BASIC TECHNIQUES to help all actors grow. An excellent course for beginners or experienced actors, wanting to strengthen their "instrument."

2 hrs. weekly

CREATING A SCENE 2.

Using the TECHNIQUES learned in Acting 1 to approach SCENES from plays. Applying improvisation to written scenes to explore EMOTIONS and RELATIONSHIPS of characters in the scenes. REHEARSAL TECHNIQUES are explored like BLOCKING scenes naturally.

BUILDING A SCENE 3.

Delving more deeply into scenes, stressing CHARACTER STUDY. Helping actors to become more VERSATILE in the roles they play and stronger in their EMOTIONAL commitment. LEARNING LINES while still making each PERFORMANCE feel SPONTANEOUS and NATURAL.

SCENE STUDY 4.

INDEPENDENT rehearsal scenes, presented to the class. Each scene is picked for the actor's needs and performed until it is SOLVED. This class is the culmination of the acting classes, allowing actors to use what they have learned. VIDEO TAPES are made for self appraisal.

2 hrs. weekly

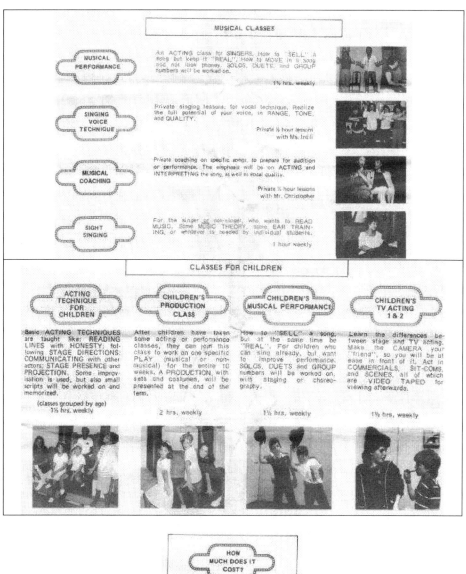

At the beginning the rates were reasonable enough for the students and because I had a large enrollment each term, it gave me a moderately good living. Nonetheless, registration for each term was a tense time, until I found out how many students would enroll and if I would be able to work out a manageable schedule to include them all. As the years went on, some of my teachers dropped out and my studio seemed to attract less students each term. As tuitions dwindled I wanted to raise the fees, but I felt that my students would be less inclined to continue classes.

Ultimately this became a major problem, but for most of those exciting years, I just walked out my back door and I was at a job that I loved, and I could pop back into the house for a cup of coffee whenever I wanted. I met and worked with some immensely talented people and some not so talented people; some actors who became good friends and some scary characters that I wished had never taken the class; some serious actors trying to enter show business, some people who just wanted to try acting out for a lark; some people who went on and worked in community or professional theater, and some who took one class and stopped.

Although I would have liked it to be a school strictly for adults, I had to make my mortgage, so I included children's classes in the afternoons. Many of these classes were babysitting for parents who wanted more free time from their kids, or who thought their little darlings would be stars, or at least should do something besides sports. I often found myself just putting up with the little ones, so that I could teach the adults at night.

My experience taught me that children are not automatically natural actors, more often they're instincts are limited and don't care to learn how to develop them; they just want to have fun after school. Though I did encounter some rather talented children, it was not the norm.

The one type of children's class that I enjoyed most of the time was the musical comedy class. This was more directing than teaching. I would put together a mini-musical by writing a silly, simple script to fit some songs together, give simple choreography to songs they'd learn, and then they would rehearse. I remember having a great deal of fun with songs like "One Brick at a Time" from *Barnum* and "It's a Hard Knock Life" from *Annie*. At the end of the term, the children would present the mini-musical for their families and friends, who always loved it no matter how it went, though occasionally these little shows were quite good.

My favorite type of student was the adult who came in with zero acting experience, completely ignorant of the process, and often shy or introverted. I found that if these students stuck with it and took it seriously for several terms, they would often grow and slowly come out of their shell. Sometimes they would be surprised and find their acting chops, doing some powerful work in later scene classes. It was beautiful watching them gain confidence and feel so much better about themselves. Those people didn't always go on to perform in theaters, but they definitely felt more at ease with themselves and hopefully that confidence and ease made its way into other parts of their lives. Seeing someone blossom like that is always the most gratifying experience I have as a teacher, whether it was in the public school system or in my acting studio.

For example a stocky guy with a beard, in his 20s, enrolled in an Acting One class with a friend. I found out later that he was depressed and was becoming a recluse, so his friend dragged him to the class, just to get him to get out of the house and to socialize with other people. Tentatively he took the first few classes, but as he got more comfortable, he started to come alive and performed some extremely amusing improvisations.

So impressed with his work by the end of his second term, I asked him to perform in a play produced by NJ Public Theater. It was Noel Coward's *Private Lives* that I was directing. I was also playing Eliot, with Linda Herman playing Amanda. He looked sort of like Sebastian Cabot, a popular British actor of the time, and he could do a decent British dialect, so he seemed like a good choice for the second husband. He reluctantly agreed and I heard later that he had to be literally pushed on stage for his first entrance. But he ended up turning out a fairly solid performance of the role.

This happened to be the time that Gary was preparing to resign from the NJ Public Theater. My shy actor was Richard Dominick who not long after *Private Lives*, bought NJ Public Theater, took over as artistic director and ran the playhouse for several years. He also went on years later to produce the Jerry Springer Show and turned it into an international hit.

One day a young man came in to register for an acting class, recently graduating from college, named Christian Fitzgerald. He was gorgeous, blond, tall, thin, with blue eyes, a big smile and a bubbling personality – and was obviously straight. He did extremely well in class and we became quite friendly, but I never mentioned that I found him to be a dreamboat.

One night we went into Greenwich Village together to see an Off Broadway play at Circle Repertory, called *Feedlot*. He wanted to go for a drink before the show, and since the only straight bar I knew in the Village was White Horse Tavern, I took him there. Then we attended the play and afterwards he said he could go for another drink, but not at the White Horse. I gave this some thought. A gay bar that I often hung out in was Julius', a macho looking bar with sawdust on the floor, boxing photos on the wall and good hamburgers, though still very gay. Nervously, I took him there, hoping he wouldn't be offended.

We sat at the bar, and after we got our beers, he turned to me and said, "I love this place – I come here all the time." I virtually fell off my stool. He confessed to being gay and wondered why we hadn't come here together before. After that night, he remained my very good friend and one of my all time favorite people.

Richard Dominick and Christian Fitzgerald rehearsing a scene.

Teaching eager actors

Christian setting up for a scene on the much-used folding cot.

A mirror exercise, with Tom Lynch (who became a good friend)

Neil Cerbone teaching dance to Judi Adams

It was early in the studio's years that met my favorite acting partner and dearest friend, Linda Herman. One day on the phone a woman called and asked about taking classes, wondering which class she should take. She sounded to me to be what I called, a "Westfield matron", the type of bored housewife who wanted to do something different. So I told her what I tell everyone, you should probably start with Acting One.

She said, "I have had some experience. I've worked in community theater".

This strengthened my view that she was a Westfield matron, so I said, "I still think it's best to begin at the beginning, so you get an idea of the style of acting that I use."

"Very well", she purred in her Bankhead/Hepburn baritone voice. And we set her up in an Acting One class.

When she walked into class, I could tell that she was someone special, with her blond hair rakishly piled up on top of her head and her warm Southern charm. When she began acting, I was immediately impressed with her talent and security in a scene. This was no amateur. It didn't take me long to realize that she was someone that I wanted to work with her. So when Gary suggested that we do *Who's Afraid of Virginia Woolf* and I told him that I had the "Martha". This began one of my finest working partnerships and closest friendships.

Linda was a mother of five, who had divorced her Exxon executive husband because she didn't want to be a trophy wife. He left her the massive Victorian home in Cranford, which was crammed-full with antiques, where she raised these children on her own. To help with the support, she worked in an antique shop, continuing the collection that of which she was so proud. As I got to know her and spend time in her home, I was not surprised to find her son's surf board sitting in the living room amidst all the treasures.

On top of raising the children and working, she built up a vast repertoire of acting experience, playing among others, virtually every Tennessee Williams female leading character.

She and I would spend hours on her vast front porch, sipping mint juleps and reminiscing about roles we'd played or planning future projects together. I loved going over to her home and sometimes brought friends just to see the wonders of it. Linda got cancer and we lost her much too soon. There is no one that I miss more than her.

Linda, her youngest daughter Tammy,
and one of her beloved two pugs

Linda's amazing home.

* * *

When one is a teacher, one hopes that there is at least one student whose life you inspire and change for the better. I think I can say, from the Facebook posts alone, that I have achieved this often in my career, and it always fills me with comforting sense of accomplishment.

On the top of that list of students is a sixty year old, woman named Clara Davis. I was teaching speech and acting to her daughter, Jean, a stunningly beautiful, black woman who was a fine singer and actress. One day she came to me and said that her mother would like to take speech with me, but she was shy and frightened by the prospect, and asked if I would I meet with her.

She told me that her mother had had little education, growing up in Alabama before the civil rights movement, and had come up to the North on a bus when she was in her early twenties, and that she quickly got a job as a maid in a hotel in New York, working there for most of her adult life. She raised a family and she and her husband made a fair enough living to purchase a house in Westfield (a neighboring town of Cranford) so their children could go to good schools. But now, her Westfield educated grandchildren were mocking the way she spoke, and she want to improve her speech.

I met with Clara and she did indeed have some terrible speech challenges. She seemed incapable of making the last sounds of any word, just rushed over those sounds or eliminated them. It was a combination of black-southern speech and sloppy diction. So we began private speech classes.

I grew to love working with her because although she wasn't particularly bright, she worked so diligently to improve. I could tell that it was hard for her to practice the exercises that she needed to do at home, but I think she waited until she was alone in the house and did the best she could. Her reading was poor, so as we progressed with her speech, I also made her read from a book as a final exercise in class. In the beginning it would take her a while to get through one page aloud, attempting to get the sounds, but also attempting to read correctly.

After about a year of working on her speech and reading, I asked if she would like to learn some grammar, to understand the language better. She was thrilled and happily obliged. So I went to my old school and asked for an English grammar book, and we began to explore nouns, pronouns, verbs, adjectives etc. It was all completely new to Clara.

When we got through the grammar book and when she was reading more fluently, the book we were reading mentioned Ancient Rome. I asked if she knew what that meant, and I realized that her grasp of history was completely lacking. She honestly believed that the world started at Christ's birth. So I got a World History book and we began back with the cave men. When we got to Egypt, I took her into the Metropolitan Art Museum to see the Egyptian collection. When we walked in the lobby to see it full of museum goers, her reaction was "Don't these people work?" All the years she was in Manhattan working at the hotel, she had never done anything but work as a maid all day and then return home.

When we got to the Roman times, I rented the VHS tapes of the British mini-series *I, Claudius*, which we watched in full. I had to pause the tapes often and explain what was going on and show her how it fit into our history lessons.

Around this time she told me that her current job, waitressing at Howard Johnson's, was terminated, so she would have to stop classes. I said "Clara, you never have to stop classes. You are a permanent honorary scholarship student, and never have to pay again."

We were reading something like a Jacqueline Susan novel when I asked her what the capital of England was, and she said, "Europe?" So out came the geography book. I said, "There is Europe, now where are the British Isles? – They are islands"

She couldn't find them, because she didn't know that the blue represented water. Thus, map reading became our next project. This was during the first Iraq War and one day she came in to me all smiles because they had shown a map of the Middle East on the news and she knew what they were talking about. She was so proud of her new map-reading knowledge, as she was with all the things we learned over the years we worked together.

One day when we were simply reading a novel together, she told me that she had cancer and would not be able to come to any more classes. We were reading a book she was enjoying, *Crazy in Alabama*, so I went to her home so she could complete it. She was too weak and in pain to read herself, so I read aloud to her. I went two more times, but we never completed the book, because she died before it was over.

One of my goals and dreams had been to take Clara to London, she would have been so thrilled, but it wasn't to be.

Her daughter, Jean, asked if I would speak at Clara's funeral. I said I'd be honored, assuming that I'd be one of many testifying about her life. I would tell a story about her, amongst the many other stories. In the church, I was the only white person in the crowded sanctuary. I looked at the program and it listed an opening prayer, a solo song, and "Speaker: David Christopher", then the benediction. The program indicated that I was the only one who would be speaking. *I was it!* The preacher did a short prayer, a woman sang a gospel version of "Over the Rainbow" and it was my turn to give the eulogy. I didn't have a clue what I would say.

I slowly walked past Clara's open coffin, up onto the pulpit, and looked out over a sea of hostile, black faces. Most of them didn't have any idea who this honky was that was going to speak about Sister Clara. I have never had such stage fright in my life. But I loved Clara, and she had loved me, and I wanted nothing more than to honor her life and speak of the person I was so fortunate to know through the many hours we had spent learning together.

I took a deep breath and, referring to the rousing rendition of the song that had just finished, I said, "Over the Rainbow. That's just where Clara wanted to go and where she is now....."

As I continued improvising, about half way through my speech I started hearing "Amen"s and "Hallelujah"s with people raising their hands in praise. I think I spoke for about 15 minutes and I have absolutely no memory of what I said, but at the end I got a rousing reaction from the whole congregation.

* * *

I'll never regret leaving a tenured position with a retirement package, even though I never really made a decent living after the first few seasons. During the last couple years, I started getting more directing work that conflicted with classes, so I had to begin cancelling sessions. This discouraged students from registering again and enrollment got smaller and smaller. I did eventually have to take a temp job to survive. And there were even times between registrations for a new term when I counted on a Christmas check from my mother to pay the bills.

I finally closed the studio, but those twenty years that I ran The Acting Studio were truly wonderful years and I wouldn't change a thing.

Fourteen

The Munro Doctrine

1979 turned out to be a momentous year in my life, in both a tragic way and a romantic way. And the two incidents happened almost simultaneously.

It started one night when Christian Fitzgerald and I went into Greenwich Village to see a play, as a farewell excursion to Chris since he was moving to California the next day. After the play, we went into a gay bar called the Ninth Circle. Coincidentally, this was the same bar I had gone to on my first trip to New York and met "Joey, Joey, Joey...". It was rather a seedy bar, but there was a garden in the back where patrons were welcome to sit and smoke a bit of weed. We started out in the garden, got some tokes from an obliging guy and then we settled into a booth indoors for some beers.

Since it was his party, so to speak, I told Chris that he was free to pick someone up and that I could get home to New Jersey by myself. He said, "And you feel free to do so as well."

"Yeah right," I said "like I ever pick anyone up in bars." And I honestly never did. But after we'd had some more beers, I looked across the crowded room and saw a young man, and for some reason in my drunken/stoned state, I was instantly attracted to him.

"That guy looks just like Montgomery Cliff", I said.

Now my "type" has always been blond, blue-eyed twinks, but this dark haired, brown-eyed guy knocked me out. I got his attention and told him with my hand actions to "get over here, cutie". He did and we had a flirty conversation, ending with me saying that I'd like to get together with him. Unfortunately, he said that he lived out in Queens and it didn't seem practical to bring him back to New Jersey. And frankly, I was in no condition for a sexual romp, anyway. After we determined that we couldn't hook up that night, I asked if I could have his number. Then he did something so sweet that I've never forgotten it. He asked if he could have one kiss to help him decide. We kissed, he smiled, and then he gave me his name, David Munro, and phone number. I told him that I was going out of town for the weekend, but would call him as soon as I got back. And that was that.

David Munro, the year I met him.

The trip I was taking was to Fort Lauderdale, Florida, in order to interview for a dream job with Eastern Airlines. If I were hired for this job, I would be going to the movies and being paid for it! I would view pre-screenings or opening showings of current movies and write a report for the airlines telling them if I thought a movie was appropriate to show on flights between New York and Florida. Even though I got the recommendation from a friend at Eastern Airline's New York office in New York, I had to go to the corporate office in Fort Lauderdale for the interview. I packed my suit and some beach clothes and went down for the weekend.

My interview was on Monday and it went very well. I was no longer teaching in the public schools, so I had free time during the day to go to screenings in New York. They seemed impressed with my knowledge of movies and I got the job. I would be paid $25 plus expenses for every movie I critiqued and I would get invitations to private screenings with the critics and theater bookers. I was very excited about this job, as I boarded the plane for home, and I was also looking forward to the forthcoming date with David Munro.

We had to change planes in Atlanta and when I got into the terminal I was paged on the loudspeaker. The message was for me to call my brother. *What in the world?* When I reached him at some unfamiliar phone number, he told me that our father had died and that I was to go immediately to where our parents had moved to retire,

Chickasha, Oklahoma, for the funeral. He didn't give me any particulars just that I had to get there as soon as possible. I was completely in shock, since aside from my father's depression problems, he was very healthy.

The airlines dug into the airplane hold to fetch my luggage and gave me the first available flight to Oklahoma City. I boarded the new plane in a daze. How had my father died? What about my poor mother? It was all happening so fast and I couldn't really get my head around it.

I was picked up at the airport by my mother's brother, Uncle Chuck, who was quite taciturn and I still was not clear on what happened to my father. Evidently, several family members were coming from around the country, so they were holding the funeral until they arrived. We drove up to the house and I went into the living room with the gathered relatives.

My mother ran into my arms, weeping and blurted out that my father had hung himself! She had gone into the garage where he had made a workshop for himself and she found him hanging from the rafters. My poor mother. Dad had left a note only saying "I can't take it any more." There was not a word about her in the note and I think this hurt her the most. But as my cousin Marianne, who was a nurse, said, "Depressed people rarely think of others, it is the nature of the disease." Still my mother had to live the rest of her life remembering the sight she came upon in that garage, and she was haunted by it and had nightmares for years.

So the funeral proceeded in a haze, I don't remember any details.

It did create a reunion with several relatives I hadn't seen in years, like my cousin Charles, who was close to my father, a sort of soul mate with his own depressive tendencies, and who was devastated by my father's suicide. Bobby, who was Jonathan's son from his first marriage to Carmen, came from New York. He had spent many vacations of his childhood with my parents and adored my dad. I got to meet my Uncle Val, Dad's brother, as an adult for the first time, and his sister Aunt Betty who I hadn't seen in years.

A story has been told that during the agonizing wait for late relatives, to break the mournful ice I demonstrated a parlor trick my father had taught me. It was an amusing pantomime of sewing one's fingers together with an invisible needle and thread – I was the entertainer even at such a sorrowful time.

After Dad's funeral
Top Row: Uncle Don Lyons, Cousin Charles, Brother Jonathan, his wife Solveig, Uncle Bill, Mother (with Miss Muffet), Florie (Chuck's girlfriend), Uncle Chuck, Uncle Val.
Bottom Row: Aunt Betty, cousin Marianne, Me, Bobby (Jonathan's first son), Irene (Val's second wife.)

    Since I could cancel my Acting Studio classes, I stayed on in Chickasha to help my mother manage her life during this dreadful time. We muddled through it, and among other things, I learned much more about the mental problems that my father had had all their married life. That's when I found out that the moving around our family did was primarily due to his inability to cope under some of his jobs and situations. I finally became aware that all the times when I thought my mother was being bossy and harsh with him, she was really trying to snap him out of one of his depressive moods. I can vividly recall her at our childhood dinner table sternly saying, "ROBert. Not Now!" He was evidently slipping into a blue funk and I didn't know what she was talking about. I had never realized how difficult it was for my mother to live with his condition all those years. They both kept the situation from Jonathan and me, or perhaps we were just too wrapped up in ourselves to realize what was really going on. I had been aware on some of my recent Christmas visits that he was not the jovial father I knew, but the fact that he was suicidal was a complete shock. I realized then that the way one dies from the disease of clinical depression is suicide.

My mother decided rapidly to spend her widowed years back in her home town of Highland Park, Illinois. I accompanied her there and immediately went apartment hunting for her. We ended up finding her a beautiful condo on the day I was to return home, and she lived there, as happily as possible, for the rest of her life. Another shocking tragedy occurred there for her, when her beloved younger brother, Chuckie, came to visit from California, and had a heart attack in her guest bathroom. She discovered him the next morning naked in the bathtub. I can't imagine how hard these two experiences were for her, but she was a strong woman and she survived.

By the time I got back to New Jersey, it was several weeks after I had promised to contact David Munro, but I called his number as soon as I got home. He was surprised to hear from me, assuming that I was just another "Give me your number, I'll call you" - who doesn't. But he seemed please and we set up a date. We met for lunch in Manhattan where he worked and since our first encounter was totally superficial, we started to get to know each other.

Up until this point, I had never dated anyone who wasn't in some way connected to the theater, and David Munro was, and still is, a clock maker. Except for a chorus part in a high school production of "Carousel", he'd never been involved in the theater other than as an audience member. Also, in the relationship I had with all of my boyfriends, whatever their age or the duration of the relationship, I always played the role of "teacher". It was obvious from the beginning that Munro had a high intelligence and knowledge in a vast number of areas in which I was completely ignorant. Here was someone to whom I didn't need to be "Auntie Mame" and "show the world", but someone from whom I could actually learn something. And it was a huge relief for me and a great pleasure.

For our second date, so that we could get to know each other more intimately, I invited him to spend the weekend in New Jersey. It was planned that he would see one of the last Celebration Playhouse plays under Gary Cohen's regime. It was an original, very silly, musical spoof of the movie *Good News*, called *Bad News!*. In it I played the rather effeminate Dean of Hickson University. and I would be coupled up with the grumpy spinster, Professor Pross, played by Judi Adams. The rest of the cast was filled with Celebration regulars, Neil Cerbone, Carol Vuocolo, Angela Intili, Lisa Minogue, Oscar Stokes, etc.

Judi and I each had as a prop a *pince nez*, which are spectacles that hang on a ribbon around the neck and are used by pinching them on the nose (hence *pince nez*). We both used them more for flourishing and sternly pointing them at people for emphasis. When Pross and the Dean got together romantically at the end, we linked our *pince nez* together, which is one of my favorite moments for use of objects.

Then we sang "The Sweetheart Stump", as part of a sextet with the other two couples. Judi and I each thought the other was the funniest person alive. So, while singing this silly song in each other's faces, we could barely hold it together to be able to sing, and sometimes just mouthed the words laughing while the others carried the song.

This was not one of my prouder moments on stage.

Probably to impress Munro, and I must have been nuts, I seated him next to the handsome Randy Hertzog, the boy I'd once had such a crush on, who came in a white suit (ala John Travolta) and looked ravishing. The musical was great fun, but I can't imagine what Munro thought about seeing me in such a silly part in such a silly play. And the theatrical evening didn't end with this, either. That night there was a midnight showing of *Women Behind Bars*, a campy spoof of women's prison movies, which featured a naked man and the head matron played in drag. At least I sat next to Munro for this one.

Between the shows, Munro was sitting in the dressing room and Angela came up to him and asked, "What high school do you go to?" David was flattered thinking of it as a compliment, as he was in his 20s, but little did he know that she asked that because of my reputation with high school boys.

Despite whatever impression he got from that theatrical evening, on our first night together we clicked, and we have been together ever since, for 34 years, so far. So I must have done something right that night.

After that, I would either go into Manhattan to see David during the week or he would travel from Elmhurst, Queens to Cranford by subway and train in order to spend a weekend together. One weekend there was a major subway strike in New York, and David Munro had no way to get to the NJ Transit train from Queens, so he walked to Penn Station. I guess he really wanted to see me – and I was very flattered.

We continued this routine for about a year, but the following February we finally decided that he should move out of his apartment and live with me in Cranford. We count our anniversary on Valentine's Day, to make it easier to remember, but I'm not sure which we count from, the year we met or the year we moved in together – it doesn't really matter after all these years, anyway.

While he was visiting primarily on the weekends, I was living with Bill Biach in the house we had bought together three years previously. Bill had his girlfriend living with us, a beautiful acting student that I had introduced to him, named Cara DenBlycker. So with David, we became a quartet and fortunately the four of us got along well. Cara and Bill had the big bedroom and David Munro and I shared the small one that I had been using. That year the four of us had a wonderful time together and it was a house full of love (Bill and Cara married a couple of years later) and we are still friends today.

As often happens when a relationship is new, the rest of the world sort of carries on around it, but it takes over one's life. I was still teaching in my studio and I was still acting occasionally at New Jersey Public Theater, but mostly Munro and I were building our life together.

He moved in with many antiques that he had acquired while in high school, like two beautiful grandfather clocks, which I learned are properly called "long case clocks". He also brought an intricately carved, handmade desk that his grandfather had built, along with the very old chest with the tools that made it. A prize antique was his grandmother's three-quarter bed, with a beautifully carved headboard. It was too small for two people, but we wanted it in our little bedroom and didn't mind the intimacy it required.

The world of antiques was completely foreign to me and this would be one of the many areas where Munro became my instructor. Most importantly, I discovered a new appreciation and understanding of clocks. Having viewed thousands of antique clocks over the years in museums, private homes, antique stores, flea markets, and of course, David's clock shop, I can easily discern a trashy clock from a valuable one. Though my taste sometimes leans towards the tacky, much to Munro's amused disgust.

Our house was built in the 1910s, but it had been gutted in the 60s, replacing all the electrical wiring and much of the plumbing. Unfortunately, all the original molding and detail was removed and covered with new plasterboard. The only original bit of woodwork is the newel post and banister to the upstairs. Also, two stained glass windows, though not particularly good ones, are still in place.

One night soon after he moved in, Munro had a friend visit from New York. While I was teaching out back in the Studio, he and his friend were perusing the house. David's friend noted, "That wall in the living room covers the chimney, and you know, I bet there was a fireplace behind it".

"Let's find out." said Munro, and he went into the basement and got a hammer and chisel, and they preceded to break through the plasterboard, and found what was once the place for a coal stove. They also uncovered a portion of the wall which was brick. At that moment I came in from my class and found them hammering away at the wall with plaster all over the floor. Before I could say a word, David said with excitement, "Look, this whole wall is brick that has been plastered over. We can easily remove the plaster and have an exposed brick wall" (which were popular in the 70s). "And I think it used to be a coal fireplace, so we could put in a wood-burning stove."

All I could do was shake my head and go along with what I thought was madness. However, this incident established our relationship for the rest of our lives. David Munro would get ideas of which I would never have conceived of, but I would blithely go along and be utterly amazed by the outcome. His philosophy is "a wall is only a suggestion." He had no qualms about totally changing anything in the house completely reconfiguring it and improving it. Over the years he has basically redone the whole house and now it is simply spectacular, and <u>almost</u> done.

The latest major addition to the house is his clock tower/pizza oven, which is next to the studio. It was a five year project that Munro designed and built himself because he bought a tower clock movement from a church in Ireland on Ebay, and therefore needed a tower to put it in. The pizza oven was an afterthought when he realized how much brickwork was needed at the foundation of the tower. He decided to make use of it by putting in a wood burning oven, which he now uses year-round for pizza and any other food he needs baking. He even designed a geodesic dome for the oven, cutting numerous fire-brick triangles to create it.

I doubt that it would be an exaggeration to assume that a clock tower/pizza oven is unique – in the world.

One element of our relationship that works beautifully is that Munro is a planner, designer, creator of projects, but he's not good at finishing them. I, on the other hand, can't stand not finishing up something that has been started. So at the end of the day, after he has done all the work of tearing down and building up, I'll happily clean up and get things back to normal so we don't live in chaos.

A good example is when he decided to completely reconfigure the layout of the 2nd floor of our house; doubling the size of the bathroom, putting in a shower, and breaking down walls in the hall to make the den more open, and reshaping the bedroom into an octagon. We did this construction only during the weekends, and the project took a couple years to complete. So my job at the end of every weekend was to clean up the unnecessary clutter and mess, making the upstairs a livable space during the week. Then, as in most of our projects, it is my job to paint the walls and finish up any small tasks that need doing to bring it to an end. This symbiotic partnership has gone smoothly for many projects, and is part of the reason that we get so much done together.

The same year that Munro moved into 189 North Avenue, he decided to leave his job working for a crazy clock dealer and start up on his own. So he found a loft in lower Manhattan, on John Street, a block away from the World Trade Center, and proceeded to make it into a clock shop. There was lots of work to do to make this shabby space into a working clock shop, which included many sheets of sheet-rock. Unfortunately, they couldn't fit in the ancient elevator, so we had to lug these heavy sheets up 8 floors, one at a time. But eventually, the clock shop was built and this is where Munro spent his working hours for about two years, until the Collegiate Church who owned the building doubled the rent.

I enjoyed those years, because we got to explore and get to know lower Manhattan and the Wall Street area whenever I came in to visit him. I could take the PATH from Newark, coming out in the World Trade Center, a block away from the John Street shop. His loft had many windows surrounding it on three sides with a great view, particularly of the World Trade Center. We could also look down on to lower Broadway, where ticker-tape parades originated.

As a "Master Clockmaker", David Munro was, and is, a world-class expert in antique clocks, particularly French clocks. He renovates high-end, museum-quality clocks, manufacturing any part needed to precision perfection. He also designs and builds beautiful clocks of his own. Many of his creations have been sold to clock collectors all over the world. In the clock-world, he is well known as a perfectionist and an artist.

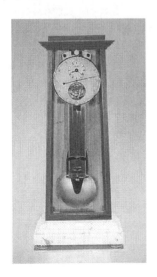  

Three Munro Regulators

After his two years on John Street, he moved his operation to the Upper East Side, 55th Street between Third and Lexington. He was lucky to be given free space in the prestigious antique store, Frederick P. Victoria's, because Mr. Victoria would collect his rent by having a master clockmaker on the premises. The space Munro was given was tiny, actually a small room that was once an elevator shaft, but it was sufficient for his purposes, and being located on the Upper East Side in this fine store, gave him much more access to wealthy clock owners. During those years he was able to work on some of the finest clocks in the world, including some in New York museums, like the Frick. His business and reputation prospered there.

* * *

That first year that Munro and I were together, The Acting Studio was going strong. I didn't do any acting that year, but I did do one significant theatrical project. I decided to direct my acting students in a full-length play at New Jersey Public Theater. So I picked an Off Broadway play that I had seen several times in Greenwich Village called, *Say Goodnight, Gracie* (it didn't have anything to do with Gracie Allen). There were five characters, who were friends, with several of them residing in a Greenwich Village basement apartment together.

I was able to cast all students from the Studio, including my friends Chris Fitzgerald, Peter Adams and Cara DenBleyker. Since they all had taken classes with me over the years, we were able to use acting techniques that we used in the Studio, including lots of improvisation. The set, being this Greenwich Village apartment, was such fun to create using so many crazy props from my collection in the studio. As my actors rehearsed and created these interesting characters, with familiar props and each other, something really special happened. They weren't just doing scene work, they were making a full production for an audience.

I had only performed for Celebration or N.J.P.T., so this was my first directing job with them, and it was a huge success. It made me realize that I could combine my acting and teaching techniques as a director, to create something really powerful in a real production.

This was the start of my directing years.

Say Goodnight, Gracie with Chris Fitzgerald, Eileen Balmuth, Cara DenBlecker, Peter Adams and David Sousy

It was around this time that Munro made a major improvement to The Acting Studio. The building consisted of two rooms, a smaller back room that was originally the 1920s garage and large room that was added on by an owner in the 60s to be used as an art studio. The big room or Acting Room was two stories high, with a balcony on one end that I used for props. The small back room was the lounge and waiting room. It had a hideous, pointed roof with a leaky skylight in the back and a tiny crawl space that I used for storage, only accessible by a ladder. Munro thought that the back room needed changing. And boy did he change it!

He felt that the entire roof/ceiling should be removed and replaced. In the basement he constructed frames for a mansard roof and then proceeded to tear down the entire roof, leaving it with just the cement block walls. It was summer and we didn't anticipate rain that week. Then step by step, with the help of Chris Fitzgerald, the roof was assembled, covered with sheathing and then shingles. Since the ceiling was now so much higher, he installed a balcony to that room, connected to the other balcony, which would be used for costumes. A new window was installed, with a column we found on the street, cut in half and surrounding the window. Sheetrock walls were put up, and even sheetrock ceiling, which was the hardest job of all! When the construction was finished it transformed that tacky back room into an elegant lounge, with the tall, column-framed window and a functional balcony.

The framing of roof. Then Chris & DMunro putting up the sheathing.

Roof done, beginning shingles.

Almost done with the shingles.

The worst job, plaster-boarding the ceiling.

Building the balcony.

Finished balcony with costume racks

The original window (below) and new one (above)

Final window, with split columns, set up for <u>Love Letters</u>.

The room was so wonderful, I decided to use it as a performance space to put on small plays for outside audiences. I wanted to inaugurate it with something special, so I mounted *Love Letters*, acting with my dear friend and acting companion, Linda Herman. On the opening night of this play, I had a surprise honor for Linda – I dedicated the room to her, calling it "The Linda Herman Room".

Love Letters with Linda   and later Judi Adams

We ran *Love Letters* for about 10 weekends, Linda doing 4 of them and then I had different students play the woman's role with me, the most memorable being Judi Adams, who was married now and hadn't acted in many years. She was wonderful in the role.

After the success of *Love Letters*, several other student productions were mounted in the Linda Herman Room, ending with *Jake's Women*, which was a challenge in that small space. I played Jake and seven of my students played the various women in his life. The production was so successful that we transferred it to a full size theater, the Edison Valley Playhouse.

Original cast of *Jake's Women*   The cast when we moved to E.V.P.

The set at Edison Valley Playhouse.

Another area where Munro was a vast help to me was set design and construction on productions I directed. Whether solving technical problems, like building a trunk large enough to fit a rotund "Indian" and myself, in my most recent production of *The Fantasticks*, or actually designing and creating the full, beautiful set for *The Cocktail Hour*.

The first set he tackled was for the second adult play I directed at New Jersey Public Theater, *The Fifth of July*. The design was complex, especially in that small theater, since the first act was inside the house, with part of the front porch visible, while the second act moved over so that the yard and porch were the main areas, with the living room only partially visible. Munro solved this in such a clever way and the audience was able to view the change over during intermission. I overheard people say that the set change was one of their favorite parts of the play. To create the outdoors feeling, two large panels were painted with trees and bushes, and erected over the walls of the theater, while the porch railing was moved over to cover the main part of the stage. It's hard to describe, but suffice it to say, his ingenuity made this production work in that space, and I was extremely grateful for his help. I've called upon his expertise and imagination many times over the years, and he has never disappointed me.

* * *

Over the 34-plus years that David Munro and I have been together, our relationship has remained consistent and has grown stronger. Our life together has been adventurous, supportive, fun and for the most part, stress free.

From the beginning we were completely different in many ways, but this seemed to enhance our partnership rather than create conflict. Munro's Scottish, emotional reserve and my French emotional bombast seem to balance each other out. We both have our separate lives – the theater world and the clock world – but when we come together, there is always harmony.

It was fortunate for me that Munro was always a theater and movie lover, so I never had to drag him with me. He is a discerning critic of theater and always has strong opinions of what we see, even the dreadful stuff to which I sometimes subject him. However, he is the one who often suggests a movie night, or slipping in a movie in-between two plays that I have tickets for in New York.

A unique aspect of our relationship, that I think is indicative of our trust of each other, is that we are each other's barbers. Early on I taught him the art of hair cutting that my father taught me, and neither of us has set foot in a barbershop in over 30 years.

I recently learned that early in our relationship, David made the promise to himself that he would never lose his temper at me – never even let himself get mad. I'm a person who doesn't often get angry either, although I never made a conscious commitment to myself. Like any couple, we often have differences of opinion, but we work them out, usually with one or the other compromising and I feel it's evenly balanced. We, of course, have moments that irritate us, but we never let them blow out of shape. We either mention this to the other without rancor, or "deal with it", which is often my motto (I even have it on a tee-shirt).

We have also kept what I feel is essential in a happy relationship: a sense of humor. Each of us can still make the other laugh, and we enjoy laughing at the same things. I can't say enough about how we've both made the other happy, feeling both lucky and pleased that we serendipitously found each other that night in The Ninth Circle.

Addendum

The Wedding

Near the end of 2013, Same-Sex Marriage was legalized in New Jersey. So after living as a couple for 34 years, David Munro and I decided to get married. There is no question that we both felt married for all of those 34 years, but now it was a question of making it official.

The way we came to this decision was initially because of Affordable Care Act. Munro had been paying exorbitant monthly rates for his health insurance, so he was eager to switch to another provider under the new system. However, because he had spent the last two years as an unpaid construction worker, rebuilding our basement and his studio after the floods of Hurricane Irene, his income was very low. So when he applied for new insurance, he found that he only qualified for Medicaid. This would mean his care choices would be severely limited, and this did not appeal to him.

One afternoon in November, he came to me and said, "We should get married" and explained his predicament. Although I had not felt the particular need to do so, it seemed a good plan. Then as we discussed it, I became more and more excited about the prospect. So we began the process for an actual wedding, not just a justice of the peace thing.

Since Munro is a Quaker (although at the time I wasn't aware how seriously he took this religion) we decided to have a formal service in the Quaker Meeting house. New Year's Day of 2014 seemed like a good day to schedule the ceremony.

The first step was to gain permission from the Quakers, so Munro took a letter of intent to the Sunday meeting. When he presented it to the clerk, she said that they had just completed their monthly committee meeting which had to okay the ceremony. But the clerk was so excited by the prospect of a wedding, particularly a gay wedding, that she reconvened members of the committee and read them the letter, and it was immediately accepted.

Evidently in the Quaker system, things move with glacier-like speed. But since we wanted the wedding in a little over a month, events happened with unprecedented swiftness. We were told to meet with a "clearness committee" (which I referred to as "Quaker vetting") the following Tuesday. So that night we arrived at the home of one of the

Quakers and were met by a lovely couple, and two others that were to be our four "wedding overseers".

They asked us several questions, but mostly they were interested in my understanding the Quaker philosophy and ritual for weddings. I felt extremely welcomed and encouraged by this meeting. They understood that I was not a religious person, and they said that there was no problem with that. They explained how the ceremony would work, and that they were there to help and guide us, but the ceremony was ours to plan as we wanted it.

We decided to have our "reception" at a China Buffet in South Plainfield (five minutes from the Meeting House). This was sort of an in-joke, since we are known to love Chinese buffets and they aren't what is normally thought of as wedding catering halls. But it was practical too, because we couldn't know the exact number of people who would attend, and this way we could accommodate for however many joined us for the reception.

Next came the invitations:

Wedding Announcement

David R. Umbach and David M. Munro

Are pleased to invite you to participate in a celebration of their marriage.

New Year's Day, Wednesday January 1, 2014 3:00pm
The Quaker Meeting House
(Rahway & Plainfield Friends Meeting)
225 Watchung Avenue, Plainfield, NJ 07060

Dinner to follow at China Buffet
Casual dress. No gifts, please.

We also included an explanation of what a Quaker Wedding would entail:

Plainfield Quaker Meeting House
Built in 1788

What is a Quaker Meeting?

Quakers meet in a plain room, in silence, without clergy or choir, ritual or creed, without fancy dress or fancy titles. The idea is that removing these distractions, there is an opening for a genuine spiritual experience.

What happens at a Quaker wedding?

The couple sits on the front bench, with the committee overseeing their marriage, facing friends and family. After a period of silence they stand and exchange promises and rings, and sign the wedding certificate. The meeting returns to silence, at which time anyone is welcome to stand and give a message. The meeting concludes with a handshake, and then all come forward to sign the wedding certificate.

If you are planning to join us for dinner afterword
at the China Buffet,
please let us know so we can have an accurate count.

davids212@verizon.net

These were sent out to about 150 people, and we waited to find out who would attend. We told the China Buffet that we'd get at least 40, and we hoped that we'd fill that number, but we weren't sure.

The reaction to our plans was astonishing! Friends literally jumped for joy, particularly our straight friends. Everyone was thrilled at the idea and more people than we ever anticipated promised they would join us on New Year's Day. As it got closer and closer, I grew more and more anxious, not about getting married, but about the event.

We were thrilled that relatives from both sides were planning to attend. David Munro's brother, Doug, and his family were coming from

Michigan (their son Daniel lives in New York and was going to be our photographer). My brother and family were coming from New York state, which would include their son Sven's in-laws from Colombia, South America, who were visiting for the holidays. We had attended Sven and Stephanie's wedding in Barranquilla and her parents were very happy to come to our wedding, even though they didn't speak English.

One of the differences in a Quaker wedding is that there is no one officiant, but everyone at the ceremony is a witness and they all sign the marriage certificate. So a huge certificate had to be created. Munro worked for hours designing a beautiful certificate with places for over 60 signatures. But when we learned that there might be even more at the wedding, he had to make a second side of the document for more signatures.

We also liked the Quaker custom of not needing to "dress up" for occasions. Their feeling is that every day is equally important and to dress for any one day, demeans the others. So dress was to be casual. But we wanted to do something special for our wedding, so we went to Charles Tyrwhitt, a fancy shirt store in New York, and bought beautiful, matching, but different colored, cuff-link shirts. But no ties.

Friends offered to help with the occasion, too. Dawn Noonan and Emily Bengels were willing to decorate the party room at the China Buffet. Eric Harper agreed to sing, with Emily's accompaniment. Michele Mossay agreed to read the wedding certificate at the end of the ceremony to the congregation. Bill and Cara Biach contributed a floral arrangement for the altar (the only decoration). And we couldn't have done any of it without the help of Bruce and Mary Harpster, Jim Birdsall and Janice Stavenick, our Quaker marriage overseers.

Then we had to plan our vows. There is a simple statement that is to be said at a Quaker wedding ceremony, which Munro chose to say. I, on the other hand, wanted to say more, and didn't feel comfortable including the "god" part of the statement. I asked him if they would be offended. He said that they would be more offended if I said something I didn't believe. Integrity is important to the Quakers – I liked that.

We had a final meeting with our overseers, which ended at the China Buffet for a "rehearsal dinner". I was also able to give the restaurant a more accurate number to plan for the party. It now looked like we may have at least 70, so I told them to set up tables for that many.

It was a cold, but clear day on January 1, 2014, and we were prepared for our wedding. I had become as nervous and excited by the event as any groom feels. When we got to the Meeting House, we were told to wait in the library while people arrived. We had no idea how many friends and family would attend. It turned out that almost one hundred showed up, which really surprised us.

This beautiful old Quaker Meeting House, built in 1788, was almost full of people when we walked in and took our seats in on the front bench. We were to sit in silence for a period of about 5 minutes, which is the Quaker way, and it seemed a very long time for me. When we felt like standing, we stood and said our vows to each other. Then we exchanged rings, which were brought up to us by my second cousin, 3 year old Owen, we kissed and sat down. We were brought a table with our Marriage Certificate which we signed, then Michele stood up and read the whole certificate. Another period of silence.

First to stand up and share his thoughts was Munro's brother, Doug. He gave a very moving speech about how he didn't react well when David came out as a teenager, but upon getting to know him as an adult and meeting me, he saw how poorly he had acted and now truly loves his brother and warmly welcomes me to their family. Then more silence.

One at a time, people got up and spoke (with silences in between). My directorial mind kept saying "Pick up your cues! You could run a truck through these pauses". But of course this was the Quaker way and everyone seemed to be very moved by it. Wonderful things were said by both friends and strangers. Eric and Emily went to the piano and he sang "The Best of Times is Now", and the theater folk joined him on the last verse, with lots of tears flowing.

When it seemed that everyone was done sharing, Bruce stood up and shook our hands, then everyone in the meeting house shook hands with people around them (this is the traditional way to end a meeting). At "rise of meeting", all the witnesses were asked to sign our certificate, even the children – they were all witness to our marriage (96 people signed it). Then they joined us for a coffee and cookie reception in the back room.

At some point we left to go to the China Buffet and we were joined by 69 guests and had a festive dinner and celebration. I can't think of a more wonderful day in my life.

Bruce and Mary Harpster

The Biachs, Chris Fitzgerald and Marcy Repp

Eric Harper sings

Doug Munro giving a testimony

Owen Umbach bringing us the rings

Stephanie talking to her parents from Colombia, Sven and Solveig on the right

Michele Mossay reading the Marriage Certificate

Signing the certificate

The rings and the kiss

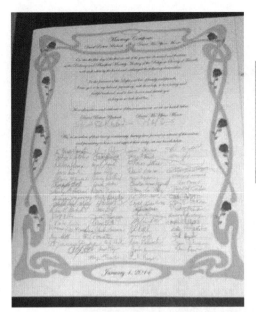

The Marriage Certificate, both sides, with a total of Ninety Six Witness' Signatures

The Munro family at the reception

People often ask "Do you feel any different now that you're married?" The answer is "Yes and No". David Munro and I have been unofficially married for 35 years, but having it on a certificate makes it feel slightly special. I'm glad we did it and the whole ceremony and day were simply wonderful, and we are both extremely pleased that we are now truly married.

Sixteen

Travelosity

To me, an important factor to a happy relationship is when partners are also compatible traveling companions. Although I loved my first trip to Europe with Reynolds, it was obvious that we didn't jibe as traveling partners. Our angry disagreements and screaming fights in train stations proved that. This was partially true because our relationship in life was "teacher/student", but in Europe, I didn't know any more about what to do than he did, so when I didn't understand the train schedule or something, he became obstinate and disagreeable, leading to severe arguments.

David Munro and I, on the other hand, turned out to be excellent travelers. Our temperaments have always seemed to compliment each other, thus we tend to want the same things when discovering the places we visit. We both have that "Let's go to Vegas" attitude, much preferring city life over countryside.

We react differently to stressful situations, thus being more able to help each other through them. For instance, I tend to worry and fret about the daily, small things, like being late or where to go or how to find our way; while Munro calmly researches these things, knows how long it will take, follows maps simply, and even figures out foreign subway/bus systems easily. On the other hand, he tends to freak out over difficult situations, like getting robbed or credit cards not working or not finding any place to eat; while in those situations I tend to remain calm and rational so I can work out the problem.

From the beginning, Munro was my teacher in our relationship, which was a huge change for me. He is much more knowledgeable about things like architecture, current affairs and history, so he opened up my eyes to things I never would have noticed. To this day, he will point out some beautiful detail of some building or a significant fact about an area, that I would have completely missed. And of course, clocks. Wherever we go, the search for beautiful clocks is always on the docket, so I've seen some of the greatest clocks in the world, and have come to much appreciate them.

Our first vacation together was a car trip up to Quebec and back down through New England. This was before internet, so referencing a book on the gay guide to Canada, I pre-booked hotel accommodations in a "gay-friendly" hotel in Quebec City. After a long, exhausting drive through pretty boring Canadian countryside, we arrived at the hotel around 10:00 in the evening, and it turned out to be, indeed, very gay. In fact it was similar to a bathhouse, where residents were wandering around from room to room with drinks in their hands, wearing only towels and looking for "love". It was obvious that a night's sleep for two weary travelers was not what this hotel offered.

So laughingly, we retreated to search for another place to reside for a couple of nights. Next door was a charming looking guest house, and we assumed that since it was near this gay hotel, it would be gay-friendly too. So we were quite taken aback when a dour, hawk-faced woman answered the door, glared at us and barked "What!?" Sheepishly we replied, "We'd like a room, please, with a double bed." Contemptuously she growled, "Two Men – Two Beds!" slamming the door in our face.

We eventually found a place to stay and enjoyed exploring the city neither of us had seen before. Driving home, back through Maine, with its endless trees and little civilization, we got to know each other's taste in traveling. Neither of us were enchanted with "scenery" for long, it was a city's charm that always drew us, and the more foreign the better.

Over the 34 (plus) years that DMunro and I have been partners, our trips have primarily concentrated on discovering new cities, exploring them and getting to know them as much as possible by enjoying their food, architecture and culture. Since we both prefer traveling to foreign countries versus domestic destinations, we've frankly seen more outside the States than inside.

When we have traveled in the USA, to cities like Los Angeles, San Francisco, Denver, Chicago, New Orleans and Miami, it was usually to visit friends or family, and we often discovered these cities with their help.

But mostly we traveled to other countries, like France, Great Britain, Germany, Italy, Turkey, Egypt, Colombia and Mexico. Lately we have enjoyed going on luxury cruises to places we've never been. The first big cruise was touring the Baltic Sea, which included Copenhagen,

Stockholm, Helsinki, Tallinn, Gdansk, Oslo and St. Petersburg. For my 75th birthday we took my dream cruise, a month in Asia, taking us to Tokyo, Beijing, Busan, Nagasaki, Shanghai, Hong Kong, Saigon, Bangkok and Singapore.

The Travel Page on my website, linking to photos of our travels.

It would take another whole book to describe all these adventures, including many of the photographs, but I will concentrate here on two particularly memorable trips: our first time in France together and our trip to Turkey.

*   *   *

Loving movies like we both do, no matter the language of the place we're visiting, we can always find a movie in English (*version originale*) to draw us in for one evening at least. Not always good movies, like a dreadful Keanu Reeves thing we saw in Prague, but any movie will do to satisfy our cinematic hunger. So our favorite place to visit is Paris, because Parisians are a movie-loving people. On our first trip there we bought the Parisian version of TimeOut, and I counted the number of V/O English language films playing in Paris that week was something like 75. *Amazing!*

Munro being an expert in French clocks, we planned our first trip to France around clock locations all over the country, and we decided to take a full month to see as much as possible. For preparation, Munro worked on his French at the Alliance Françoise in New York, but I decided to study it on my own.

I happened to have a student from Paris in my acting class at the time, George LaFone, who was a business man on an exchange program. He had come here for a year with his high school age son, and since Cranford High School was considerably behind the boy's Paris high school, George brought along a young woman to tutor his son so he wouldn't fall behind. When I told George that I needed help with my French, he introduced me to his au pair, Cathy Dumazeau. She had plenty of time on her hands and said that she'd love to teach me French.

Cathy and I became close friends and spent lots of time together that spring. However, very little French was studied, because mostly we talked in English, laughing, gossiping and going to the movies. She happened to be a lesbian, which was a complete surprise to me, but that made our friendship even more agreeable. Little did I know that knowing George and Cathy would have a huge impact in our upcoming trip to France and consequently in our future lives.

A few years later, Cathy met a married woman named Christine Buxereau who had an infant son, Thomas (pronounced Toe-mah). Christine wanted to leave her husband for Cathy, but in order for them to get custody of Thomas, they had to meet very secretively for a year until the divorce was final.

When Thomas was five years old, the three of them came to visit us in Cranford. We decorated the attic bedroom for him with posters of Disney characters so he would have a friendly place of his own in this strange country. I was amazed at what a serious and intelligent little kid he was. They would spend full days wandering museums and specific parts of New York City, and this little boy never complained. In fact we sometimes had to drag him out of a room in a museum, because he was so infatuated with a certain painting.

They came to the States again when Thomas was 10, and I introduced him to musical theater by taking them to Plays-in-the-Park's *Annie Get Your Gun*. He was thrilled with the play, because they have nothing like it in France. He was too shy to talk in English, so I didn't know how much he understood, but he seemed to love it. I made a tape of the music to give to him when they left.

*Thomas at 5,
with a parrot from Linda Herman*

Christine, Thomas & Cathy

Thomas at 10 with his mother

Six years later, Thomas, who was now an openly gay teenager, and definitely a show-queen, asked to spend the summer with us by himself. I was worried about how much English he knew since he never really spoke it as a boy to us, but when he arrived I was relieved to find that he spoke perfect English, with little or no trace of a French accent.

Over that summer David Munro and I became his "Fairy Godfathers". He was amazingly intelligent and funny, and he loved to go to the theater. That first summer I had lots of free time so we spent much of it together either in New York or buzzing around New Jersey. I was astonished at how much this 16 year-old French kid understood about American culture. When I showed him the movie of *Who's Afraid of Virginia Woolf*, I expected him to have questions when it was over, but his first comment was "It reminds me of Ionesco's *The Bald Soprano*." And when I took him to see Alan Rickman in *Private Lives*, he caught all the subtle Noel Coward humor, laughing at all the right places. He was a delight to be with, and I grew quite fond of him.

Thomas came for a stay with us the next three summers and our friendship grew as he matured. He became a regular at the summer theater I worked in, Plays-in-the-Park, a groupie of all the shows whether I was involved with them or not. He attended every rehearsal when I directed *Hello Dolly!* and he even ran the follow spot for *Wizard of Oz*.

On one of his visits we saw our friend Chris McGarry in a play that starred Cherry Jones. Afterwards, while we were talking to Chris, Thomas went over and introduced himself to Ms Jones, and they became rather chummy. So a couple years later, when Chris was understudying in *Doubt* with Cherry Jones on Broadway, we took Thomas to see it on a night when Chris played the role. Going backstage, Cherry recognized Thomas and they had another jolly chat. She was also enthusiastic when she found out that my uncle was the photographer in her home town, who took all the school pictures of her. She is a gracious, delightful person and a great actress.

Thomas went on to finish his university studies with honors and began working and living in Sydney, Australia. Cathy and Christine later separated and went on to new partners. Though I don't communicate much with Cathy anymore, Thomas and I are still very much in touch, and he visits the States whenever he can. And some day, I fervently hope to visit him in Australia.

Teenage Thomas
on his first summer with us.

His second summer

When we visited Limoges
with Cathy and Christine

A recent visit to New York
with his Fairy God Fathers

* * *

George LaFone told us that he was going to be bicycling around the Loire Valley the summer we were going to France, and he generously offered us his apartment to stay in for our two weeks in Paris. This was an amazing opportunity and we gladly accepted his kind offer. The apartment turned out to be in Levalois Perret, a section of Paris right outside the center city, which was easily accessible by the Metro.

The day we arrived, we found the place easily and climbed up the four flights of stairs (France's third floor) passing the concierge on the way up, who greeted us as we passed. When we walked into the apartment we found a young woman on her knees scrubbing the kitchen floor and an older woman vacuuming the carpet. They jumped up and introduced themselves as George's girlfriend, Sylvie, and her mother, saying that they hadn't finished cleaning the flat for us yet. They didn't speak much English, and since together we spoke only novice French, our initial conversation was brief. They appeared upset since they were still working on the flat. To ease the discomfort, we said that we'd leave our bags and go downstairs to get some lunch.

When we reached the street, we saw the concierge shopping and we said *Bonjour* to her. She asked what we were looking for and we said some *dejeuner*. She told us to follow her and she preceded to take us from one restaurant to another, for a half an hour. She would read each menu in the window, rejecting them and moving on, covering the whole neighborhood. She told us that she wanted us to have the perfect restaurant for our first meal in Paris. Finally finding one that suited her, she took us inside and instructed the *maitre de* to give us a fine meal, and left. We were quite boggled by the hospitality of the folks we had met that first day.

The apartment was huge with high ceilings and tall French doors that opened onto a balcony that overlooked the whole area. So from this amazing vantage point, we spent the next 2 weeks exploring Paris, and then coming home to Levelois Perret. On our first day of sightseeing, after coming back on the Metro, we stopped for a coffee at a small outdoor cafe. Next to us was a man with a long baguette of bread, completely unwrapped, leaning on his chair. The waiter came by to serve us our coffee and accidentally knocked the bread over onto the sidewalk. The man picked it up, leaned it back on his chair again, and continued drinking his coffee, the waiter sort of shrugged and went back into the cafe. *Ah, Paris.*

After our happy introduction to the French, we continued to fall in love with them the whole month, which included some traveling around the country. One mildly negative, but typical, incident happened when we arrived in Orange by train and wanted to rent a car to tour Van Gogh's countryside. In the train station, there was an booth that advertized car rentals, and when we went to the guy behind the counter and asked about renting a car, he shook his head and pointed to his watch saying *"Dejeuner, retournez vous a deux heures"*. It was noon, so we knew from experience that French places seriously closed down for lunch. We grabbed a sandwich and went to the local park to wait the two hours. When we returned to find the man at his counter, we asked again about renting a car, and he told us that we had to go downtown – he didn't do that there. *Couldn't he have told us that at noon?*

Our month in France ended with the most amazing example of Parisian hospitality. When we got back from our little tour, George was back in his apartment, so we got a small hotel room. But George told us that they had gotten tickets for us to see *Cabaret* in a large theater, directed by a famous French stage director. The production would be in French, but the songs would be in English. We know the play well enough so that seemed like a terrific idea. He also told us that after the play we were invited for dinner at a friend of Sylvie's apartment. Unlike Parisians, we like our dinner at "normal" dinner hour around 6:00 PM, and we knew we'd be starving by the time the play was over, so we had a sandwich in a café near the theater before the play. George and Sylvie saw us and were surprised that we were eating so early, but didn't say anything.

The production was long.....very long, and in our opinion not very good, but the audiences went wild, with curtain calls going on for almost a half an hour, definitely the longest curtain calls I've ever seen. It was close to midnight when the group of about ten of us made our way to the apartment of Sylvie's friend whom we had just met. We pulled George aside and said that we had to get up pretty early to make our flight back to the States, so we'd just skip the party – feeling kind of odd going to the home of strangers, who didn't even speak much English. George was horrified. "What do you mean, this party is in your honor. You can't miss it!" So we went, not knowing what to expect.

When we arrived at this rather elegant apartment, there was a long banquet table stretched out the length of the living/dining room, full of a veritable feast. Bottles of wine, bowls of fruit, dishes of raw oysters, plates of meats, baguettes of bread, trays of cheeses, and pastries beyond belief. And all of this was in our honor. The crowd talked to us as much as they could considering the language barrier, and the party went on for hours it seemed. We would be saying good bye to George and Sylvie and their incredible kindness, so we chose to stay as long as we could. But finally we had to get back to our hotel and prepare for our departure from the most wonderful first trip to France anyone could imagine. And what a send-off it was. Our first impression of the "rude" Parisians has never been changed. We absolutely love the French!

David Munro on our first trip
to France –
on top of Notre Dame.

On top of the
Roman amphitheater
in Arles.

On the Quai de L'Horloge
(clock makers)

* * *

Surprisingly enough, we were also extremely impressed with the country of Turkey. Because of economic tightness that summer, we needed a country that was not only cheap but had a good exchange rate. Portugal and Turkey were the best choices, and since Portugal seemed a bit "Catholic" for my taste, we chose Turkey, even though we knew very little about it. This was at a time when it was rare for Americans to travel there, so naturally everyone tried to talk us out of it. The main source of opinions came from seeing "Midnight Express" with Brad Davis stuck in a horrible prison. But this didn't deter us and I'm so glad, because we absolutely loved visiting Turkey.

Our first impression of Istanbul came during the hotel-supplied car ride from the airport into the city. It was a beautiful weekend day and the drive was along the coast of the Sea of Marmara, and we passed long beaches with families out enjoying the sun and sea. As we approached the minarets of Istanbul, it was like seeing a Disney set, and different from any skyline we'd ever seen. Our chauffeur spoke perfect English and explained things as we went. We fell in love with the city immediately.

Early views of Istanbul

    Our hotel was connected to the walls of Topkapi Palace. It was so romantic and reminded me of Milena Mercouri and Peter Ustinov breaking into it that palace for the crown jewels. After settling in, we decided to take a stroll to familiarize ourselves with the area, and the first place we came across was a park, also connected to the outside of the palace where some sort of festivities were going on. As we wandered in we slowly realized that it was a family carnival and decidedly not for tourists but for locals only. We worried that we would be shunned or mocked since everyone looked at us a bit strangely at first. But it turned out that people were pleased that we were sharing this local festival with them and they were eager to show us the various games and foods that were on offer. It was a great way to get to know the Turks and their friendly ways.

    In the days that followed we were enchanted by the whole city, so beautiful and exotic, with the mosques and rug sellers. We would explore the poorest sections of the city and never feel the least bit threatened. An there was virtually no begging. Oh, everyone was hoping to sell something, from expensive carpets to some old woman's handmade handkerchief, but if you said "no, thank you" they would immediately let you alone.

We noticed one thing about the Turkish men. Young men could be handsome as hell, but something happened to the men over 30, when they seemed to become downright ugly. From this paradox we coined our use of the phrase "Young Turk", which we use even today, and not just about Turks.

The Blue Mosque

Overlooking the Bosphorus River flowing to the Black Sea

A "Young Turk" with stuffed goat and a live kitten

A beautiful slum in Istanbul

Inside the Blue Mosque

Rainbow over a fortress

One of the biggest adventures in Istanbul was at the Grand Bazaar, a humongous indoor market, with thousands of individual shops mashed together in a rabbit warren of a place. The noise and chaos of the place was amazing, but again we never felt pressured or threatened as we passed shop after shop full of wonders. I bought a few things including a beautiful plate that had the Arabic signature of a sultan. It spent years on my kitchen wall until it was knocked down one day and broke – I miss it.

We came to a shop that had some clocks in it, so of course Munro stopped to look. There he saw, among the schlock, a beautiful, gilded French mantel clock from the 19th century, made for the Turkish market with Arabic numerals on the enamel dial. He realized that this was something special and asked the shop keeper about it. The shop owner shook his head and pointed out other clocks, which were obviously much less in quality and more "affordable" to the typical American tourist. But Munro insisted that this was the one he was interested in and asked again for the price. Again the shopkeeper shook his head and pointed elsewhere. Finally Munro convinced him that he was only interested in this particular clock and the man gave him a price. Now, in Turkey, one is always expected to bargain for a lower price, but the shopkeeper insisted that this was the lowest he could possibly go. Munro realized that this was very low price compared to what it would cost in the West, though it was still expensive for our wallets, so he told the owner that we'd go out to lunch and think about it.

I'm sure the shopkeeper either thought that it was too expensive for these tourists or that it was a bargaining ploy. But when we went to lunch and Munro said to me, "I know that's expensive, but if I pass this up, I know I'll regret it the rest of my life."

So back we went. He told the guy it was a sale, which seemed to really shock him. He said that he'd had it in the shop for many years and it had never sold. So he and Munro proceeded to take it apart and pack it. The shopkeeper immediately sent his minion out for tea for us as well as a free travel bag for us to pack it in. I decided to take a stroll around the bazaar while they were doing that and after awhile I realized that I'd never find my way back. Another shopkeeper saw my panic and said that he knew where I was headed and showed me back to the clock shop. News travels fast in the bazaar, and our sale was famous for blocks around. That day we obtained a wonderful clock that now sits in our living room and we consider it the best clock in our collection.

A tiny portion of the Grand Bazaar

The French Clock with Arabic numerals.

We had some time left before our flight home and we felt we'd explored Istanbul enough and we wanted to see more of Turkey. So we found a local bus to take us to a seaside resort called, Kusadasi. Suddenly we realized that we were in a situation where no one dealt with tourists, therefore no one spoke a word of English. But just like the first time we mingled with the locals in the Topkapi Park, everyone was friendly and helpful. We were impressed that the bus had a stewardess who handed out drinks and hot towels.

The bus driver stopped outside of the town of Kusadasi and indicated for us to get out of the bus there. He pointed down a road that would lead to the center of town and waved us goodbye with a friendly smile. When we arrived to the center of this charming town, the first sign we saw was in front of a bar that said "BIG BEER, 10,000 lira". Soon after we found a pleasant hotel and settled in for this part of our journey.

It was a touristy shore town catering to Germans and English tourist, with lots of open-air restaurants and stray cats everywhere. However, there wasn't much to do besides go to the beach and not being beach people, we decided to take some tours out of the area.

We booked bus tours for two major tourist attractions one for Ephesus and one for Pamukkale. Ordinarily we like to explore on our own, but we felt we would get more out of it if we had someone to explain just what we were seeing in English, and the rate for car rental was very high.

Unfortunately, the Tour Guide, who was the same on both these tours, took us for much more than a ride.

*   *   *

<u>The Saga of the Bizarre Tour Guide</u>

When we got onto the bus, we met the tour guide. He was a nice looking young man, with a pained expression on his face. He told us in halting English that he had a toothache and he would accompany us to Efes but then an expert guide would take us through the ruined city, and he would join us after he went to the dentist. He didn't say a word until we reached the Ancient Greek city, Ephesus.

Efes, in Turkish, was a seaport beginning around 300 BC, where it remained a modest shipping center. But around 50 BC the Romans took it over and enlarged it and built large impressive city on the Aegean coast. Sometime later, around 300 AD the Meander River, which flowed into the Efesian bay, silted up, moving the ocean far away from the city, so the inhabitants abandoned the city. In modern times, archeologists have uncovered the city and have found extensive treasures from the Greek and Roman period. Most of the great sculptures and artifacts were taken to big European museums, particularly Berlin (much to the Turk's fury) but the remains of the buildings and the foundations of the town are still there, in all their glory.

When we arrived we were introduced to an fascinating guide, an older Turk who spoke rapid, excellent English, and who took us on a whirlwind, breathtaking tour of the city, from the public baths and toilets, to the brothels, to the libraries, and the huge Roman theater, along roads lined with pillars -- we were duly impressed. Pictures do not truly capture the grandeur of the place nor the feeling that we had standing (or sitting, as in the case of the toilets) where Romans had been during the Roman Empire. Names out of the bible and out of "I, Claudius" were mentioned and I felt as if I were in another century, long ago.

The old Turkish guide at Ephesus

Our young guide returned for the end of our tour, accompanying us to a place where we ate our tour-included lunch. We were seated at a large table, with all of the others in the tour (not a friendly lot) and got a so-so lunch. I mentioned to the guide, who had talked a bit on the bus to us about the local places we drove through, that the word "fabric" means 'factory' in French and German, and means 'cloth' in English, and thus was confusing his English speaking crowd. In truth, his English was extremely poor and he limited his comments to very fundamental phrases which he repeated a lot (i.e. "this city has an auto fabric and a pottery fabric", clearly he wanted us to know that Turkey was industrial). We were relieved that he was not our guide in Efes.

The tour then went to the House of the Virgin Mary, which we could have skipped (and not gotten a free lunch), but we thought, "What the hell?" By far the most worthwhile part of this excursion was the bus ride up the mountain, which wound around incredible vistas of the countryside as it went higher and higher. We're not going to speculate on how Mother Mary (*Meremana*) got up this steep grade, or how she got supplies to her house on the top where she resided, or why this particular mountain was any different from any other of the numerous mountain tops in the area, so that the blind, German, invalid nun envisioned this particular mountain in her dream – we did not address any of these questions. But apparently hundreds of tourist make this trek every day and a loud mass was being held outside of the tiny house that was built on the 'very spot' that Meremana lived in 50 AD or so. To this day we refer to the place as "The Virgin Mary's Retirement Condo."

Our guide seemed as uninterested in the Christian shrine as we were, giving almost no information about it, he just wandered off allowing his charges to explore the house, and of course the gift store, on their own. We followed him and as a small group of us waited for the rest of our group, where we received the most interesting and passionate speech that we heard from him. He began to talk about the social problems of Turkey and how the people are being cheated by the government and how it was going to be no different after elections, etc. His English was still poor, but at least he was telling us things in an animated way, albeit not "tour-guidish" things. On the journey back to Kusadasi, he said almost nothing the whole way.

Early to bed to get ready for our longer bus tour the next day and the continuation of the Bizarre Tour Guide Saga. Again we waited for our tour bus to pick us up and were greeted by the same young man, whose name we were never told. I inquired about his toothache and he looked at me with a questioning look and then finally said that it was "O.K."

We now had a three and a half hour bus ride ahead of us and we'd hoped that it would be enhanced by a guide's comments, but our dour guide only mentioned some of the city names as we went through, telling us about the *fabrics* that existed there. When we went through a particularly poor section of farm country, with peasants in shacks, he said with a sneer that these were the "Greece people". Several other times in the day he mentioned, with obvious hatred, the "Greece people" and we assumed he meant Greeks.

He also made a major grammatical error by saying that this town has "too much" restaurants or "too much" factories, when he meant 'many'. Some of the mountainous scenery was fine and the towns were interesting to some degree, but our guide was no help making the long trip more interesting. There was a half hour rest stop for food and whatever, but it was a long time to be on a bus.

During the rest stop, we had another chat with our guide and I mention to him (ever the speech teacher) about the difference between 'too much' and 'many'; he seemed pleased with the knowledge. But then he started grumbling about how he could never take a vacation to London, because the government had tax for leaving the country that was far too expensive. Also, he said that in three weeks the tourist season would be over and he would be out of a job and wondered how he would he support his family. He seemed to resent the tourists, but tried to cover it up with a smile, occasionally.

As we approached the area of hot springs, of which Pamukkale is the most important, we saw a sight of a bubbling hot spring, running like a creek, and women washing their clothes, carpets, and hair. They were used to tourist buses stopping to take their pictures and were extremely friendly.

A hot spring creek where the locals did their laundry.

When we reached Pamukkale the guide told us that we would have two luxurious rooms in a hotel to change into our bathing suits, one for men and one for women. They weren't at all "luxurious", just motel rooms, and having 20 men trying to change clothes in that room was not a joy. Our guide made a point of telling us to keep all our valuables in our rooms, not to take them to the springs or to the pool, that he would be there to protect them. He said this in his halting English and most of the people on our bus were Dutch or German, so not everyone understood him.

The famous White Springs of Pamukkale, which in the 1800s was a resort spot famous for its flowing, hot water, rushing over the salt deposits. But they were a bit of a disappointment by the 1990s. The beautiful white, salt-solid waterfalls, with the pools of warm spring water are still there, but a bit greyer, because very little water is left in the springs. It is full of people sitting in the pools and walking on the white salt formations and mostly just taking pictures. We stayed a while and then went back to the hotel to swim in the nice pool at the top of the springs.

The White Springs of Pamukkale

Then I asked Munro to go to the room and get some money to buy a drink and maybe a snack. He got the key to the room, which was just sitting on the hotel front desk and when he returned he gave me my empty wallet and said that we'd been robbed. All his cash, in dollars and lira, and two credit cards were taken. All my cash was gone, but Thank Zeus, my credit card and bank card were untouched.

We looked for our guide, as did the man at the desk, but he was nowhere to be found. We learned that at least two other people, who had understood his English instructions, had also been robbed of their cash. We now had to wait until the meeting time for all the group at 5:00pm to figure out what to do since no one was helpful at the hotel.

When it came time for the bus to leave and everyone was on board, the guide was still nowhere to be found. The bus driver, who spoke no English, went out to look for him, but came back shrugging. Finally, an English speaking guide from another tour with the same agency came on board. She was fluent in English and German and told us that our guide had been in an auto accident and that our bus driver would take us back to Kusadasi. I told her about our robbery, as did another English couple, and she was shocked. She said that we should meet with her at the rest stop, where she would call the agency.

That two hours ride to the rest stop was not pleasant. We were thirsty and hungry and angry. We actually hadn't lost that much money (about $50 in lira and $20 in dollars) but the feeling was that we had been betrayed by a guide, who obviously wanted to make a strike before he was laid off for the season. Since the Germans didn't understand his instructions or were two smart to follow them, he didn't make much on his heist, and he couldn't go back to the agency for any more tours to rob.

At the rest stop, I saw the woman guide calling up the agency, agitated, pacing back and forth -- it was obviously a big shock to everyone at the agency. We felt extremely deprived that we couldn't buy anything to eat or drink. A British couple offered to lend us some money, but it felt uncomfortable since we wouldn't be seeing them again. The last hour and a half on the bus was even more unpleasant. The bus driver went another way and we were sure the whole bus was being abducted, but it turned out that he just didn't take the scenic route through the mountains on the way home.

We had to stop off at many other hotels before we finally reached our hotel, where we were met by an agency person who told us to come immediately to the office. We went to the hotel first for a drink of bottled water and a wash up then I proceeded to the tour agency. Munro was in no mood to handle these people, so I went by myself. The people at the agency couldn't have been nicer. They cashed some credit card money for me because the banks were closed, they took my statement and vowed to follow up the best they could. They called American Express in Istanbul to cancel Munro's credit card. And they offered us a free meal at the Toy Restaurant, across the street. I got Munro from the room and we had a delicious, expensive dinner on the agency, which made us feel much better.

The first thing Munro did the next day was to go to the local police to report the incident, in case his credit cards were used. Unlike the police in "Midnight Express", they were extremely cheerful and friendly about the whole thing, but they couldn't be much help, because it didn't happen in their district; but they did record the robbery, for the credit card people. On his way to the police station, the carpet seller, that he checked prices with on Saturday, stopped him to ask what had happened the night before. When told, he was most sorry, as was everyone who heard, it seems that this was a rare and unusual incident. We were told by other tourists the night before, that you expect these things to happen in Italy or Spain, but not Turkey.

We vowed that we would not let this incident spoil our trip, or our feelings about Turkey, and if nothing else, we would have a good story to tell.

* * *

For our last day in Turkey, we wanted to do some independent touring, *with no guide*. While Munro was at the police station, I was picking up a rental car, so we could get as early a start as possible. Our first destination was a little town called Didim, down the coast. It was a lovely drive through quaint villages and farmland, with the blue Aegean always off to the right.

The reason we went to Didim was to see a ruin highly praised in the tourist books -- and were the books ever right. A Greek temple of Apollo lies in the middle of this small town that was the most awe inspiring archeological site I've ever seen, including Efes. 103 of 109 pillars of this temple are still at least somewhat standing, though only 3 to their full height, and these pillars are superbly decorated. The flutes on all these columns were amazingly deep and large, like a dinner plate-size scoop was used to cut into the whole length of the marble. And the bases were enormous and each one was ornately and differently decorated. Even though this dates back hundreds of years BC, the detail in much of the carving was impeccable, not worn at all. One pillar had fallen and they had left the huge sections of it laying like a whole line of dominoes, with each circular domino, a 6 feet wide and 2 1/2 feet thick slab of marble. There was also a large face of Medusa that was quite stunning. We left this place very happy that we had made the trip south to see it.

The amazing ruins of Didim

Our next goal was to go to a tiny village on Lake Latmos, called Heracleia, where there were ancient monasteries. It wasn't much of a village (we were glad that we didn't wait to eat lunch there) and the Roman ruins and monasteries weren't as wonderful as others we'd seen, but the people of the village made it memorable. First a boy, about 12, wanted to be our guide, though he spoke no English and only a little German. He pestered us until we made it clear we could explore alone; at least we thought we could. He shrugged and went on his way. It was a very hilly village and the Roman buildings were spread throughout the town.

We started up one path, which lead no where, then a woman beckoned to us to follow her. We wended our way down a path, to a hidden ruin, and she waited as we viewed it and waved us on. Along the winding path, she stopped and offered us some lace to buy. We said, no thanks, she shrugged and led us to some more places. We expected her to ask for a tip, but while we were viewing something, she wandered off.

We ended up on top of a hill with a big square building, obviously old, and an old man approached us as we looked at it. He ascertained our language and then handed us a very clearly written card, in English. It said that he was the keeper of this Roman fort -- he kept the rocks safe and fed the dogs -- that his needs were few but this was his only job -- could we help. He lived in a shack next to the building, and the dogs were friendly; we gave him some lira. After we looked at this plain edifice for a while, he showed us to the path down to the lake. In the lake was an island, where the monastery was, unreachable but picturesque. Then we wandered our way back to our car, which we had left open (not realizing that we'd be gone so long and so far), but of course, nothing had been touched.

The village Heracleia

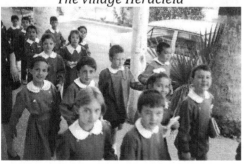

As we drove north, through more marvelous mountains, there was one more ancient delight to be seen before we headed to the highway for the airport. Understand that on every other hill and dale one could see remnants of the Romans, the sight of them became almost routine. But just before we hit the highway, we noticed a Roman bridge over a gully by the side of the road. We pulled over to take a picture, and I'm so glad we did, because when we got out we realized how big this bridge was. It took three giant arches to span this ravine and it was still in perfect shape and being used today.

A perfect finish to our glorious Turkey Experience.

Seventeen

Relative-ity

My Mother's side of the family, the Guyots, consisted of her two brothers, Chuck and Bill and they all lived in Illinois, so I was closest to them in my youth. My cousins, Marianne and Charles, lived in Highland Park, so whenever I lived there, I spent lots of time with them. Chuck and Marvine were their parents. My Uncle Bill and Aunt Annie lived in another suburb of Chicago, Lombard, which is to the west, as opposed to Highland Park to the north. Their children were Billy, who was a half a year older than me, and Susie, who was several years younger. We only saw that part of our family when one of us made the trip to visit the other family.

*Adults: Uncle Bill, Aunt Marvine, Uncle Chuck, Mother, Dad and Aunt Annie
Children: Charles, Marianne, Billy and me (Susie was not born yet)*

When I was young, there were several summers when my parents sent me to Uncle Bill's house for a week or even month, because they assumed that I'd want to be with my cousin Billy. They had a brick house, where the bricks were purposely set jaggedly, and even as a little kid I found it ugly. I hated going there because it was an excruciating experience every time and all I could think of while I was there was, "When can I go home?"

Uncle Bill was a hyper-intelligent, highly neurotic man. He worked as an engineer in some company that made gadgets that I never understood. I learned early on never to ask him about anything, because he would go on and on explaining it in terms way beyond a child's brain. To be polite I once asked him how television worked and that was big mistake. He gave me an in-depth explanation that went on for what seemed like hours and I didn't understand a word. He had a huge hi-fi system, extremely advanced for that era, and he was wildly proud of it. He would play records (always classical) at the top of the volume scale, blasting out any possibility of conversation or listening to my favorite radio programs. He was also allergic to all kinds of basic foods, like wheat, so the diet at their house, catering to his allergies, was pretty awful. I vividly remember the loathsome, wheat-less bread that Aunt Annie made. Choking down those sandwiches was always a dreaded experience.

Aunt Annie, I was told by my mother years later, was jealous of me, because I was so much more advanced than her precious son Billy, who was several months my senior. I walked and talked before he did and I got much better grades in school and was more animated and engaging. It was because of this jealousy, that Aunt Annie never gave me any affection when I was staying there, she just ignored me most of the time.

Billy and I never much cared for one another, but we learned to tolerated each other since we were contemporaries and had to spend so much time together. We always had to play what he wanted to play, which was not at all what interested me. All he wanted to play was soldiers, either with toy soldiers or running around the yard pretending to shoot each other. I know he had enormous pressure from his parents to be bright, but he just wasn't.

The only interesting memory I have of Billy was when we went out in the prairie across the street and in the tall grass we played a "you show me yours and I'll show you mine" game. This interested me more than it did Billy. However, it caused quite a stir with Aunt Annie when she noticed that I'd left my belt out in the prairie and Billy told her what we'd been doing. And so at the age of eight, I undoubtedly faced my first encounter with homophobia.

That was the summer of VJ Day, the end of World War II. I was desperately homesick so when on the phone with my jubilant parents, I wept and pleaded for them to come and bring me home. They did and I begged them not to make me spend any more summers with that family. To this day Lombard always reminds me of those wretched summers, even though now it has become a yuppie town, the prairie covered with condos and the hated, brick Guyot house long since torn down.

Billy grew up to be a bitter, lonely man, working in a box factory, making just enough to keep a small apartment in Florida. Last heard from has had a stroke and is in a nursing home. I have not seen Billy for at least 40 years. For awhile I sent him Christmas cards, but he never responded, so I stopped.

The most powerfully, dramatic story from that family comes from Billy's little sister, Susie, that we ignored on my visits because she was so young. She and I had absolutely no contact as adults, and I have not see her since she was a little girl. Calling herself Sue, she got married, had 4 children, and then a divorce. Two of her college-aged children, a boy and a girl, went to visit their grandfather (their father's father). We can never know what triggered this, but the boy got into a violent rage, took a hammer and killed both the grandfather and his sister.

He went to prison, but since the affair was psychological and a drug-related, blackout situation, he was released long before I would have thought practical. He and his mother actually visited my mother soon after his release. I hear that they sat there in Mother's apartment, Sue smoking (a real "no-no") and the boy making pleasant conversation. Mother even found him charming. She thought that they would ask for money, but they didn't. I believe Sue died recently from lung cancer and the boy is living in Chicago.

I am quite fond of my cousin Charles, Marianne's brother: a large, lovable eccentric and a quiet genius with a huge moustache, who long ago he married a petite Spanish woman named Paqui. Together they make a colorful and unique couple. When they were younger, they would travel all around the country on a motorcycle. They often move to various foreign countries, like Spain, France or Peru, according to Charles's whim; usually where he believed he could live the cheapest. He is purported to have done well in the stock market over the years and has accrued quite a lot of money, but no one really knows how much or its location and he is loathe to spend it.

Marianne tells the story of the day he arrived at her house on a motorcycle and deposited a package of gold bars in her freezer. Two days later, without a word to Marianne, he took off with the bullion on his motorcycle for parts unknown. He sometimes takes trips to Switzerland and we all quip, "to visit his money".

Charles is also an extremely talented artist, and he paints brilliantly colored works, many abstracts and some even quite violent in nature. Occasionally he will do more realistic paintings, and they are always are done in bright colors, I believe. He won't sell any of his works, but he loves to give them away to friends and family. A lot of his more disturbing work I don't particularly want to hang in my home, but I was able to attain a more conventional pair of chalk drawings, one a self portrait and the other depicting his wife, Paqui.

Charles and Paqui in my den.

Charles and Marianne at Cathy's Wedding

Marianne and I are the closest of the cousins. I lost track of her after she graduated from nursing school and became a practicing nurse for most of her life, later managing entire hospitals. She moved to California and married a man, and had a daughter, Cathy. It was not a particularly good marriage, though I don't know the details, and she left him, taking her daughter, and moved back to Highland Park. There she reconnected with an old school friend, Ray Cimbalo, and they fell madly in love and got married. Ray is a kind and quiet guy (the opposite of her first husband), who is a major golfer and caddie. Now in his eighties, he still caddies for longtime customers who request him.

Ray took up painting after he retired, though he had never done anything like that in his life, and turned into an amazing, realistic artist. Every time I visit their home I see new paintings filling up the large den in the basement and I am in awe of what he has accomplished. I was lucky to receive my favorite painting (so far) as a Christmas present, depicting poppies growing through a white bench. You can't see in the photograph, but the painting continues around the edges of the canvas. It proudly hangs in my living room.

Ray's beautiful painting that hangs in my living room

Marianne was very close to my mother after she returned to Highland Park as a widow. Both avid readers, they would give each other abundant amounts of books, especially at Christmas time. Both Mother and Marianne loved Christmas over any other holiday, though neither was particularly religious. They just loved the giving of gifts and all the trimmings. David Munro and I spent one Christmas with mother, but Christmas Eve and Christmas morning were spent at the Cimbalo's home. The stacks and stacks of presents under the tree were astounding, and most of them were for Mother; many many books from Marianne but also gifts from Mother's students and friends. It was rather embarrassing, but I know Mother loved it. And of course, Marianne went overboard on decorations and an elaborate Christmas breakfast, which included the English tradition of "poppers", so we all had to wear those silly hats and compare the silly gifts that came in the poppers.

Mother at Marianne and Ray's home for Christmas breakfast

Marianne in Xmas-management mode with Charles

The two of them traveled all over the country and knowing them, there wasn't a silent moment in their conversation-filled time together. Their trip to Washington DC was a highlight, I know, both of them being ardent Democrats immersed in politics.

The story goes that when they went to lunch in the Senate building they met Illinois Senator Paul Simon in the hallway. Marianne introduced Mother to him by saying, "This is Mary Umbach and she is a democrat from Lake County." They shook hands and then she said, "I'm Marianne Cimbalo and I am the other one." As Lake County is very Republican, he laughed and they had our picture taken with him.

One summer I joined them in Florida for a few days at Disney World and Epcot Center. The three of us acted like kids, going on rides, traveling to all the countries of Epcot Center, and doing lots of laughing.

But the most memorable trip I did with the two of them was to the Chautauqua Institute in New York.

One time when Mother was visiting us, she nostalgically mentioned to David Munro about a pleasant childhood memory; how she and her family would attend Chautauqua tent meetings. Munro said, "Do you know they still are going on, and in a permanent place in New York State?" She did not know this and was fascinated by the fact.

A few months later, Munro made the suggestion that we spend a week at Chautauqua with Mother and Marianne that coming summer, and I thought it was a splendid idea. So I suggested it to them and they were thrilled. I made arrangements, by reserving our place for one of the weeks that they operate. I also had to make the living accommodations and I found that the Grand Hotel was already booked, so I reserved three rooms in one of the boarding houses on the site. Although I organized the trip, I had no idea how historic and extensive this place was and the enormous amount of activities that would be on offer.

Chautauqua Institution is a walled community on the shores of Chautauqua Lake that has been functioning since the Nineteenth Century. Visiting there is like time travel to another era, featuring leafy street with gingerbread-trimmed Victorian houses, the grand old hotel and hundreds of dilapidated, clapboard rooming houses, along with concert/lecture halls and various performance spaces. Each summer it offers a mix of performing arts, lectures, interfaith worship and educational activities and over the course of nine weeks, more than 100,000 visitors come to Chautauqua and participate in these varied programs.

Choosing the right week was tricky, because each of the nine weeks of the summer features a different topic, like next year offers: "Our Elegant Universe (science), "The Next Greatest Generation" (religion), "America" (politics), "Model for the Middle East" (international), "Health Care" (reform) etc. Therefore the speakers and lectures during a given week will be centered around a specific theme. I picked a week that was more political and less religious, which seemed best for the four of us.

Cranford and Highland Park are about equidistant to Chautauqua, so we planned to meet at the boarding house where we would be staying. Munro and I arrived first and when I saw the place I had booked I was horrified. *It was a dump!* Marianne and my mother were used to staying in fairly high-class hotels when they traveled and this was a rickety old wood-frame house. The bedrooms were tiny and without any comfortable furniture besides the beds, which were wrought iron framed with lumpy mattresses. And, we would all be sharing the single bathroom with the other guests. *Mother will kill me!*

However, when they arrived Mother took one look at the place and became all nostalgic about her "days in Summer Bible School Camp", because this was just the type of houses they lived in. She didn't complain about the bed or the shared bathroom and she genuinely loved the place. I was extremely relieved. We all actually became very fond of the place, despite it's rusticity, and the other guests in the house were delightful. Since there was a small kitchen we often enjoyed breakfast, lunch or afternoon tea sitting on the second story porch.

The atmosphere was like living in a small town in the 1940s. Children ran free in the streets and everyone offered a warm greeting as you passed them on the sidewalks. My mother always liked to take her afternoon constitutional walk by herself and she would wonder aimlessly around the complex, often getting lost in the similar looking blocks. Friendly folks recognized her and always guided her back to our home, engaging in an animated conversation along the way.

Chautauqua had no shortage of activities. Our house was a couple blocks from the main meeting auditorium where from 8:00 AM to 11:00 PM there were lectures, church services, and concerts all day, every day. And there were other venues as well where arts and crafts were taught or dance or aerobics or guitar lessons or children's activities. We would consult the daily schedule and plan our days accordingly.

Often the four of us would go our separate ways to seek out our own interests, but then we would gather at one spot for something that we all enjoyed. At night there was a college-based theater company that performed in repertory. We were able to see *She Loves Me* and *You Can't Take it With You*. They were fairly good productions, primarily due to the enthusiasm of the troupe of actors which was infectious. The whole atmosphere of the place made for much scintillating entertainment. The grounds also had restaurants (which were always crowded) and stores (which sold religious and tourist schlock), but mostly we went from place to place soaking up "culture".

I will always thank David Munro for suggesting this trip, because it was a perfect choice for Mother and she genuinely loved it. Also it was the last time she was able to make one of these extended journeys and I was able to share it with her.

Where I had hope we'd be staying at the Chautauqua Institute

Where we actually stayed

When my mother was in her late 80s and her traveling days were almost over, she made a framed poem for Marianne, that expressed her gratitude for their friendship and all the places that they went to together.

TO MARIANNE

If it weren't for you I would never

Have been to Galena, Illinois
Or to Dorr (Dore?) county, Wisconsin
Or to New Orleans
Or on a Mississippi River Steamboat... The Delta Queen, even !.
Or to a Guyot reunion in Noble
Or to OSPEC (or whatever) and Disney World
Or to Williamsburg
Or talked all the way to Quebeque and back
Or got to visit Nellie ...on her farm or in her house in Olney or in the nursing home.
Or ridden cross-country on Amtrac to Glacier National Park (where all those wild flowers are and where two persons can nearly freeze to death on one of those red buses)
Or gone by boat to that island off Cape Cod
Or visited Seattle and Victoria and flown ACROSS the PUGET SOUND
Or had dinner at the motel with the Snively Boys....
Or had cake and strawberry ice cream at their house, either.
Or have visited Washington D.C. and all that that entails ...TWICE
Or....oh, My Goodness, on and on and on ....such richness over all these years!

I was able to join them on their trip to Disney World

*Marianne and Mother at my father's funeral.
Upper left is Uncle Bill and on the right Uncle Chuck,
with my nephew, Bobby, holding Mother's dog, Muffet*

Marianne's grown daughter, Cathy, is married to Dave Goldberg and now has two teenage children, Sarah and Brian. Gramma and Grampa Cimbalo have recently moved to a western Chicago suburb to be close to their grandchildren, and life in the remaining Guyot family is good.

Cathy, Brian, Sarah and Dave

*   *   *

My mother and Munro's mother, Bea, together for the first and only time.

My father had a brother and a sister, my Uncle Val and my Aunt Betty (who later changed her name to Beth), so there were also two families of cousins on the Umbach side of the family.

The whole Umbach family around 1954
Me, Mother, Father, Grandfather Milton, Uncle Val, Jonathan, Uncle Don
Aunt Christine, Valerie, baby Kit, Barbara, Donna, Doris and Aunt Betty

Uncle Val lived in Paris, Tennessee, with his wife, Christine, and two children, Valerie and Kit. I saw very little of that family, only on special family occasions.

The only photo I have of my father (right) and his siblings, together.

Val's daughter, Valerie, and I didn't really get to know each other until we were adults, but she did visit our house a few times when she was a child. My primary memory of her was as a cute little pre-school girl in my kitchen proving to us that she could read. She pointed to the name on our refrigerator and boldly spelled out in an adorable Southern accent, "F-R-I-G-I-D-A-R-E --- *Icebox!*"

I reconnected with Valerie and her mother, Uncle Val's first wife Christine, at an Umbach reunion several years ago. Val had passed away by this time. Since then I've visited Valerie in her home in Smyrna, Georgia several times. She was married, becoming Valerie Luke, and was an airline attendant for most of her adult life until she retired. She has a daughter, Amanda, who graduated from college and became a teacher. Quite recently she adopted a 17 year-old senior in high school, Jessica, who plans to go into the theater.

At the reunion I also met for the first time, her brother, Kit, who was several years younger than she was. He was married to Barbara and had two adorable children, Sam and Will. Kit died tragically, very young. He had Hodgkins disease in his early twenties and the radiation he was given damaged his heart and lungs, which showed up when he was in his fifties. It was the treatment for the Hodgkins that saved his life at the time, but eventually killed him.

The primary way I keep up with these Southern cousins and their families is to follow each of them on Facebook.

At the Umbach Reunion in 2005

Kit, Barbara, Will and Sam

Amanda and Valerie

Kit and Will shootin' pool

More recently, Amanda with her adopted daughter, Jessica

*   *   *

My Aunt Betty and Uncle Don Lyons lived in Rochester, New York and my mother and father were more friendly with that family than the Val Umbach family. Therefore I became familiar with their daughters, Donna, Doris and Barbara, when they were young. Our families took some vacations together on the Finger Lakes and we would visit them in Rochester on occasion, as well.

As we grew up, we cousins saw each other at family functions like weddings, and I always enjoyed the three girls a great deal. I also had warmer feelings for Aunt Beth (ne Betty) than any of my other aunts. Still proximity made intimate friendship with the Lyon family difficult.

It wasn't until more recently when the family moved to Connecticut that I was able to spend more time with them. We have since become quite close. Donna and Doris live in Simsbury, each are divorced and now have man-friends. Doris had two children in her marriage, Jennifer and Stuart. Jennifer recently married and is now Jennifer Theodoratos, and has a new baby girl, Alanna. Also in Simsbury is Aunt Beth, now in her nineties, living on her own and doing amazingly well.

Donna, Barbara, Aunt Beth and Doris in Donna's home with her dogs.

Barbara, Stuart and Doris

Jenn and Donna

A four generational photo with Beth, Doris, Jenn and Alanna

Barbara is the one sister that didn't stay around, but instead went to Mexico after she graduated and married a local man, Alberto Perez, and resides in Oaxaca, Mexico with daughter, Elissa and her daughter, Olivia. Barbara's son, Roberto, lives with his wife, Leah, in Connecticut.

One Christmas David Munro and I visited Barbara's family in Oaxaca for the holidays and it was a delightful trip. Barbara and her husband own a small hotel in the center of Oaxaca where we stayed. At that time Barbara was responsible for making breakfast for the residents and those breakfasts in the charming outdoor courtyard were scrumptious. Oaxaca celebrated Christmas in lavish ways, because the outlying towns in the province of Oaxaca came into the city to celebrate. The colorful festivities were endless, with parades every day, bands playing and a general party atmosphere for several days around Christmas, reserving Christmas day to be more solemn in its celebration.

A particularly surprising evening for me was the night we went to Alberto's family home for a Christmas Eve potluck dinner. It was so moving that this Mexican family, most of whom didn't speak English, welcomed David and me into their home and made us feel like family.

Barbara and Alberto's hotel in Oaxaca

Preparing breakfast

The Zocola with Christmas festivities.

The Perez family on Christmas Eve

Roberto, Elissa, me, Barbara and Alberto

* * *

My closest relatives are my brother Jonathan and his family. During their early marriage, he and his lovely, Swedish wife, Solveig, lived in Manhattan in a huge loft on 23rd Street, right in the middle of the flower district. I loved visiting them there because they hung out with a fascinating, artsy crowd. After their first son, Sven, was born, followed by Oliver, they felt the desire to move to the country. So they left their loft and built a house in hills around Warwick, New York, a town right over the boarder of New Jersey.

Jonathan and Solveig in the 23rd St. loft

At Sven's baptism, w/ mother and Bobby

Sven and Oliver grow up in the country

As my nephews, Sven and Oliver, grew up, their interests centered on modes of transportation: first skates and skateboards and then automobiles. Both of their passions still include cars, which they can dismantle and rebuild with ease, as well as drive fast. In their early teens I was determined to broaden their scope of interests, since their country life was rather narrow. Jonathan and Solveig rarely took them into the city any more and I wanted to introduce them to some more culture. So I decided to give them both a trip to a Broadway play for Christmas.

I asked Solveig if the boys had seen the movie *The Rocky Horror Picture Show*. She said that they'd seen it on TV, so I figured that the new stage musical revival would be a good choice for their first Broadway play. I knew that the movie was very popular with most teenagers because of it's bizarre sexiness and I assumed that Sven and Oliver would also feel that way. As we sat in the theater I asked them how many times they'd seen the movie, and they said that they may have seen bits on TV but didn't remember it. *What?! Oh My God!*

In their rather provincial upbringing, they were completely unprepared for what was to follow. I got the feeling as I watched them watch the show, that they were unclear of what a transvestite was or had had any real awareness to gay life at all. Their mother kept them innocent of my relationship to David Munro for most of their childhood (which always pissed me off) and I didn't think they had any contact in their school. So I was quite worried about their reaction to the play and to theater in general. They didn't say much about it afterwards, but I think they liked it, in their teenage way, because it was so raw and new to them.

Over the years I've taken them to a Broadway show ever year, and they have become more and more sophisticated in their taste. They've told me that their favorite so far was *In the Heights*, which makes me happy, since it was one of my favorites, too.

A few years ago, when the boys were around 30, they surprised me by both getting married in the same year. First Oliver married Brieanna, who had a little girl already, Maddie, and Oliver's son was well on the way. At the wedding David Munro referred to her as "the bulging bride". Their son, Owen, was born soon after and he was, and is, a charmer.

Brieanna, Jonathan, Oliver and Owen at Thanksgiving
(Maddie in the background)

At Oliver's wedding, Sven announced to me that he too was getting married to a gorgeous Colombian girl, Stephanie, and that the wedding would be in Colombia later that year. So David and I made plans to attend, giving us our first South American vacation.

When wedding time came, we landed in Cartagena and spent three days exploring this historic town, which we enjoyed thoroughly. We then took a bus down to Barranquilla, where Stephanie's family lived and the wedding was to take place. Jonathan and Solveig were already there, along with Oliver and a few friends of the boys who had made the trip as well. Stephanie's parents, the Castros, were delightful and even though they spoke little English, they welcomed us into their family wholeheartedly. They were impressed how we had welcomed Stephanie into our home for Thanksgiving the year before. They put the Umbach guests up in a beautiful, posh hotel, across from a huge, modern mall, very different from quaint Cartagena.

The wedding took place in a rented beach house, so we assumed the ocean breeze would keep us all from melting, despite the tropical heat. We were wrong. There was not a whisper of a breeze for the entire wedding,. But that didn't stop the festivities from being joyous and exuberant. Drinking and dancing went into the night and the heat didn't seem to bother anyone, but us Northerners. And despite the heat, it was truly a beautiful wedding.

We accompanied the newlyweds, with Jonathan and Solvieg, on a short honeymoon around the coast of Colombia, ending up back in Cartagena, leaving them there to finish the honeymoon alone.

The Castro and Umbach families uniting on the beach at the wedding.

Above the newlyweds a double rainbow appeared

*Me, Jonathan, Stephanie and Sven
on the honeymoon in Cartagena.*

Sven and Stephanie had to wait for months for her to get a visa to move to the States as the wife of an American, but she finally got it and now they have their own apartment now near Warwick. Sven is a salesman-manager of a store there and Stephanie is a social worker. When our home in Cranford was flooded by Hurricane Irene, Sven was one of the first to come to our aid, bringing a gas pump, to evacuate the six and a half feet of water in our basement. And a year later when Hurricane Sandy hit New Jersey, both nephews frantically went searching for gas generators for our house.

For about a year everything look to be perfect for my two nephews; Sven and Steph leading the life of young couple in love, working during the week, but partying hard on the weekends. While Oliver, who had gone to school to learn the mechanics of BMW automobiles and had become a master repairman of these vehicles, was happy to be a father of two lovely children.

Then misfortune struck poor Oliver, he hurt his back while at work, badly messing up his spine. He was in agony for months, not able to stand, or walk. When they finally got workman's comp insurance to treat the condition, he underwent an horrific operation which was supposed to fix it, but two of the pins broke leaving his back in pain again. Being out of work and workman's comp being minimal, Brieanna had to take a job, leaving Oliver to care for the kids. This has been over a year now and the situation put a major strain on their marriage. Recently, Brieanna has left Oliver, taking Maddie and leaving primary custody of Owen to his father. That is the situation at the moment, and although Owen and his father are very close, it isn't a happy time for that family.

Oliver and Owen

Jonathan and Solveig with their grandchildren

Last Christmas I took my nephews and their wives to see a Broadway musical, *How to Succeed in Business without Really Trying*. It was the wives' first Broadway show and they seemed to really loved it. Oliver was in pain, but still able to enjoy the play.

Oliver, Brieanna, Stephanie and Sven, with David and Michele after our Broadway excursion

* * *

For many years Jonathan's family and ours have alternated Thanksgivings, one year in Cranford and the next up in Waldwick. One of my favorite traditions has been that whenever we had the feast at our house, we took a family photo on the stairs, so we could watch the family grow over the years. Here are some of the pictures from the years that Mother was able to join us.

All photos include Mother, Jonathan, Solveig, Sven, Oliver, me and David Munro

with Bobby & girlfriend

with Bobby

with Marianne

with Bobby

with Marianne & Ray

Mother's last Thanksgiving with us

* * *

The Munros have been a wonderful addition to my life, beginning when David's brother, Doug, and his wife, Tina, invited us to visit them in Cairo, Egypt. We were treated like kings, given first-rate tours to all the Egyptian antiquities as well as their beautiful home to stay in while we were there. That is when we met their children, Daniel and Catherine, who were both in grammar school at the time. Doug worked for GM Motors, International, which required the family to live in Sao Paulo, Brazil; Zurich, Switzerland; Cairo, Egypt; and Dubai, United Arab Emirates, spending little time in the States.

The Munro Family in Cairo, Egypt

When the Munro family moved to Dubai, the children attended an American High School there. When they graduated, they both wanted to go to the States for their college experience. Daniel was the oldest by a year, so before he graduated Tina, Catherine and Daniel came to the States to look over colleges for Daniel. Since he was interested in studying film making, he settled on New York University. Munro and I showed them around New York and Greenwich Village, so they spent quite a bit of time with us, and it was so nice to get to know them more.

One of the days that they were touring the city was Gay Pride Day. We didn't accompany them that day because we wanted to go to the parade and weren't sure how they would react. It turned out that the Munros were standing on the same corner of the Village watching the parade as we were, but we didn't see them. Their reaction was completely joyful, when the talked about it to us afterwards. Nothing like that ever happens in Dubai, for sure, so it was a totally new experience for Daniel. From then on he became an ardent advocate for Gay Rights.

When Daniel entered the University we became his only family near to him, because his mother had to go back to Dubai for Catherine's senior year in high school. His father had been moved by GM to South Africa for the year, thus not around at all. So we made sure that Daniel had a family to help him through the major adjustment of living for the first time in the United States. In the fall, I took him shopping for winter clothes, something he had never had before. It was such a lovely experience buying him scarves, gloves, a winter coat and a warm hat – I felt like a father taking his son shopping.

That November he came to Cranford for his first Thanksgiving in America. It happened that year that the leaves were late turning color, so he was awed and ecstatic to see the beautiful trees of our town because he'd never seen this phenomenon. Being a photographer enthusiast, he took hundreds of photos. It happened that we also had our dear French friend, Thomas, visit at that time, his first Thanksgiving, too. And of course the Umbach family was there and Sven brought Stephanie, who also experienced her first Thanksgiving. It was an extremely memorable event for us all.

A Thanksgiving photo with Daniel on the bottom, Thomas on the top, and Stephanie in Sven's arms

Daniel is now graduated from NYU's film school and is a freelance film sound engineer, living in Queens. We get together with him whenever we can to see movies or plays in New York, and he comes and stays in our house often. Catherine has graduated from Washington University and continues her medical studies, so I don't see much of her. Tina now lives in Michigan and visits us often, and we have gone to Michigan for several visits, as well. And at the moment Doug is teaching in Kuwait at a university.

The Munros when Tina visited Daniel at NYU

I am very grateful that I have cousins, second cousins, even third cousins, nieces, and nephews in my life now, from the Guyot, Umbach and Munro families. They all enrich my life.

Eighteen

The End of Bobby

When my brother Jonathan was just a kid staying with me in New York City, he got involved with a girl from the Dominican Republic named Carmen. She became pregnant and the two decided to get married. My father flew out to the East to make sure that Jonathan wasn't getting coerced into a marriage he didn't want, but it seemed legitimate and the wedding happened.

Jonathan and Carmen had a son, Bobby, and they lived in an apartment in the Bronx, near the zoo. When Bobby was about four, the marriage ended and Bobby went to live with his mother in an apartment in a Dominican section of upper Manhattan, with her fanatically religious mother and aunt. In the midst of this harsh neighborhood and three strict, domineering women, Bobby spent his childhood.

He was such a sweet little boy and one of the joys of his life was to visit his grandparents in Illinois and his uncle in New Jersey. My mother and father doted on him and he spent some happy summers in suburbia with them. When he visited me, I would take him *down-the-shore* and we would ride the bumper cars over and over, because it was his favorite thing to do.

As he grew older, one of his guilty pleasures was to listen to the recording of *Jesus Christ, Super Star,* because he knew how much his Dominican grandmother and aunt would be scandalized by this blasphemy. He played it over and over when he came to my house.

Unfortunately, as he became a teenager, the temptations of the Dominican neighborhood seduced him and he became involved in drug use, and unbeknownst to the Umbach family, he became addicted to heroin. Carmen tried to deal with this problem because Bobby truly wanted to improve himself. During his teens and early twenties he seemed to be functioning well, landing a job in a florist and attending community college. He visited me often, though I was never aware he had a drug problem.

But at some point during this period, he hit bottom and was placed in a detox and rehab. When he came out of this, he told his grandmother and me about his problem. He swore that he was "cured", and went back to college and to his work in the florist shop, where the owner was a friend and supporter. One day Bobby asked his grandmother for money to "help pay the rent", and she entreated me to give it to him. David Munro tried to talk me out of it, knowing that an addict needs money for only one thing, but I blithely took him the money. I don't know what he did with this money, but I hoped it was for the rent.

Through all these years he remained a loveable, charming young man, but a man with a serious problem.

Down-the-shore.

At his grandfather's funeral.

Gramma adoring Bobby

When he was about 25 years-old, he was arrested for drugs and spent time in jail. The Umbach family never heard about this but when he was released, Carmen took him down to Florida, to get him away from the temptations of New York in an attempt to clean him up. It was evidentially successful and he improved in Florida with nothing but optimistic plans for a rosy future. He was supposedly clean of drugs for over a year and was became involved with a girlfriend, named Irma.

Bobby and Irma decided to take a road trip that would end in their marriage. They planned to visit his family; me first, then his father, then his grandmother in Illinois, then some relative of Irma's in Iowa, and finally off to Las Vegas to get married and settle down. They set out with all their worldly possessions, jammed into this beat-up, old Buick, which Bobby loved and had poured $1300 into to make it safe for their vacation/honeymoon. The two of them set off for this adventure, happy and in love.

After driving up from Florida they stopped first in New York City. Bobby took Irma around, showing her the city for her first time. Irma was a 19 year old, Mexican girl, who spoke limited English, with a lovely, happy smile. Bobby's last stop in New York was to his old neighborhood in Queens. He brought Irma into a restaurant and told her to wait while he went to "do something" -- to buy two packets of heroin, as it turned out. Then they drove out to New Jersey, to "surprise Uncle David".

They arrived on Tuesday night, at 10:30 PM. I had finished classes and was watching "NYPD Blue" and David Munro was in bed, so the house appeared to be dark. At the last minute Bobby must have chickened out, figuring that a surprise visit at this hour was not a good idea, or perhaps the call of the little white packets in his pocket was too strong. Irma begged him to give me a call, but he decided to find a motel for the night. In all honesty, I probably would not have been too pleased with that late night surprise, not having heard from Bobby in at least six months.

Finding out from a gas station attendant that motels in the area were expensive and that they were cheaper down at the shore, they went down the parkway and ended up, for some reason, an hour away in Long Branch, New Jersey.

After they got a room, Bobby got out the heroin. Irma was aghast. She pleaded with him not to do it, as he had promised her to never, ever do that again. She had known that he was an "ex-junkie" but believed he was cured. He promised her that it was just "one last time and then never again". She was furious and told him she didn't want to see him do it, so he went into the bathroom. Desolate, Irma crawled into bed and fell asleep.

When she awoke at 4:00 AM, she found he was not in the bed. She went out to the car, and finally into the bathroom, where she found him on the floor, dead. Hysterical, she got the night manager to call the police, but it was too late. Either from bad heroin or an over-dose, his life was over. Then her nightmare experience continued. She was alone in New Jersey, far away from her home and not able to speak English very well. Her happy marriage plans were shattered. The only person she'd ever loved, and who was supposed to take care of her, was now dead in a morgue. She would not to see a familiar face for two days.

A kindly detective put her into a motel, after all the questioning, where she spent a sleepless night. Finally she called him, weeping that she couldn't stand being alone, so he brought her back to the police station, where she remained in the dingy, depressing lobby until the following evening, when I finally picked her up on Thursday.

All during the day on Wednesday, phone calls were flying around from the police and Irma in Long Branch, to Bobby's mother in Florida, to Irma's mother in Mexico City, and to Bobby's father, Jonathan, and finally from Carmen, Bobby's mother, to me. Jonathan's second wife, Solveig, got the news before Jonathan and had called me about the rudimentary situation, even before she told Jonathan.

By the time Carmen called me, she was so hysterical that I still didn't understand exactly what had happened. Nevertheless, I planned to skip work at Merck on Thursday to begin making arrangements, but when Jonathan called me later that night, he said that we should wait for Carmen to get up from Florida and we would all go down to Long Branch together.

I went to Merck for a full, and fortunately busy, work day. When I got home, I got a call from poor, weeping Irma, begging me to come and pick her up. I told her that I was waiting for Carmen and Jonathan, and would get there as soon as they arrived. They got to my house around 6:00 PM and the three of us took the solemn, one hour drive down to Long Branch.

I expected Carmen to be an out-of-control mess when she arrived, but I was surprised to find a strong, capable woman, who had lived with hardship and dealt with Bobby's drug problem for years, handling herself and the situation with grim fatalism. I think it helped her that her main job now was to take care of Irma and help her through this devastating experience so that she wouldn't be psychologically ruined for life. I was also proud of Jonathan for handling himself with dignity, and even some decisiveness, through the whole affair.

It broke my heart to see the face of that dear, little girl when she first saw Carmen after her two days alone. They rode back together in the back seat of my car, with Irma bawling and talking in Spanish and Carmen trying to calm her and convince her that it wasn't her fault. Irma felt that she had let Carmen down by not stopping Bobby, but both Carmen and I tried to tell her that none of us could have stopped him from taking that heroin. He was obviously determined to get the stuff as soon as he got to New York.

It was a pitiful drive that I will never forget. Behind us Jon drove Bobby's Buick, packed with all his things, back to Cranford. That wasn't an easy task, I'm sure. The rest of the night was devoted to getting Irma to eat something and get some sleep, as she hadn't slept or eaten in two days. She went to bed with Carmen in the guest room and Jon went to the bed in the attic, but none of them got much sleep.

The next day we had the grim job of driving down to the Coroner's office to take care of Bobby's body and arrange some sort of funeral. Freehold, New Jersey, where the Coroner is located, is also an hour away from Cranford. At the morgue, Jonathan, Carmen and Irma went in to view Bobby. I refrained. Irma insisted on taking part in every aspect of this gruesome day.

From there, we went to a local funeral home, which was a ghastly experience, sitting and talking with the funeral director trying to plan Bobby's funeral arrangements. Both Jonathan and Carmen agreed that it should be done as cheaply as possible. Poor Irma sat whimpering the whole time. We insisted on comparing the price of a cremation with that of a ground burial, but when the costs were not too far apart, Jon conceded with the latter, because Carmen's religion really was against cremation.

When we left there, the painful process was not over, because I offered to go to a clothing store and pick out burial clothes for Bobby. I was told by the funeral director to get a dark shirt or sweater, since his autopsy scars would show through a white shirt. This shopping excursion was particularly horrible, probably because I hadn't anticipated it (and because it was, ironically, at Bob's Store).

After delivering the clothes, we left Freehold and stopped for lunch in a diner, everyone somewhat relieved that this part was over. Irma was now able to get her mind off the tragedy for a time and it was wonderful to see her smile, recalling happier times, before she would be plunged into sorrow again.

I had some good conversation with Carmen and Jonathan that night. They were handling this all very well and getting on well together, too. I haven't seen Jon that decisive and secure with himself in a long time; Carmen had a good effect on him. Much of their conversation was about Solveig, and it wasn't kind, from either of them. Carmen definitely blamed Solveig for Jonathan's dropping Bobby for his other two sons, and subsequently helping him to become an addict.

Bobby's feelings were definitely anti-Solveig, in that she had treated him shabbily since her sons were born. Carmen blatantly hated Solveig and Jon wasn't too fond of her right then, either. This didn't bode well for the funeral the next day, where the only other participants would be Solveig and Bobby's step brothers, Sven and Oliver.

Saturday morning was grim, even though it was a glorious, Spring day. We had to leave for Freehold by 9:30am to be at the funeral home by 11:00, counting on heavy, shore traffic. Carmen dreaded the anticipated arrival of Solveig and the boys, who were forced to get out of bed very early to arrive by 9:00am.

They arrived sullen and sleepy, but subdued. Carmen stayed in her room during breakfast (Solveig was worried because "the boys wouldn't eat before they left!"). We got started on time, believe it or not, Carmen and Irma with me and the Umbachs in Solveig's mini-van, with Sven driving. I had to drive slowly down the parkway, because Sven was a new driver, but we were in no hurry, because there wasn't the expected traffic. As a matter of fact we were half and hour early, so the Umbachs and I went to a diner for more breakfast, leaving Carmen and Irma in the parking lot of the funeral home.

Carmen and Irma were already in the viewing room when we got back and they were in terrible shape. Bobby looked pretty bad, with bruises on his face and a dark complexion that must have matched his Florida tan that looked extremely fake. We had the viewing room for an hour, which was more than enough time. Sometimes we left Irma and Carmen alone, sometimes we sat quietly in the room. Sven and Oliver were quiet, and chose to remain the entire time. Sven showed no emotion, but Oliver was visibly moved and before we left, went over to Carmen and hugged her and cried; Carmen was touched by this, because she knew that Bobby liked him best. To everyone's relief, Carmen ended the viewing fifteen minutes early and we went to the parking lot to wait for the hearse.

After an interminable twenty minute wait, we followed the hearse to a nearby cemetery, where the usual arrangements had been made. Four chairs were placed under a canopy, in front of the grave. The pallbearers, Jon, Sven, a funeral director and I (Oliver couldn't do it), placed the plain, pine coffin onto the straps above the grave. I led Carmen and Irma to the chairs and indicated for Jonathan to sit. He started to give Solveig a chair, but I stopped him because I knew that Carmen would have become quite upset. Then, since no one seemed to know what to do, I asked Carmen if I should say something. She nodded, so I stood up and said, "We are here to say good-bye to Jonathan Robert Umbach (he had been named Robert after our father). He was one of the sweetest people that I have ever known. We will all say our prayers and good-byes in our own ways, in our own hearts."

It wasn't much of a eulogy, but it seemed to suffice. After a few more minutes, we got into our cars and left. Bobby's remains were, and still are, in a plot of ground in Freehold, New Jersey, not the ending Bobby, or any of us, would have planned.

On the way back, Carmen and I talked about the impending gathering planned at my house, a barbecue. Jonathan had wanted his family to spend some time with us and suggested it. He had gone to the supermarket the day before and bought all sorts of food for the event. I wasn't particularly looking forward to it, and Carmen was outright dreading it. I told her that she could stay away from it all, until Solveig left, which she did.

David Munro, of course, had made all sorts of preparation for the barbecue while we were gone, so it went smoothly, and by the time the food was prepared, we were all hungry, again. It was a subdued, strained, but fairly, congenial afternoon. Irma had come down for some of the food and was somewhat coming out of her depression. We talked about her home, Mexico City, where Jonathan and Solveig had been.

After this rather awkward conversation, the Umbachs decided to leave, and Carmen came out of hiding. She had said good-bye to the boys, but she refused to say anything to Solveig, literally hiding behind a bush when their van pulled out. Jonathan was driving Bobby's green car, which he hoped to sell and give the money to Irma, and I know it broke her heart to see it pull away from the curb.

Carmen said that she would take Irma into her apartment, to live with her 14 year-old son, Michael, her ailing aunt, and her mother, until Irma could either get her own place or goes back to Mexico. Irma said that she would try to get into a school and learn better English. I got the distinct feeling that she was a strong and resilient girl, and that she would ultimately survive this ordeal.

As the evening went on, I asked if they would like to go to a movie (my panacea for everything); they declined, but David and I went because I wanted to get away from the trauma of the weekend.

Early the next morning, I took the two of them to the airport, with two of our suitcases and 4 boxes, full of Irma's belongings. It was a teary good-bye. I had become fond of Irma and my feelings for Carmen had changed and strengthened. Irma swears that someday she'll come back to visit me and Bobby's grave. I doubt she will. I swore that if I go to Florida, again, I will definitely stop by to visit Carmen. I never did.

*   *   *

This experience and the suicide of my father were the two great tragedies of my life. It is coincidental that they involved two family members that I not only loved, but who deeply loved each other. Bobby and my father had a great bond since Bobby was a young boy. They seemed to empathize with each other more than with any members of the family. I know that my father's death was devastating to Bobby and when he came out to Oklahoma for Dad's funeral, he was completely shattered, even though they hadn't seen each other for several years.

One of my favorite pictures of my father was taken after one of Bobby's visits when he was a young boy. Bobby had been so enchanted with the fact that there were so many birds in Grampa's yard that he wanted to catch one for a pet. So he built a "bird trap" in hopes of doing so. Of course, it never fooled any birds, so Bobby went back to New York disappointed. After he left, my clever father took a photo of himself as a "bird" to send to Bobby, showing him that his trap was, indeed, successful.

Bobby and Grampa at the zoo.   *Grampa as a "bird" in Bobby's trap.*

Nineteen

Playing In The Park

Having performed and directed in many local New Jersey theaters over the years, the one theater that more or less changed my life was Plays-in-the-Park in Edison. It is an out-door summer theater that produces at least three large scale, high quality musicals each summer season. In the mid-1980s, admission to these performances was free to audiences, and they came each night by the thousands to set their lawn chairs on the hill in front of the stage to enjoy a professional level production.

Though the technical positions and musicians were hired and paid, the actors were all volunteers, but its reputation for quality professional productions made it a prestigious theater in which to work, so much so that hundreds of actors auditioned every year. My friend Gary Cohen, who would later become the artistic director, had directed a few of their productions, but in 1987 he was not the artistic director yet. The philosophy of the theater back then was heavily balanced toward the singing, so that actors were chosen primarily for their vocal talents, but not necessarily their acting abilities. This meant that I, being an actor more than a singer, didn't have much chance of being cast.

But in 1987, Gary was directing *Camelot* and knowing that *Camelot* features a non-singing role, King Pelinore, I decided to go out for it. And I was cast. It was a sumptuous production, with gorgeous medieval costumes designed and built for the whole company on the premises. It included elaborate sets and special effects. My costume primarily consisted of full (plastic) armor, over my bald wig with straggly hair at the bottom, and drooping white mustache. I also lead around a dog, which was written to be a St. Bernard, but in this production was Gary's tiny Scottie. To justify this, I, as King Pelinore, explained "he got caught in the rain and shrunk". It was a terrific comic role and I truly made the most of it.

My first role at Plays-in-the-Park, King Pelinore (upper right)

Since the orchestra and all of the audience are outdoors and under no cover, rain is always a major factor at Plays-in-the-Park. So the minute it begins to drizzle the union orchestra packs up and will close the show for the night. *Camelot* was plagued with lots of rain. Out of the ten scheduled performances, five were rained out.

One night the rain began during the overture, so we actors were all ready to go on when it started, and we heard over the loud speakers that the show had to be stopped. However, it was only a drizzle, so the powers-that-be decided that the orchestra would come up on stage and the cast would stay in costume and sing the show for hearty audience members who wanted to stay in the mist. Gary always liked to do this if it happens early in the run, because it is a good rehearsal for the orchestra, and they would get paid whether they did the show or not.

Here I was in make-up and full armor, which was not easy to get in and out of, needing a dresser's help to do so. Since I did no singing in the play, I asked Gary if I should get out of costume and go home. He told me, no, that I should stay in costume and narrate the play for the audience, filling in what was going on between the numbers. So wacky old King Pelinore took the hand microphone and proceeded to tell the story of *Camelot*, from his own perception. It was an actor's improvisational dream and I had a ball! In all humility, I have to say I was hilarious. People have told me over the years that they saw and remembered that night as a highlight at the theater. It has been said that it was the "King Pelinore Show" and that King Arthur was none too happy about it, either.

Due to the five rain-outs that year and given the show had cost so much to mount, they decided to give five more performances the next summer, adding it to the front of the season. This was somewhat stressful for me because that summer I was also cast as Captain Hook, in *Peter Pan*. As arduous as that summer was for me, I was happy that I was now accepted as a singer and a comic actor.

The rehearsal process for *Peter Pan* was not a pleasant experience; the director was not my favorite. Not only did he terrorize the Pirates and Lost Boys, he gave me absolutely no direction. I was left entirely on my own to create Hook and I just had to muddle through and deal with it. When the show was finally transferred from the rehearsal space to the theater, we were seen by Gary Cohen, who was now the Assistant Producer at PIP, and he was not pleased. I asked him for some advice, as he had always known just how to push me into being better in my roles that he directed.

He said that I was a funny Hook but not a scary Hook. The audience needed to be worried that the children would be harmed by Hook and that the fight with Peter should be exciting, not just silly. I was basing my interpretation on Cyril Richard, who played it rather campy in the Mary Martin version, which I had only seen on TV, not on stage.

One of the problems, Gary told me, was the hook itself. The prop department had given me on of those plastic hooks from a Halloween shop, and I knew that in the huge PIP venue it would be lost, so I made one myself. With David Munro's help (of course), I bent a long piece of aluminum into a large hook, and secured it into a tin can to cover my hand. With it I was able to do all sorts of silly manipulations like picking my nose and scratching my back – cute schtick. But Gary said that a moving wrist was impossible if a person has had his hand removed, so moving the wrist wasn't believable or scary. I went home and reconstructed my hook so that metal straps went up my arm and my wrist couldn't bend at all. This inhibited me from some of my silly schtick, but it definitely made Hook's hook scarier.

I worked hard in the two rehearsals I had left to add "scary" to my Hook and achieved it in my scenes by Opening Night, but unfortunately, I feel my songs still landed more on the silly side. After a couple of performances I melded the two areas and created a completely scary and funny Hook. But I learned two lessons: directors make a difference and so do props.

Captain Hook, with the great actor Oscar Stokes as Smee (lower right) I regret that the night of the photos, I forgot to wear Hook's hat.

It was through these parts that I got a reputation as a qualified actor/singer, so the following year when Gary was set to direct Sondheim's *A Little Night Music*, I got the part of Fredrik, the leading male role. I had played that role for Gary back at Celebration Playhouse, and I loved it, but the thought of doing it with a full orchestra, in front of a couple thousand people each night, terrified me. Lyrics have always been the hardest for me to learn, and I've been known to screw them up, but never in a venue this large.

I was most frightened right before the first number I sang every night, "Now". Sondheim's lyrics for that song are extremely repetitious at the beginning of each line: "Now, as the sweet imbecilities tumble so lavishly on to her lap... Now, there are two possibilities, ………". Every verse begins with "Now…" and it's easy to slip into the wrong line after that – and the damn orchestra is not going to stop and fix it the way a pianist can. Plus, during this number I had to do a strip tease and get into a night shirt. This was a nightmare for me every night, but happily, I got through it successfully in every performance. Once that song was over I was able to relax and enjoy the rest of the show and it turned out to be my favorite musical theater experience as a performer. It was truly an opulent and flawless production.

"A Weekend in the Country" from <u>A Little Night Music</u>, a glorious production!

Soon after that, another of my favorite Sondheim musicals was scheduled for PIP, *Sweeney Todd*. Again, Gary had directed me, as Sweeney, a few years before in an exciting, intimate, environmental-theater production and he wanted me to play the title role this time, too. But let's face it, I may be able to act the hell out of Sweeney, but to sing it at Plays-in-the-Park standards would be difficult. I wanted to do this so much, that I went to a vocal coach for 6 months before auditions to train for the role. I wanted to know the score backward and forward, and I was sure that I hadn't learn it correctly when I did it before.

Off to open auditions I went. I received a call back for the role of Sweeney and felt fairly confident. When I arrived, a little late, to the call back audition I found that there were eight potential Sweeneys standing around the piano practicing the audition song. I joined them as they sang "They all deserve to die, tell you why Mrs. Lovett, tell you why.....". I felt like I was in the middle of the Mormon-fucking-Tabernacle Choir. These booming baritone voices around me made my heart sink. Still I belted out along with them. When the solo audition came, I acted my brains out and sang it with every ounce my being, as well as I could.

When everyone had sung, I did a scene with several Mrs. Lovetts, including Lisa Cohen (né Minogue, now Gary's wife), who was my Mrs. Lovett when I had done it before. Then it was over. We all had to go home and wait until the director, the musical director and the choreographer came to a decision as to the cast.

Gary called me on Saturday night saying that he and the musical director could not come to a meeting of the minds. The musical director wanted the actor that sang better and Gary wanted me, who acted the role better. He asked me to come in on Sunday for a Sweeney Face-Off, to help them make a decision. The actors should prepare the comic number about meat pies made from human flesh, "A Little Priest" and would do the scene preceding and sing it with Lisa Cohen, who was cast again as Mrs. Lovett.

After a sleepless Saturday night, I arrived at the theater hoping that I could pull it off. I'd been preparing for this for six months, and I really wanted that part. So Lisa and I did the scene and song – I acted it better than I ever had and sang it just fine. Followed by the other actor who sang his brains out and made it through the acting all right.

Then suddenly Art Neil, who had been already cast as Pirelli and who coincidentally had been King Arthur, walks into the room. He heard about the Sweeney Face-Off and had asked if he could try out for Sweeney again. He got up and acted it terrifically AND sang it magnificently. As the production team conferred, I knew what the outcome had to be. Gary came over to me looking miserable. I waved my hand saying, "Don't say a word...I know what you are going to say...If I were the director, I'd say the same thing...Art got the part."

That's Show Biz.

Lisa Cohen and I in the <u>Sweeney Todd</u> that I did do

After I didn't get Sweeney and there were no particularly good roles for me in the next season or so, Gary asked if I wanted to direct at PIP. "Sure!" I said and he hired me (directors get paid!) to do a non-musical, *California Suite*, just to get my feet wet at this venue. In those days, the early 90s, Gary added a fourth production each season which was a straight play. They had to be plays that could be broad enough to reach this vast "auditorium" without music. Some audience members were sitting so far back that Gary called it "Radio with Pictures". I acted in two of these plays, both comic villains: Dracula in *Dracula* and later Jonathan in *Arsenic and Old Lace.*

We rehearsed *California Suite* in a small rehearsal space and I was ecstatic with my cast. A broad, Neil Simon comedy though it may be, I got some beautiful, nuanced performances from my actors. I couldn't wait to show Gary when we moved to the Park. So the actors assembled on the huge stage, which was way bigger than our rehearsal space, and Gary and I sat up the hill a bit at about the 4th row, which would be 10th row in a normal theater.

As my dear actors were doing their praiseworthy acting, I was thinking: "Where Is My Play?" It had completely disappeared into all that vast space. Gary didn't look happy at all. He told me that at Plays-in-the-Park you had to reach hundreds of people which were far away from the stage. So I went to my actors and said, "I hate to say this but, everything you are doing is great, but it's invisible. So you have to make it bigger, louder, broader – but don't lose the honesty you have". They were stunned, but by the next rehearsal they nailed it.

My cast of California Suite at Plays-in-the-Park

The next season when I played Jonathan in *Arsenic and Old Lace* I had learned my acting lesson. When Gary directed me to be "bigger, louder, broader" than I had done it for him at Celebration Playhouse, I knew what he meant and I enjoyed creating an entirely new character from the one I'd done earlier. It worked well, except for one thing, my scar make up. I made a three dimensional red scar, with large black stitches. Up close it was hideous and I was sure it would read perfectly for Jonathan's plastic surgery and his grotesqueness, until a friend in the fifth row said after the play, "What scar?" More lessons learned. We were all happy with the PIP version of this play, but it was one of the last straight plays to be done at the Park. They just didn't draw enough crowds, because everyone wanted musicals.

Subtle Jonathan at Celebration   *PIP's Jonathan, with Susie Speidel*

Gary tried one more time with a straight comedy, with music and dance, *Stepping Out*, and asked me to direct this play. Now I had seen this in London and knew it to be a wonderful ensemble piece about a tap dancing class for adult beginners. The comedy was my favorite type, character based and real, not full of jokes and gimmicks to get the laughs. The dancing was secondary except for the finale, when the class of amateurs finally performs the number that they've been "rehearsing for months". And there was one solo dance done by the dance teacher. I really liked the play and happily accepted the job. It turned out to be the only truly unpleasant experience I ever had at Plays-in-the-Park.

The crux of the problem was that the only production of the play Gary had seen was a community theater version, where the comedy was done in broad strokes with caricatures rather than characters. He thought that this was what it was supposed to be and therefore perfect for PIP audiences.

In that version, the tap teacher was played by an excellent, local choreographer. Her husband, who was known for slapstick comedy, played the one male class member. Gary hired this woman to be my choreographer and needless to say, she and I saw the play entirely differently. In casting the play, she pushed towards dancers who could ultimately do the final number perfectly, while I pushed for actors who could really play these characters and maybe learn to tap by the end of the rehearsal process – like the characters do. The cast ended up half and half.

But the real disaster came when casting the dance teacher. No one auditioned that seemed right so we needed to reach out. Someone heard that an alumni from PIP, who had played several leads, including Evita, and had gone on to be in *A Chorus Line* and *Cats* on Broadway, was back in New Jersey and might be available. When I called her she didn't seem much interested and told me that she had commitments that would make her miss several rehearsals and be late to all of them. I told this to Gary, but he urged me to cast her, because he felt that she was perfect and didn't need all that rehearsal time, "She's a pro!" Thus I cast her. Coincidentally, she had choreographed my *Camelot* many years before, but I didn't remember her since King Pelinore didn't dance.

And so it began. In one of our early rehearsals I tried to incorporate a mini-version of a rehearsal exercise that I had often used in ensemble plays. I liked to ask the actors in an ensemble-type play (which I considered this to be) to improvise a party in character, to get to know each other's characters and build relationships, before even getting to the script. This had been particularly successful for plays like *That Championship Season* and *Brighton Beach Memoirs,* when the actors were excited about how strongly their relationships became with each other after the full-evening party concluded.

I realized that with this cast, made up of half musical comedy/dancer actors and half straight play actors, it would not serve us to dedicate an entire rehearsal to this exercise. But I told them at the end of one of the first rehearsals that it was the "pianist's birthday" (a character in the play) and there was cake and soda, which I had provided, in the wings. I told them to have a party, in character, and just see what happened. They tried, and many actors got into it and conversed in character and played this theater game properly. But many just took their soda and piece of cake and watched the others, not knowing how to improvise. I stopped it after 15 minutes and asked them, as I always did, to tell me what they learned. Some gave a few good ideas, but many just stared at me like I was some kind of nut.

This theater game polarized the cast into the "with me" and the "against me" groups, which lasted through the whole uncomfortable rehearsal process. One actress who was in the community theater production and who interpreted her part as a cartoon character, out for nothing but laughs, drove me mad. I tried to change her direction, but to no avail. This turned her friends and my choreographer even more against me.

I was surprised to find that the professional actress that I had hired for the lead, fell into the "against me" group. One would think that someone who had studied acting and worked with professionals would have understood what I was doing. But this gave me my first insight into this professional's lack of professionalism. She was the last to learn lines. She refused to "lead" the ensemble, as the character of the "teacher" should have done. She just mumbled her lines, not interacting with anyone. She told me that she was taking a TV acting class and was told to keep her acting internal and subtle. *At Plays-in-the-Park?*

I always like to invite friends of the cast to the last rehearsal before going to the Park, so I asked some friends of mine from out of town who had never seen my work. It proved to be an extremely embarrassing experience, about which I am still nagged today. The rehearsal was a shamble, primarily because the leading lady couldn't remember her lines or be heard on the lines she did know.

Needless to say, getting on the main stage at the Park pulled things together, and as soon as there was an audience the "star" started to perform. But she never really was part of the ensemble. The outcome was a compromise, I suppose, between the choreographer and me, and the audiences seemed to enjoy it. My favorite moment of the whole experience, however, was one night when the teacher was performing her solo number and a pigeon shat on her hat. Sometimes the critic gets it right.

The year before *Stepping Out* I was hired to direct *West Side Story*, which was a major turning point in my directing career. Outside of Roselle Park High School, I'd never directed a musical, especially in a venue as professional as Plays-in-the-Park. In those days, the philosophy of PIP was not so much "recreating" the original production (as it is today), but more allowing the creative team to go in different directions. This was especially urged of us for *West Side Story*. Gary asked us to have it not look like all the copies that we've seen over the years, but to invent our own unique style for the piece. I remember playing with the set model, trying to invent exciting ways to make the production different. I had such fun sliding the panels around to create different looks on the stage, like playing with a doll's house.

My favorite creative moment came from the balcony/fire-escape scene. Rather than keeping the fire-escape stationary, when Tony climbs up to sing with Maria, I had it break away, move to the center of the stage, and spin around as they sung their passionate duet. It gave a cinematic effect of the camera circling the actors as they sang. I'm sure this has been done in other places, but to me it was original and I loved that moment.

<u>West Side Story</u>, *the first major musical I directed.*

Over the years I was honored to direct eight exciting musicals at Plays-in-the-Park: *West Side Story, Hello, Dolly!, My Fair Lady, Oliver!, Kiss Me, Kate!, Aida, Thoroughly Modern Millie* and *Singing in the Rain*. Every one of these was a joy and a success. The thrill of directing a large bunch of enthusiastic actors, all pulling together to make a big musical come to life is unlike any other directing experience. Yes, we have to live through horrific tech weeks, which are my least favorite time in any show, especially musicals – because I'm so bad at them. But when it all comes together and the crowds roar with approval, it's like nothing else in the theater.

A major life moment that happened while directing these musicals was meeting Michele Mossay. It started with *Oliver!* when Gary was searching for a choreographer. He asked me into his office to meet a possible candidate. He introduced me to Michele and I was immediately taken with her and urged Gary to hire her on the spot. He did and right away asked us to take a road trip together to Pennsylvania to see a community theater production of *Oliver!*, a production that would be using the same script we would use and on a set built by the same designer we would have.

This trip required Michele and I to be together for the long drive out, a dinner, the show, and the long drive back. I suppose this could have been an uncomfortable experience for two people who didn't really know each other, but it turned out to be a pure delight. We hit it off amazingly well and by the end of that day we knew that we'd work well together. I don't think we stopped yakking from the moment we got into the car to the moment I dropped her off at her home.

As it turned out, Michele and I became a terrific team, true creative partners. We both saw the musicals we did together in exactly the same way; she handled the movement and dance and I handled the acting and production, and we never clashed. Both of us know that the story is the thing and that every element of the play must serve the story. I was so happy when I saw that her choreography wasn't just "dance" per se, but always served the plot or characters. Believe me, this is not always the case with choreographers. I like to think that each of us is accomplished in our own fields, but together as a team we excelled. I've never had a choreographer that I enjoyed working with as much, and I don't think I ever will.

Out of this partnership came a lifelong friendship. We no longer stage big musicals together, but we remain the best of friends who are particularly fond of attending New York theater and have traveled together to Key West and Chicago.

The four musicals I directed with Michele Mossay as my choreographer.

Oliver

Aida

Kiss Me, Kate.

Thoroughly Modern Millie

    Plays-in-the-Park is still going strong, having celebrated it's 50th Anniversary. It still produces quality musical theater, even though the cost of a ticket has gone up to an exorbitant $8.00.

    To find out more information about the theater, visit their website at: http://www.playsinthepark.com/

Twenty

ARBAD-A-CARBA

Once I was a magician. I know, it's crazy. I have always loved magic shows but I never thought I would ever be a real magician.

It all started when a rather nebishy high school student of mine decided that he wanted to be a magician when he left high school. He became The Great Benzini. He must have had lots of financial help from his mother, because within a few years he had accumulated many, expensive, major illusions and was doing his act all over the state. Unfortunately for him, he was never the real showman he should have been to pull all of this together to make a terrific magic show. He had lots of help from the lovely young women and men who were his assistants, but most of the time he just waved his hands saying "Abracadabra" and let the assistants do the work.

This was during my Acting Studio days, so one day he contacted me and asked if I could direct his show and give it some pizzazz. I had never seen his act and I was excited to be let in to the mysteries of the magic, so I accepted.

One night I went down to his basement where they were rehearsing to see what I had to work with. I sat in a folding chair and two feet in front of me was the frame of a large fish-tank box, without its glass. I talked with Ben and the assistants for awhile about what they wanted to show me and how I could help them, then they started their act.

The first illusion involved this fish-tank, The assistants put in each of the four walls of Plexiglas, and then the top piece, making a clear, empty box. Ben directed all of this by waving his hands over the box as they did this, then he helped cover the box with a cloth. They spun it around a couple times and then Ben whipped off the cloth. And, poof, right before my eyes, the box was filled with a girl.

Now, I'd been two feet from this box, and never had a clue that anything was going to be in it. I was flabbergasted. My fascination with magic had been struck to the heart – I was in love. Of course, I learned later that the girl had been scrunched into the false bottom of the box all that time I was sitting there. Thus, the first of many magical illusions was shattered.

As they proceeded with their show, it was obvious that the illusions were notably impressive, but the showmanship of the whole troupe was terrible. I gladly took on the task of directing and sprucing up the production.

The first thing I did was make them all come to my studio and I gave them "pizzazz lessons", teaching them how to do gestures and movements with style and flair. These classes were great fun for us all – certainly different from what I taught to my other acting classes.

After that when I started to direct the magic show, the "pizzazz lessons" made all the difference. Though Benzini never completely stepped up to the mark, it was his show and his money and his illusions that were the selling points. His assistants, however, made the show exciting, and the bookings started to come in as his reputation increased.

Then their biggest booking came. They were contracted to perform the show for a whole summer at Kennywood Park outside of Pittsburgh. Ben wanted to add several new illusions and costumes to create a truly impressive show, so he asked me to come to Pittsburgh and direct the whole shebang. Since I could make my own schedule for the studio, I took off the summer that year and hit the road with the magic show.

Kennywood was a huge, old amusement park, that had been around since the early 1900s. Known still today for it's impressive number of roller-coasters, both the ancient, wooden ones and the modern, metal ones. The stage we were assigned was beneath the giant octopus ride, called the Monongahela. And we would be sharing the stage with a musical show of young singers and dancers from Georgia. We would perform five half-hour shows a day alternating with the five musical shows.

Being at Kennywood was a joyous time for me since, once the show had been mounted, I was spending every day in an amusement park, for free, riding all the rides I wanted. At that time I was nuts about roller coasters, and especially enjoyed the one that was next to a deep ravine, so that the initial, steep drop was not proceeded by an uphill slog – surprising and thrilling. I was able to take in the carnival-like atmosphere as well as actually being a part of it.

Ben's biggest, most expensive and impressive addition was a large water tank illusion. One "lucky" assistant submerged herself into the tank that filled up to the top with water and was visibly swimming in this glass tank for the audience to see. Then the tank was padlocked with a chain and covered with a cloth. A large clock counted down the minutes for the assistant to escape, and a park security guard was on hand with an ax, in case she couldn't. This added to the suspense for the audience and performers, as it was quite the scary illusion. When the cloth was removed, a male assistant was swimming in the tank and the girl was gone. So, when they un-padlocked the tank and he stepped out and the female was revealed on the other side of the stage, dry as a bone. It was an excellent illusion, but hard for the assistants.

I planned to stay at Kennywood for several weeks, until the show was running smoothly. But then Ben asked me to remain longer to take over the magician's job for two weeks, while he and his main, male assistant went to a magician's convention.

When I found out that I would replace Ben, I practiced all the magician's moves trying to make the show run as well as it had the first month with Ben. Since the magician's job was primarily to "flourish", not much magical skill was necessary, and it was all up to the expensive illusions and the hard-working assistants. However, the opening part of the act was the magician performing small illusions by himself and chatting up the audience. I worked diligently on the opening of the show doing some hands-on illusions, like a three rope trick, a disappearing dove in a box, and a card trick with large playing cards; all of these called for sufficient dexterity.

The opening monologue also required amusing patter and audience participation, with which I was quite comfortable (more so than Ben). One night, during the monologue, I invented the phrase "Arbad-a-carba", which is Abracadabra backwards. It received many laughs and I made the audience repeat it after me. I found it warmed them up and got them involved, so I kept the phrase and it became the focus of my opening act.

My favorite part of in the show was actually participating in the "trunk switch" illusion. It was the same idea as the water tank, but different enough because the magician actually did the trick. The process was that a female assistant was handcuffed and put inside the trunk, then the magician would stand on top of the trunk. Two assistants would raise a concealing cloth around the magician and the trunk. Then with a flourish, they lowered the cloth to reveal the magician still on the top, who says, "One". They raised it to cover the magician again, then lowered it with a "Two" and covered the magician again. When they lowered it on "Three" they would reveal the female assistant standing on the trunk and a seemingly missing magician. They then would drop the cloth and open the padlocked trunk to find the magician inside, handcuffed. Though it was a challenging illusion that moved quickly and required agility, I loved performing it every night.

Since then, I have watched famous magicians perform the same trick and I sat knowing exactly how they are doing it because I had done it. I am still sworn to secrecy, and as a policy, I never reveal any of the magician's trick that I learned. Though, nothing thrills me more than watching a magician's act where I cannot even begin to understand how the illusions are done.

Incidentally, Ben's assistant was Chris McGary who later became an actor who went on to understudy the role of Father Flynn in the Broadway production of *Doubt* with Cherry Jones, and even performed the role with her in the national tour. Since Ben took Chris with him to the convention, it was necessary for me to find my own assistant. So I asked a young Georgia boy, Harry Christian, who was in the musical show that alternated with us.

We got to know each other because we both resided in the seedy hotel called the PennMckee. We recognized each other as soul mates, with the same sense of humor and love of movies, new and old. He was tickled to do it, even though it involved swimming in that damn water tank illusion, so we signed him on.

His first time doing the water tank illusion was genuinely frightening. After he was revealed in the tank, they couldn't get the padlocks opened. He was inside, holding his breath much longer than rehearsed. He told me later that he'd never been so scared in his life. I was nervous, as well, just standing there waiting for the locks to be opened. The security guard didn't know what to do, since he couldn't actually smash open the tank, because it was Plexiglas not glass. When Harry finally got out, we all heaved a real sigh of relief, not the fake one that was rehearsed.

"Arbad-a-carba" I say as assistant Fran is "cut into 3 pieces". My male assistant, Harry, stands to the side and watches in awe.

Harry and I got along famously and I told him that if he ever came up to New Jersey, I would cast him as The Boy in *The Fantasticks*. Well he did, and I did, and we've been best friends ever since.

Given the successful run as the magician that summer (more popular than poor Ben ever was), Ben asked me to do some magic shows back in New Jersey that he set up during the Halloween season. He had a Magic-Costume Store that he managed, so he couldn't do the Halloween shows.

I went to malls all over New Jersey doing a campy show known as "Draculuv the Magician", because Ben thought that the name "Dracula" would scare the kids. It was primarily aimed at children and was pretty silly, but I had fun doing it.

The music that introduced the act was Michael Jackson's "Thriller", which was popular at the time, and the finale was "The Monster Mash". In between, in my Dracula make-up, teeth and black cape, I would lip-synch to a jolly/scary voice-over with more fun house/disco music, while I performed simple magic tricks with my assistants who were dressed as witches.

Besides performing the show four or five times a day, I would wander all around the malls during breaks in my Dracula costume interacting with the shoppers, especially the children. It was amusing to see the faces of the shoppers as I surreptitiously entered stores and pretended to shop.

Draculuv introduces his assistants
(the tall witch in the pink hat is Chris McGary)

One year I was actually booked in a mall in New York, across from Macy's. So I can honestly say that I performed Magic in Manhattan. It was a new Manhattan Mall that ultimately failed in the building that was once Macy's rival store, Gimbals. I loved doing this and the shoppers were much more sophisticated than the New Jersey malls. With one exception.

Across the street was a SRO (Single Resident Occupancy) hotel, for homeless people, and often the audience was made up of children from this place. It was lovely making some of these woebegone kids smile and look at me with awe, probably having never seen a live show of any kind.

One day a sweet looking boy of about 10, who had attended at least three of the showings, came up to me after the performance and wanted to chat. I talked to him awhile in character but he didn't seem as giggly and impressed as other children. Then his mother approached me and offered to "sell" him to me for an hour. Aghast, I shooed her away.

I often wonder what ever happened to that boy.

After a few years my career as a magician dried up, mostly because Ben ran his inherited fortune and life into the ground. Drugs, phone sex and rent boys caused him to lose his house, his store and saddest of all, all his expensive illusions. I went on to other things, but Ben didn't.

My love for magicians hasn't let up over the years. I have found that learning how the tricks are done is not always a good thing, since the wonder and surprise is lost when I see some illusions. I recently saw a famous magician perform a big Vegas show, and he included the "trunk switch" – I was disappointed in the rest of his show after that. But the big guys, like David Copperfield or anyone who does close up, card or coin magic, will still thrill me – as long as I can't figure it out.

On a recent cruise there was a brilliant magician who performed close up magic in the bar. When he did a show in the big room I couldn't wait to see it. He blew me away with every illusion.

The best was his final trick, where I had the pleasure to take part. He brought a man on stage who happened to have a one hundred dollar bill in his wallet. The magician had the man write his and his wife's name on the bill, then roll it up into a tight cylinder and put it in a paper sandwich bag. Then he came out in the audience and picked me to hold another paper bag that contained a sealed plastic bag with an orange and several marshmallows. He instructed me, when he asked, "Where's the bag", to stand up on one leg and say in falsetto, "Yoo Hoo, I have the bag". He also picked a woman who was to say in a low voice, "Yo, I gotta knife".

He then went back up on stage to the man with the $100 bill, and told him to guess which of the three paper bags he held up had the rolled up bill in it. The man choose one and the magician said he trusted his decision, and took the other two bags and set them on fire. Then he asked the man to take his bill out of the bag he chose, which of course was just rolled up tissue paper.

At that point he called, "Who has the bag" and I got up and shouted my line, getting a big laugh. After the woman did her part, we were both called up on stage with our objects. I took the plastic bag out of the paper bag and the orange out of that. The orange was completely unmarred. The lady with the knife was asked to cut into the orange, eventually cutting it in half. And there, inside the orange, was a rolled up $100 bill. When it was unrolled, we all saw on the soggy bill the man's name was written there along with his wife's. I was the one with the orange and I stood right next to it as it was being cut open, and I have no clue how he could have accomplished such an amazing feat.

That's what I call magic.

Twenty-One

Coming Out to Mother, in Europe, Yet

Around the time I was playing the magician, both David Munro and I took our mothers, separately, to Europe. Munro's journey was not pleasant, because he wasn't particularly fond of his mother, and their interests didn't jibe at all. "Queen Bea", as she has been called by her family, had just been widowed and wanted to travel. She offered to pay for the whole trip if he would accompany her, so it seemed like a good deal. I don't know all the details, but I do know that most of the trip was spent going from shop to shop looking for porcelain and china – pretty boring stuff.

On a previous trip to Europe, Munro and I had enjoyed the campy Victorian décor of Brighton Palace enormously, ogling and laughing throughout the whole museum. So he took his mother on their excursion, thinking that she might also enjoy the place. She walked through it stone faced, looking neither left nor right. But when she got to the gift store, she bought post cards of all the things she hadn't bothered to look at during their tour. This pretty much exemplified their trip together.

In contrast to that, my mother and I had similar tastes and we always got along famously, so I was tickled when she suggested the same sort of trip. She and my father had traveled some in Europe, particularly when they spent a year in Amersfort, Holland, but she always regretted that she hadn't really explored the British Isles. Being a fanatic reader, she particularly wanted to visit the literary highlights in England, like Shakespeare's Straford-upon-Avon and Jane Austin's Bath.

Taking a cue from her literary interests, I planned our trip starting in London, which I knew rather well, moving up to Stratford, onward to Edinburgh, across to Northern Ireland, then down to Dublin, stopping along the way for any and all English literary milestones. My mother had recently lost her husband too, so she was ready for some traveling to get her mind off the loss.

In London we stayed in my favorite area, Bloomsbury, but in a much fancier hotel than I had ever used, The Imperial Russell Square Hotel. I had only stayed in the tiny bed-and-breakfast hotels in the same neighborhood, but I knew that mother would love the famous Victorian hotel, and she did.

I contacted Peter Barkworth and he was gracious enough to invite us to lunch in his charming Hampstead home on Flask Walk. I had told mother what a lovely visit I'd had with him back in the 60s and she was thrilled to be able to meet a distinguished English actor and see his home. In Peter's charmingly British way, he showed mother all through his house, pointing out oil paintings he had collected and photographs of actors with whom he'd worked. But she was most delighted when he escorted her down into the tiny, beautifully decorated dining room in the basement and served her a typical English luncheon, worthy of Oscar Wilde.

We had time to catch two West End plays. First I got us tickets to a new musical version of *Front Page* which started off entertainingly, until the plot involved someone hanging themselves. I'd forgotten this aspect of the story and when it happened, my mother stiffened and became quite upset, bringing back her finding my father who had hung himself. This twist was unbearable for her to cope with, so we left at intermission, with me profusely apologizing. Fortunately the second play I took us to was *Noises Off*, the original production with Patricia Routledge, before it was known in America. Thankfully, it was a hilarious play, and brilliantly done, so it made up for the *Front Page* fiasco.

On we went to Bath and environs. I had rented a car and the intimidating aspect of driving on the "wrong" side of the road made the trip scary, but exciting. I had driven in England before, so I became acclimated to it fairly quickly. With no GPS to help us we traveled the villages around Bath, trying to find the Holy Grail of mother's literature, Jane Austin's birthplace. We found Bath a beautiful city, and located Jane Austin museums and her later homes, but the humble home of her childhood seemed impossible to find. Along the way we even stumbled upon the grand house of Alfred Lord Tennyson and explored that, but it wasn't what was most in my mother's wishes.

Finally, we discovered the tiny village we were looking for and there it was. My mother melted with pleasure. It wasn't much to see, but it meant so much to her that I was happy we had taken the time to find it.

Mother finds her Holy Grail

We then moved on to Stratford-upon-Avon for some Shakespeare lore and on up to Edinburgh for some Bobby Burns. My primary memory of Scotland was that the people were nice, but I couldn't understand anything anyone said. Leaving Edinburgh we had to drive down to Cairnryan on the coast to catch a ferry to Northern Ireland. I ditched the car in Cairnryan, breathing a sigh of relief, and we boarded the ferry. The Irish Sea gave us a bit of a jostle, but we arrived safely in the port of Belfast. The Irish Troubles were in full swing at that time, so we didn't know what to expect. What we found was a city that seemed in the midst of war. Machine guns and barbed wire were everywhere, soldiers lined the streets and the people scuttled about without looking left or right.

We found that the train station where we would get the train to Dublin was on the opposite side of town from where we disembarked. We asked the best way to get to the station and were told to take a certain city bus that stopped outside the terminal. That bus ride was one of the most horrifying things I've ever experienced. Mother and I sat holding hands as we bumped and bounced across the entire city of Belfast, seeing bombed out buildings, begging street urchins, mothers clutching babies, dour soldiers with machine guns and barbed wire everywhere. We had never experienced war before, and I hope I never know that dreadful feeling again.

Once we got onto the train to Dublin, we breathed a sigh of relief, settling in for a four hour ride to what we hoped would be a nicer city than Belfast. Upon arrival, we found the city to be the exact opposite of the Northern Ireland city, charming, friendly, clean, vibrant with life and good will. However, the small hotel in the center of the city, which we had booked over the phone from England, was not as nice as we would have liked. The two cramped rooms were on different floors but shared a bathroom in the hall – this was not to mother's liking at all.

Hungry, we went to a restaurant in the downtown area, and as we began our first course, the owner came over to us, and in that charming brogue, welcomed us to Dublin. He was friendly and genuinely interested in us. He even sat down with us and blathered on and on about how he hoped we'd love his city. When we off-handedly mentioned that we weren't thrilled with our hotel, he was appalled and immediately wrote down the name and address of another hotel in the area that he knew would be more to our liking.

We finished our delicious meal, which was lamb and three kinds of potatoes, and left the restaurant to explore the city. We got halfway down the block when the owner rushed down the street after us with the hotel address in hand, which we had forgotten on the table. That would never happen in a New York restaurant.

I rented a car again, and we did some driving around Ireland and truly fell in love with the people and the countryside. On one of our excursions, we saw a sign for a castle that we decided to explore, so we ventured off the main road. This lead to a bumpy, winding, narrow road up a hill, but no castle appeared. When we stopped at a field, about to turn around, we saw a donkey walking towards us. With no human around, it seemed that the donkey was just taking a stroll down the road on his own. He approached the car and casually put his head in the window, snorted a "Hello" (and I'm sure it was with a brogue), and continued down the road towards his donkey business. We laughed and laughed over that donkey for the rest of the trip.

At a country restaurant we ordered breakfast and my mother asked the waitress if she could have the eggs over light. The waitress looked at her and cheerfully said, in the most adorable Irish way, "It's you that'll be eatin' it." I still use that expression.

Our happy vacation ended in Dublin, where we caught the plane ride home. While waiting for this flight in the airport, my mother and I had a painful falling out.

(I have to preface this by explaining that my life on the East Coast was totally "out of the closet", being more open in my gay life than many of my gay friends. But I had never come out to my parents or family in the Midwest. All the time I visited them, I just never felt comfortable talking openly about my relationships or life, thinking that I would hurt them. Though, I brought Reynolds with me when visiting my parents, even when the were in Holland. And my mother had visited Munro and me in

Cranford, but I stupidly just assumed that she was "ignorant" of my personal life.)

While having a meal in the airport restaurant, Mother brought up Christmas and asked when I would be coming to Illinois. Ever since I was an adult, I have been indifferent to Christmas, but to my misfortune Mother loved it so much that I always felt obligated to go "home" every year. Resentment had obviously been building up in me over this and it burst out of me at that table.

"Don't you understand," I said "I have a *home* in New Jersey and I'd like to spend it with *my* family there!" And I went on from there with an admission of my relationship with David Munro that had never been spoken aloud to her before this moment.

The emotional air was very chilly for our entire trip home, almost spoiling the great time we had spent together in the British Isles. I regretted my outburst, but I didn't regret my finally being honest with my mother no matter how much she would be disappointed in me. We covered up our feelings, but I was sure that our beautiful relationship would be tarnished from then on. How wrong I was.

A few weeks later, while working a temp job, a woman talked cheerfully when telling me that she was having a "coming out party" for her son – a big bash to let the family and neighbors know that her boy was gay. I was thrilled to hear this. I called my mother and told her of this, saying "Isn't it wonderful how times have changed, and wouldn't it have been better if I could have told you when I was a kid about my being gay?"

"I always wished that you would tell me," she said. "I knew you were gay before you did – when you were in Junior High School."

"What?" I said.

"Your father and I discussed it then and hoped that you'd have a happy life, even though you were "that way". Your father never thought you were as happy as you always seemed to be when you came to visit. I hoped that Reynolds and now David Munro, would be good for you. And I wish we'd had this talk many, many years ago, but I didn't think it was my place to bring it up – I was waiting for you."

I burst into tears.

* * *

My mother and I continued our loving relationship the same as before. Munro became a beloved part of the family and everyone in my family embraced my "married" situation with open arms.

Twenty-Two

Equity and Inequity

I've spent most of my theatrical life in New Jersey, and I've been fortunate to work in some excellent professional theatres as well as amateur ones. The Bickford Theatre in Morristown was where I had my first professional directing job and my cast consisted primarily of Actor's Equity Members, the union for stage actors. I had directed several high quality plays there before it became an Equity theatre, including *Mornings At Seven,* which had one of the finest amateur casts I've had the pleasure to direct. Occasionally over my career, I would cast actors who would belong to Equity, but worked under assumed names in non-professional productions.

But the first play I directed at the Bickford after it became a union house was *Sylvia.* The characters in this play include a husband and wife, their newly acquired dog (played by a female actor) and a character actor who must play 3 different roles: a butch man, an androgynous psychologist and the wife's female friend.

Beginning with the auditions, I learned that there are lots of rules in an Equity production that I hadn't been aware of before. First of all, the financial requirements for Equity actors are very stringent and it makes these productions necessarily more expensive. In all other previous plays I had directed, the primary consideration at auditions was: Who is the best actor for the role? But I found out that in an Equity production other factors are just as important, and it irritated me a great deal.

The role of Sylvia, the dog, is a popular role for comedic actresses, so many auditioned, both union and non-union, and lots of them came in from New York City. My favorites were among the union group of actors, because the experience and training of these actors made their auditions very impressive. The husband and wife roles were difficult and there were no non-union actors that that seemed up for the challenges. For the multi-character role I needed someone who was not only versatile but had tremendous comic timing, and there were none acceptable in the non-union group at all.

My producer told me that, due to the budget, I could only cast two union actors. Since there were a several non-union actresses that could play the role of Sylvia, that wouldn't be a problem, but it hurt having to automatically eliminate all my favorite choices. There was one non-union actress from Brooklyn who was quite good for the part. There were two excellent Equity actors for the husband and wife and we couldn't see casting anyone else. That left the male, multi-character role. There was one Equity guy who was excellent, so the producer said that if I cast a Sylvia who lived locally (not having to pay transportation from Brooklyn) he would put in for another Equity contract. Therefore, I ended up having to pick a third choice of non-union actress for that role. This was not the way I was used to doing things, but luckily that actress turned out to be excellent, as did the final production.

During the production I learned another "rule" that I was not happy about: some Equity actors don't like videos of their plays, due to the fact that they might get sold without remuneration. I have DVDs of almost every play I've worked on in my library and I treasure them. When I told the cast that I'd be filming the next production (expecting them to be pleased), they shooed me out of the dressing room, had an Equity meeting. Then they sent the Equity stage manager to tell me that this was forbidden.

I also learned that once the play has opened in an Equity production, I was unable to give notes to the actors. I must tell the stage manager my note and he/she will pass it along to the actors. *What?* During that production I also felt like a 5th wheel after the show was running. My job was done. The actors were doing a fine job, it's their profession, but they didn't need me any more.

The superb non-Equity cast of "Mornings at Seven" in one of my happiest directorial experiences

The cast of "Sylvia", my first Equity play

Before the Bickford Theater went union, I had one cast made up of several professional actors. The play was *That Championship Season*. I was somewhat nervous when the day of the first rehearsal arrived, because I wondered if they would treat me differently because I wasn't a union director. But from that first rehearsal these five fine actors gave me total respect throughout the whole experience. After the read-thru, I told them that the next rehearsal would be at my house. I said that it would be a *party*, and they were to come *in character* and remaining so the entire evening. The play is about a reunion of a winning high school basketball team at the home of their brutal, racist, vulgar, but beloved and now retired, coach. One of the players does not show up to the reunion. This rehearsal party was to be another "reunion" and I would play the missing player.

The artistic director of the Bickford at the time, Walker Joyce, wanted to play the coach, but I cast him as the rather dumb mayor, which was actually perfect. He did not particularly like the idea of an improvisational rehearsal, being primarily a musical theatre actor. I provided liquor and food for the party and as it began to roll, all of the actors got into the swing of things beautifully, interacting as their characters, developing relationships and delving into their parts. The actor who plays the "drunk" played his part so well that we had to carry him home. But the actor who shined most in the improvisation was Walker. He barged around as the boisterous mayor, telling stupid jokes and having a ball. He thanked me afterwards for one of the most enjoyable rehearsals he'd ever had. He also was happy that I'd cast him in that role instead of the coach.

That Championship Season cast
(Walker and Chris McGary to the right of the Coach)

But not all of my experiences at the Bickford were entirely pleasant. The first of two negative encounters with Equity actors was when I directed *Deathtrap*. The lead character in the play is a failing playwright who reads a young playwright's work and decides to steal it for his own. The actor playing this large part has to be witty, conniving, funny, diabolical (since he ends up murdering his wife) and he must carry the play. I could only hope that someone would come who could fill this role. At auditions an actor, whom I will call Ned, showed up and he had exactly the right look, distinguished with a white beard, and played the scenes with great panache. We were overjoyed because he seemed to be a perfect fit. He had just come up from Florida where he had played in many dinner theatres (this should have been a clue) and was now trying to get work in New York. We eagerly cast him.

When rehearsals started I began to realize that the Ned's main objective was to be funny and please his audience, like he would in dinner theatre in Florida. He charmingly ignored any direction I gave him, primarily wanting him to show the cunning, diabolical side to the character. Getting laughs was his main objective.

He had an irritating habit of adding a physical gesture after the laugh lines to get a second laugh out of the audience. He did it with all his lines, which was bad enough, but he also did it on other actor's lines. For instance, the character in the play that is a psychic, has a scene with him where she describes the experience of going on a teenage date and how she could read the minds of the boys she dated. After she says this speech, which is indeed funny, the actor would rotate his hands like massaging breasts to emphasis what she was talking about, in order to get a laugh of his own. Several times I told him that it was her scene and he should not hog the joke. He finally desisted.

The actress playing his wife was a fine actress and needed time to absorb the evil that he was planning, so she rightfully took moments to feel. Ned told her to pick up her lines, to not slow down the comic pacing, and when she didn't he would jump in with his next line, cutting off her moment. I repeatedly told him not to do this, but he paid little attention. I kept telling him that although the character was clever and witty, he was also a villain – a cold-blooded murderer, but he continued to play him like a matinee idol comic.

The night the play opened I sat in my seat and watched this "professional" actor blithely go ahead and ignore all my direction, including the offensive breast rub with the psychic. He also forgot lines and improvised scenes, throwing off his fellow actors. I sat in the audience seething. Unfortunately, the audiences did love him just like he wanted. Even the critic praised his funny performance. But they didn't see the play as it was written or directed. By this time the entire cast openly hated this guy, but we were stuck with him for the four-week run.

But after the after the opening weekend, Ned came to me and announced that he would not be able to complete the run of the show because he got another job in New York that he couldn't pass up. He said he would play the second weekend, but that would be his last.

I was conflicted in my reaction. One side of me was panicked and thought how could we possibly find another actor to take his place. The other side of me was overjoyed to see him go. I believe he felt the dislike of the cast and myself and was the kind of man that needed to be loved, so he found a reason to get out of the situation.

The producer contacted Equity and luckily found an actor, George, who had recently played the role and who was free to do the last two weekends. He arrived on the Saturday night of the last performance of the original actor to watch our production and to study how he could fit into it. After that performance, Ned walked off stage, out the stage door, and left without saying a word to me or anyone in the cast.

That night we had a read through with George and he indicated to us that he was appalled at what he had seen the other actor do. The next morning the cast assembled and ran through the play with the Richard, getting ready for the matinee that day. I didn't have time to give him direction besides basic blocking, but he picked it up quickly and was obviously understood the role.

When he gave his first performance that day, he was brilliant. The whole play took on a completely different feel, accomplishing what it was meant to do. The cast and I were ecstatic. We urged our friends, who had see the first two weekend performances, to please come back and see it again with the George. Now I was proud of the play.

George giving the play the menace it needed while strangling Harry and Darlene trying to stop him.

A happy cast with Richard. Mary and Howard fill out the cast

The other unhappy experience was also at the Bickford and was much more emotionally distressing. The play was one of my favorites, *A Thousand Clowns*. Many years before I had played the leading role, Murray, who was Jewish intellectual living in Manhattan with his 13 year old nephew. I had also see Jason Robards do the role, both on stage and in the movie of that play, so I knew it very well. When I took the job of directing the play, I was told that I could hold auditions for all the roles in the play, except for Murray. It was pre-cast by the producer, given to a friend of his, whom I will call Malcolm.

I was able to assemble a solid cast of professional actors, including a bright and talented 13 year old to play the nephew. At auditions, Malcolm had read with the actors and from the beginning I didn't feel he was right for Murray. He was too Irish, if nothing else. But I had seen him in several plays and he was a good actor that the Bickford audiences liked, so I hoped he would work his way into the role.

At the first read through, I immediately felt hostility from him, and I couldn't figure out why. We had worked together on a preliminary reading of *Barrymore* where he had read the off-stage prompter, and I thought we got on well. But I noticed him avoiding my eye and not seeming to pay attention as I spoke to the cast. The rest of the group of actors seemed excited and eager to start rehearsals.

At the first blocking rehearsal I got a taste of what was to come. I like my actors to freely block the scenes with me, running through a scene, moving where they feel is right. Then I comment on what they have done and give suggestions and directions and have them run it again a few more times until we all are happy with how the scene is blocked and we write it down and move on to the next scene. The first scene we worked on was with Murray and his nephew and after the first time through I commented that I liked when Malcolm sat on the bed next to the boy at one point. On the second run, we came to that part and Malcolm walked to the other side of the stage. I stopped them and said to please try it again but end up on the bed as he had done before. Malcolm walked to the front of the stage and, in front of all the other actors, said loudly and belligerently, "Are you going to keep stopping me in the middle of scenes? How can you expect me to act like that? Just let me do it my way."

Naturally, I was flabbergasted. No actor had ever spoken to me like that and certainly not in front of the other actors. I said, "OK. Let's start the scene again, and I won't stop you until it's over. But please try to capture the moment on the bed as you had done in the first reading."

They did the scene again and Malcolm literally stomped over to the bed at that moment and sat down, completely losing the reality of the moment with the boy that had been so tender before. When the scene was over, he glared at me and said, "How was that?"

This set the tone of all the rehearsals. He showed me no respect and blatantly and obviously ignored my directions when he disagreed with me – which was often. I ended up not bothering to give him any direction at all. The other actors were aware of this, obviously, but were always pleasant with me and worked diligently in the scenes, following all my directions. I mentioned this to the producer, who told me, "Yes, Malcolm can be hard to work with, but he's a fine actor and will do the part well."

I didn't think he was doing the part well at all. I didn't think he had the right quality for Murray, particularly with the actress who played the social worker, with whom he has an affair, but there was no purpose to give him direction, because he wouldn't have taken it. This is an Equity actor. If I had been the one to cast him, I would have fired him long since, or at least brought him up on charges, but since the producer hired him and was his friend, I had no recourse but to go along and work with him the best I could. We hardly exchanged a word for the remainder of the rehearsal process.

During one of the final dress rehearsals I realized that the final scene wasn't working and I knew it needed major fixing. So before the rehearsal I called the actors up on stage to work on those final moments. The producer was in the theatre watching this, waiting to see the dress rehearsal. They started to run through the scene and I stopped them and suggested a way it would work better. Malcolm turned and yelled at me, "Stay out of it, we're fixing it." It was like a punch in the stomach, and I got actually weak in the knees and had to sit down.

I said to the producer, "Do you see what I've been putting up with?" He nodded, but said nothing. I've never been so humiliated in my life.

Gary Cohen attended the opening night with me and was appalled at how wrong Malcolm was in the part, and of course he had heard my tales of woe before the show. I saw the play that night and, although I really liked everyone else in the cast, I never went back to see it again. I just couldn't put myself through the reliving of that experience. And to this day, just seeing his face puts butterflies in my stomach.

I've seen all the other actors in different productions since then and we have a very good rapport, but we never mention Malcolm and how unpleasant that production was for me and embarrassing for them.

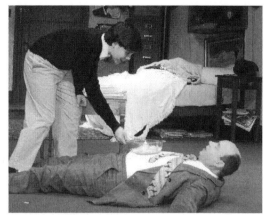

Four excellent actors in
A Thousand Clowns

Those two unpleasant incidents are by no means my only memories of working with professional actors. Other plays at the Bickford were joyous experiences, like the aforementioned *That Championship Season*, as well as *Educating Rita* and *The Subject was Roses*. These actors were true professionals, in every sense of the word, and it was a total pleasure creating these successful plays with them.

"The Subject Was Roses"   *"Educating Rita"*

*   *   *

An old friend of mine from the Celebration Playhouse days, Mike Driscoll, has been running a semi-professional theatre company called Alliance Repertory Theatre. Many of the company are Equity actors and I have been happily able to both act and direct for this company. Every experience there has been highly fulfilling. Initially I did two large acting roles for Mike, who directed them: the role of Toby in

Match and the title role in *The Champagne Charlie Stakes*. Although I was non-Equity, my acting partners were pros and it was a thrill for me to be on stage and act with these talented people.

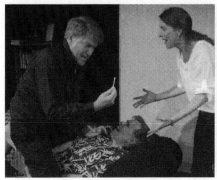

Match with
Wayne Harris and Beth Painter

Champagne Charlie's Stakes
with the brilliant Noreen Farley

Then I had two opportunities to direct for Alliance Rep. and both of these experiences were joyful. First I directed *According to Goldman*, which was a perfect play for me because it was about a teacher of film writing and his student. Movies and teaching. The twist was that the professor weaseled his way into collaborating with the young man on his script, but the young man, who was shy and timid at first, turned out to have inner demons which came out at the end of the play. Strong stuff. But I needed a young actor and a seasoned older actor, and this isn't always easy to find.

Fortunately, I had connections with Kean University and knew of a young actor who would be perfect. After negotiating with the head of the drama department, I was able to get permission for him to do an outside play. Then Mike Driscoll saw a production in another theatre that had an older man who could be good in the teacher role, so he asked him to audition. He did and was superb. One of the Equity members of the company was just right for the wife of the professor, so I had a cast that that made me very happy. And the play came off as quite a success.

I recently directed *The Dream of the Burning Boy* for Alliance Rep. and I assembled another cracker-jack ensemble of actors, including the young man in *Goldman* and my old friend, Judi Adams. This was the first time I'd directed Judi in a non-musical role, and strong emotional one at that, and she did a splendid job. David Munro did the set for me and created a very clever, rotating unit that used the pole in the center of the stage to move fluidly from a classroom to a guidance councilor's office. To my knowledge, it's the first time the pole has been used, instead of just masked in some way.

But my favorite Alliance Rep. experience (so far) was with the play *The Temperamentals*. This is a five-actor play that deals with the founders of the Mattachine Society, the first gay activist movement, back in 1950. Two of the actors play the leading founders, Harry Hay and Rudi Gernreich, while the other three play multiple characters until they finally become the other founding members. I was extremely lucky to cast five top-notch actors, including two Equity members, who made this complicated play come alive.

The play is cinematic and moves rapidly from one scene to another. I needed the simplest set so it would flow smoothly and not confuse the audience. I felt that they wouldn't always know where all the scenes took place, so I mentioned this to David Munro and he came up with an ingenious concept of street signs swinging into place for each scene, announcing the location. He then designed and built a stylish, abstract set, with only five folding chairs as furniture. It not only looked strong and classy, but was just right for the play.

We were thrilled that the playwright, Jon Marans, and the original New York director, Jonathan Silverstein, came to see the play. They stayed for a half hour talk back after the play, answering a number of interesting questions, and they seemed very pleased with the production. The director thought the swinging street signs were quite clever, since he was constantly telling the playwright to clarify the scene's locations in the script.

According to Goldman
with Angela Della Ventura,
Richard Gilmartin and Jason Gillis

The Dream of the Burning Boy
with Anna McCabe, Rachel Brown, Jason Gillis
Jeff Maschi and Judi Adams Laganga
(and Ryan Correll)

<u>The Temperamentals</u>
Jim Morgan, Dustin Ballard   Eddie Capuano, Michael Lasry, Gus Ibranyi

* * *

Another professional company that I have enjoyed working with is Dreamcatcher Repertory Company. This is an all Equity repertory company that selects it's plays for its members, with an occasional non-Equity actor filling in roles. I had been familiar with their excellent work because I knew many of the members and saw most of their plays. They asked me to be in a play called *Wonder of the World* which gave me a chance to meet and perform with the Artistic Director, Laura Ekstrand, and perform with her, Noreen Farley and Angela Della Ventura for the first time. And it also gave me an opportunity to act with my dear friend Harry Christian, whom I hadn't shared a stage with since *The Fantasticks* many years before. It was the worst set I've ever played on and the finest comic acting ensemble of I've ever been a part of.

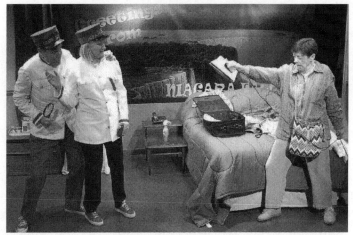
"Wonder of the World" with Angela Della Ventura and Noreen Farley

A couple years later, Laura asked me if I would direct one of their shows. I was thrilled because it's an extremely prestigious theatre and a fairly closed shop. The play she wanted me to direct had the unfortunate title of *This*. And when I read the play I was put off by the pretentious way the playwright had formatted the script – in verse form with no punctuation. Upon studying the play, however, I found it to be a realistic, contemporary, emotional, and amusing play about human relationships that I liked a great deal, once I got past how it was written. I accepted the job and set about to reformat the script, combining all the broken up lines into sentences, eliminating all the phony pauses that were indicated by the playwright, and turning the 120 page document into a 65 page script that actors could read more comprehensively.

The next major adjustment I made was to the theatre space. It's an odd space, which in the past had only been configured into a thrust stage arrangement with the audience on three sides. I thought it would be interesting to bring one of the audience units to the other side of the room and make it theatre-in-the-round. When Laura and I dragged the platforms to the other side of the room, we walk around deciding where the various scenes in the play would take place. It meant that most of the furniture could remain in place and lighting would move from one area to another, making little need for schlepping furniture to change scenes, something that I always dislike.

The next hurdle was to find an actor who spoke fluent French, or at least could fake it well. The role was of a handsome, charming, Parisian doctor with Doctors Without Borders and none of the company fit this description at all. The character has a full page telephone conversation in French, plus had to have a believable French accent throughout the play. So although the rest of the characters were cast from the company, we had to audition for this one role. Being an Equity company, auditions must include union as well as non-union actors, although for financial reasons we preferred non-union. Auditions were held for an eight hour period and actors were scheduled in 20 minute blocks.

By the end of the long, frustrating day we had only seen one actor who could fake a French conversation fairly well, who was as good looking as we wanted, but he was too young. Then just as we were packing up to go, a man walked in named, Chris Miller. He was tall, handsome and the right age. Laura and I crossed our fingers that he could struggle through the French monologue convincingly. He stood up to read it and began to rattle off the monologue in rapid French like a native Parisian, which he turned out to be. He had moved to the States when he was a teenager, but had French relatives whom he visited regularly. And he was non-Equity at the moment. Frankly we didn't know if he could act well at all, but we didn't care, and with great relief we cast him on the spot.

As it turned out, not only was he an excellent actor, but he was a musician who helped us enormously with the jazz song (a bad one) that the playwright had written for the play. He recorded a believable jazz combo to back up the live singer. On top of all this, he was a sweetheart. We certainly lucked out on that one.

The publicity man for Dreamcatcher is a talented guy who designed a beautiful poster for the play, which I think was one of the reasons this ill-named play got the large audiences it did. It didn't hurt that we received glowing reviews across the board. I believe that it was the first time that Dreamcatcher was so sold out that people were actually turned away at the door. It was a huge hit and remains one of the plays of which I am most proud.

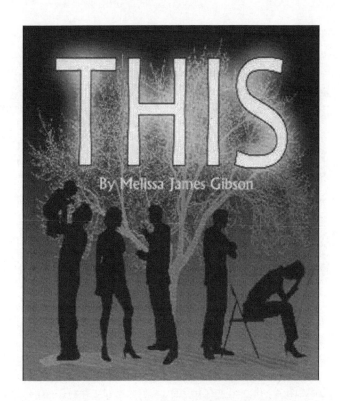

Nicole Callendar and Scott McGowan
"Frenchman" Chris Miller
Laura Ekstrand and Harry Christian

I directed another play for Dreamcatcher Repertory the following year, *Shooting Star*. The primary joy of this much simpler, two character play was working with Harry Christian and Laura Ekstrand. Both of them are consummate actors and watching and helping them create their characters, which were very different from themselves, was inspiring. They played college lovers who meet again in a snowbound airport 25 years later. The reality they created in the complex relationship of the characters touched audiences hearts much deeper than we expected, and the play was extremely popular. It proved another sold out hit and one that they loved performing and I loved watching.

<u>Shooting Star</u> with Laura Ekstrand and Harry Christian

All these fine professional New Jersey theatres have added a new dimension to my theatrical life for which that I will always be grateful. The fact that I decided in my early career not to join Actor's Equity never seemed wrong to me, but I'm glad that I have been able to function successfully in that milieu, nonetheless. I have found that being a "professional" actor does not necessarily mean that your are better than the amateurs, it just means that you are trying to make your living in the business. I have worked with extremely talented and dedicated actors both amateurs and professionals, as well as the opposite. If anything, I enjoy the excitement and pleasure that amateurs bring to the table. You rarely see professionals weep when a show closes, they are too busy looking for another gig to pay the rent. Show business is a tough business and I admire anyone who has the gumption to live their life that way.

Twenty-three

Merck Work

Near the end of The Acting Studio when finances were getting very low, I decided that I would use my free daytime to make some more money. I went to Kelly Temp Agency to see what jobs I could land. This was tough on my ego going back to being a Temp Typist like I was in my 20s, when indeed, I was in my 50s, but, I had little choice if I was going to pay my mortgage.

Being able to type and use a computer, which not everyone could do in those days, gave me somewhat of a leg up, but I'd had no real office experience for thirty years. Therefore the jobs that I was sent on were menial and boring, and always short lived.

I decided I would take a course in desktop publishing. I figured that it could lead to interesting work. The class was in a computer program called Quark, which I had never heard of before, but seemed to be used in business a great deal. Right after I added that to my skills, the temp agency called me and asked if I *really* knew this program. I said that I did and so they sent me on a job to replace someone going on vacation. The job was at the pharmaceutical company called Merck, in a nearby town. The commute was only fifteen minutes, as opposed to the up-to-an-hour I'd been traveling heretofore. The job was for two full weeks, so I gladly took it.

I replaced a woman whose sole job was to create the back page of *The Daily*, an in-house paper that was distributed to everyone in this vast company - daily. The page she worked on was nothing but local want ads from the employees – things to sell, give away, promote, or announce to their fellow employees. Hundreds of requests would come in every day and my new job was to select the interesting ones and enter them into the publishing page for the next day – on Quark. Evidently, the year before the temp replacement did not know the program well and screwed up the page badly, so they wanted someone who could do it correctly.

I ended up enjoying this job and found it easy and interesting, and it seemed that I performed well for the two weeks I was there. Unfortunately for me, however, the woman returned from her holiday, so I was out of work again. But my supervisor said that he would recommend me highly for other work at Merck, which he did and within a week I was sent up for another job there. I didn't know this, but working at this company was considered one of the best places to work in the country, and temp jobs there were extremely hard to come by.

This time I reported to one of the buildings where all the drug research was done, which was much more intimidating than the small office building I'd worked in before. The Merck campus was huge, with green lawns and sculptures and building after building – one needed a map to get around.

I followed my map to the office of University Relations on the top floor of one of the research buildings. There I met the formidable Cindy Zarsky. A handsome, tall, butch, blond bombshell, with a strong handshake, sort of a taller Joan Blondel. She seemed friendly, but I had my doubts. She set me up in a small office of my own and the first job she gave me was to make copies of some checks to universities, make envelopes for them, stuffing them with the letters and checks, and send them out. Handing me the checks and the letters, she left me in my tiny office and closed the door. I glanced at the handful of checks and none of them were under $10,000! I was flabbergasted – what kind of trust did this mean for me, a brand new, temp employee? I made the copies and envelopes and brought them into Cindy assuming she'd want to be sure I'd done it right, but she just waved me away and said, "Drop them off in the Merck mailbox on your way to lunch."

This started an easy one-year job in a pleasant workplace. The function of the department was to liaison with universities around the world, giving grants for research and coaxing young scientists to come to work for Merck. This meant that I spent much of my time writing letters to the universities and doling out thousands of dollars in grants.

Cindy and her crew were a real family and I quickly became part of it and felt completely at home, though the simplicity and routine quality of the job made it rather boring in the long run. But the atmosphere was so positive that I was sad to hear that the department had lost funding and had to let me, the extra worker, go after the first year. Cindy was saddened too, as we had become friends in that year and she was unhappy to let me go. She was a warm, salt-of-the-earth, funny lady, and a wonderful boss - I miss her still.

I figured that I was now out of work and that another Merck job, as good as Cindy's department, would be hard to come by. But, thanks to Cindy, this didn't prove to be true. While at a gathering of scientists, she ran into a guy that was the head of a research department who told her that he had lost his secretary and needed to hire a new one - fast. Cindy told him that he should call me right up, because I'd make a great secretary, that

I was smart and congenial and that he'd love me. So he did. I was at home, licking my unemployed wounds, and I received a call from Dr. Gregory Kaczorowski asking me to come right over to his department, as soon as possible. On Cindy's recommendation he hired me without even meeting me.

I hopped to it and entered the biggest research building on the campus finding the Department of Ion Channels, which was to become my place of business for the next seven years. Dr. Kaczorowski was a pudgy little man with a goatee and thick glasses. He greeted me with panicked relief, since his office had been unmanned for a week and he was rendered helpless without a secretary. I told him that I'd never been a secretary (or technically, "office assistant" to be PC) but he said he didn't care. Cindy Zarsky had said I was bright and could do anything.

He showed me to my desk which was surrounded by filing cabinets and had a Macintosh computer and a multi-lined telephone. He told me as much as he could, but was in a huge rush (as he always was) for a meeting and I'd have to work it out on my own. He flew out of the office and there I sat, feeling utterly lost.

I was soon to find that the Department of Ion Channels consisted of 25 scientists, divided into six labs, each controlled by the laboratory head with three or four assistant scientists. Most of the upper level scientists had their doctorates and were well known in their fields. And my job would be to handle them all, but particularly Dr. K.

One of the heads scientists was Dr. Maria Garcia, who I found out was Dr. Kaczorowski's wife and an internationally known expert on ion channels, as was her husband. They had written many highly regarded articles in prestigious journals (which I always called "magazines" much to Dr. K.'s irritation and amusement) and lectured around the world in scientific conferences regularly.

Dr. K. was in the middle of writing one of these papers when I arrived, and he couldn't type. So, he scribbled on legal yellow pads, and it was the secretary's job to decipher these squiggles and type it up on the computer. The first time he gave me one of these yellow pads, I thought it was in hieroglyphics, because even the words that I could read, I had no idea what they meant.

As time went by, I learned to read all the letters of the long words and figured out the subject and verbs on my own. I could make some kind of sense of the sentences, even though I had no clue what they were about. Having been a teacher, I was accustomed to reading sloppy writing, so I quickly was able to figure out his scribbling. I would type up a rough draft of what I thought it was supposed to be, and he would then correct it, since it was now at least typed double spaced, and I would have another go. This went on until we finally had a paper that made sense, to him at least.

As I got to know the scientists, I found that they were a completely different brand of human being than I had ever encountered: brilliant in scientific thinking, but often immature and childish in the daily dealings of life. I had to treat them like junior high school students, demanding that they hand in reports, prodding them to get to meetings on time, and listening to their silly jokes.

I grew to like most of them, once I understood their make up, and my office became a happy place where everyone would congregate. I was pleased that my being gay was an open and completely accepted thing. I became sort of the peacock in the middle of all of these hard working farm animals, and everyone enjoyed chatting and joking with me. I was the only male secretary in the building, so this made me stand out too.

Greg Kaczorowski (front and center) with his department of scientists. His wife, Maria Garcia, is to the right of him.

Dealing with Greg, as I came to call him, was a complicated but rewarding experience. Not being a real secretary (he called me his "acting secretary", because I was an actor and acted the role so well) I treated him with humor and laughter, whereas most secretaries would never be allowed to do so. I could calm him down when he was in one of his panics like no one else. He loved me and our relationship was, and is still, quite close.

I coerced him and Maria into going to the theater in New York, of which they became very fond, so I became the theater critic and ticket arranger for them. Greg like heavy drama best. When I got them tickets for "Death of a Salesman", with Brian Dennehy, he wept with masochistic joy, apparently identifying with Willie a great deal. Also, they attended anything I performed in or directed while I was there, and they still do so today.

Although Merck drove him crazy, the one thing that kept Greg somewhat sane was his passion for trains and train memorabilia. Once a year he would go off for a week's vacation with his BARF buddies (Brotherhood of American Railroad Fans) and chase trains. In the heat of the desert or the chill of the mountains, they would stalk trains in an SUV and take hundreds of photos. Then they would sit around drinking and smoking cigars and talk trains. He would come back to Merck burned from the sun, or frost bit, but happy as a clam.

Greg is also a food and wine connoisseur. One time he heard that my mother was friends with Didier Durand, the well-known French chef in Chicago who had just opened a new restaurant. She had been his English-as-a-second-language teacher when he first came to America, and they remained friends. So Greg said that I was to arrange a dinner at this restaurant, Cyrano's, telling Didier that cost was no object - he should serve Greg and his college friend from South Bend the best dinner he could prepare. Then Greg said to me, "When was the last time you visited your mother? You should come to Chicago with us and I'm inviting you to the dinner at Cyrano's before you go to your mother's."

So I arranged the flight for all of us (on Greg's dime with him in first class and me in economy) and off we went. We hit a major rain storm on route and the plane was quite late, so we arrived at the restaurant close to closing time. Didier welcomed us warmly, despite our tardiness, and we began what was undoubtedly the greatest meal I've ever had. Greg wanted to be surprised by the selections that Didier created, but before each course he asked what type of wine should accompany it, and he ordered an expensive bottle for that particular course. There were many, many courses, each one scrumptious. However, I never drank so much wine in my life, and I have no memory of the last courses or dessert, because I was really drunk by then. Greg and his friend weren't even fazed by the wine and enjoyed the whole meal, complimenting Didier after each course, then opening another bottle.

They put me into a taxi, and somehow I got on to the train to Highland Park. As I rode in the coach, I had the unpleasant feeling that it was spinning around me, and I hoped I could keep that glorious meal in my stomach.

When I arrived at my mother's condo, she had stayed up for me and took one look at my pale complexion and bundled me off to bed. The next morning I was able to regale her with what a great evening I had had and how gracious Didier was to my boss.

I got to know and respect the other scientists in the department, but the ones with whom became friendliest, were the visiting scientists. Given Greg and Maria's international renown, we often had scientists from all over the world to work in our department for a week, a month, and sometimes a whole year. They were not just interested in science, however, they also loved the idea of New York City and all the cultural experiences they could gather up. The regular Merck scientists didn't give a hoot for New York, and since I was the one who planned all the visiting scientists' hotels et al, and I love New York, I would often take them into the city. This task allowed me to become close with several of them and therefore have enjoyed their hospitality in other countries when I visited there, too.

For example, on a recent trip to Japan, we stayed in the home of Dr. Ana Rosa Linda Arias, a Spanish scientist who worked for Merck and now lives with her husband and two children in Yokohama. And several years ago, a renowned scientist in Innsbruck, Austria paid for our stay at the Mozart Hotel and drove us to Italy because the weather was rotten in Innsbruck.

As I approached my 65th year, I was determined to retire from any "day job", because as much as I liked the Ion Channel guys, I was tired of the work. When I reached that birthday, I left Merck, ending a marvelous run. It was invigorating to enter an entirely different kind of work place and to get a feeling for these people and the amazing world of pharmaceuticals. One impression that was instilled in me was the huge amount of money that was spent to find a single drug.

When thinking of the salaries of all 25 scientists in my department, the PhDs as well as the lesser college grads, the colossal amount of money spent on equipment and chemicals, trials, experiments etc., it boggles the mind. This department was in existence for at least 20 years and they never came up with single, viable drug. Millions of dollars, and no drug. So, when a successful drug is introduced and people bitch about the cost, they don't realize how much of it is paying for further and failed research.

I have tremendous respect for the mind of the scientists I worked for. The fact that Greg and his scientists worked on their one goal for that many years, trying experiment after experiment, but never completely arriving at a satisfactory ending to that goal, is amazing to me. We, in the theater, will work our asses off to get the show up and running, be it a success or a failure, but then it's over and we move on. I don't think I have the mentality to ever do what those scientists do.

Unfortunately, Merck had done a huge purging of scientists recently and the entire department was eliminated. Many of these scientists were just fired, some were moved to other departments or forced to go to other Merck sites around the country if they wanted to keep a job. I attended the final "lunch meeting" with the whole department, it was a sad occasion. They ordered up the same sumptuous sandwiches, brownies and cookies that I had ordered when I was secretary and Greg basically said goodbye to everyone. It was a true love-fest and I was proud to have been included.

Greg and Maria have since retired and spend time consulting with companies around the world, giving lectures and writing papers on Ion Channels based on the vast material from the experiments made in their laboratories. We have remained friends. They come to my productions, I advise them on Broadway shows, and they have prepared some splendid meals for David Munro and myself. I think Greg is much happier now, with the pressures of Merck off his back. He still has his trains.

Now retired, Greg Kaczorowski with his trains   *and Maria Garcia in their home.*

Twenty-four

Spin Your Partner, Do-Si-Do

Acey **Deucey, Peel the Top, Cut the Diamond**, Teacup Chain, Explode the Wave. These are all square dance calls, and I wouldn't have known any of them if I weren't such a fan of the *Norman Conquests*.

Being ardent theater-goers, David Munro and I decided to see the three plays of Alan Ayckborn's trilogy *Norman Conquests* all in one day. They were playing in a small Off Broadway house, 2 flights up from 45th Street. There weren't many others in the audience, so we choose seats in the third row. But before the play began we realized these seats were rather cramped, so we decided to move up to the front row with more leg room. Also sitting there was a guy named Dave Torrey, another ardent theater lover. Our conversations with him lead to going to dinner between the second and third play, which then led to a long and interesting friendship.

Besides going to countless plays with Dave over the subsequent years, he introduced me to a new hobby that I found great pleasure in for several years – Gay Square Dancing. Dave prodded me to go to the open house of a group known as Times Squares to see if I'd like it. He told me that Times Squares was the New York club affiliated with the IGASDC (International Gay Association of Square Dancing). Cities around the country and even the world had similar clubs, but that Times Squares was one of the biggest in membership. This group meets in grade school gym, PS 3, on Hudson Avenue right off Christopher Street in the heart of Greenwich Village.

Dave brought me to the group's annual Fall open house that they use to recruit new members. Upon entering the gym, I found over 50 men and women, noshing and schmoozing in a gay (in both meanings of the word) atmosphere. I was welcomed into the friendly gathering by several people and immediately made to feel comfortable.

Then a caller told everyone to find a partner, male or female, and stand in a large circle with him or her. Dave took me as a partner while other members of the club partnered with "Newbies" or each other.

Once everyone was matched up, the caller, Nick (who turned out to be my first year teacher), put us through simple square dancing calls, with campy humor and clear instructions, giving us all confidence that we could succeed as square dancers. The "Angels", the seasoned members, helped all the new guys and gals enjoy a fun time and feel at home.

Most of the men were partnered with men, and the women with women, but that wasn't always the case. Nick told us to decide whether we wanted to learn the "girl" part or the "boy" part (no matter what your biological sex might be), putting "girls" on the right side, "boys" on the left. He put us into "squares", which consisted of four couples, and we got to know the six other people with whom we would be dancing.

Nick began with simple calls but as they got more difficult, I realized that learning these wouldn't be easy, but it could be lots of fun. There was always a sense of enjoyment, even when one did something wrong. One thing that totally surprised me was the music. I'd imagined that it would be all hokey, blue-grass, country music, but not with the gay square dancers. It was show tunes, pop, and disco.

By the time the night's dancing was over, I wanted to be a part of this congenial, fun-loving club, so I signed up for classes. Beginners class, called Mainstream, would last ten months and in that time we would learn the movements to 70 calls. When we finished this course, we would graduate. After that we could dance anywhere in the world. I was raring to go.

When I attended my first Mainstream class, I found that there were only 10 new students (a low number I was told). Our class members quickly formed friendships and my closest buddy from that first class, whom I still see often, was a woman named Amy Marcus. I assumed she was a lesbian, as most of the women in the club were, but I found out at one of our dinners before class that she was straight, she just loved dancing and found gay square dance clubs were more fun.

As the classes continued, it got more and more complicated as we learned harder and harder calls, but it was also quite rewarding when we accomplished them.

The most important thing that square dancing helped me with was the art of listening. With square dancing, you don't know what call will come at any given time. The caller is in complete control, calling the next move, whatever it may be, just seconds before you have to carry it out. Your body has to respond at a moments notice, which way to move, which hand to use, which member of the square your are to connect with and with what action. If you let your concentration lapse for even a second, you will get lost.

The Times Squares, Square Dance Club

*Amy Marcus and
Perry Shore, friends from my Mainstream class*

When we were about halfway through the course, we were told that each Mainstream class had to create their own Prom, before their graduation. Since most classes in the past had been considerably larger, it was a challenge for us to do all the planning, choosing the theme, making the decorations, deciding and ordering the food, selling the tickets, etc. for a big, successful prom.

Collectively we decided to rise to the occasion. We chose the theme "Life is a Beach; Move to a Wave" (the name of a dance call). We needed something to cover up the ugly gymnasium, so over several weeks we painted a mural of sky, water and sand to cover the whole side wall. The tops of the columns were to be palm trees, and over the dance floor would be twinkling lights and lots of hanging fish.

Main course food was catered with "beach food", like hot dogs and baked beans, but one class member, Emad, was a great cook and made a dessert table full of scrumptious goodies. Everyone was expected to come in some kind of beach attire or costume, so we had lots of beach bums, skinny bathing suits, and there were also pirates and mermaids.

Nick, our teacher and the caller for the night, always dressed in drag for these events and was terribly amusing. All in all, our prom was a huge success. And the members of class were now proud graduates of Mainstream and we were ready to move on to lots of dancing in the future.

Our caller, Nick. in class   and at our Class Prom

Decorating the gym for the Prom   *Jack, who did most of the painting of the "Life's a Beach" mural.*

Pirates on the Beach   *Dancing with Dave Torrey*

Once we graduated it meant that we were now able to go to dances at any club in the country and be perfectly prepared to dance with anyone who knew the 70 Mainstream calls. Our first opportunity was to go to the Philadelphia club's fly-in in the Poconos. A "fly-in" is a weekend dance that each club throws once a year, that is open to everyone, so people fly-in from around the country and even Europe and Japan. Philly's club was called Independent Squares and they traditionally held their fly-in in a lodge in the Pocono Mountains. Amy, my companion for many fly-ins, and I drove out to our first of many dances around the country.

What fun! This whole lodge was reserved for the square dancers, about 100 of them, and all the ballrooms were full of different levels of dancers, as well as different callers. We were accustomed to Nick calling, so it was a new experience reacting to someone else's voice and rhythms, but they all used calls that we knew, so we fit in quite easily.

One thing that the gay clubs are known for is keeping a good sense of humor and support for all dancers. Anyone can miss a call, or go the wrong way, or generally screw up and "break the square". The eight dancers then just go back to "home" and wait for the caller to catch up, and then off we go again. It is my understanding that in straight groups, everything is more serious and they often don't suffer fools gladly. They also tend to wear those silly costumes like frilly, crinoline skirts and matching cowboy shirts. But anything goes in the gay groups.

The best part of the Philly fly-in is the "pool dance". After the big Saturday night, costume dance where everyone dances in the same big ball room, many of the dancers change out of their dress clothes and into bathing suits. They meet in a big pool, that doesn't have a deep end, and square-up in the pool. The callers then call dances, while the dancers are up to their waists, at least, in water, so it's all very slow, and wet, and fun.

The callers and about 100 dancers at the Philadelphia Fly-in

The wet, slow and fun "pool dance"

Over the years I have attended fly-ins in Atlanta and Chicago, two National Conventions, in Denver and Washington DC, and of course our own Times Squares fly-in, "Peel the Pumpkin", which for many years has been held in Asbury Park, on the Jersey Shore. I also went on to take the next program of dancing called, Plus, which added another 40 calls to my repertoire.

When I attended my first convention, in Denver, it was held in a beautiful, new, posh hotel that was completely taken up with the square dancers and their mates. David Munro accompanied me, because he had clock business in Denver and he had never seen the city, so we were able to work in some sightseeing as well.

I was thrilled and amazed to see the number of dancers from all over the world that attended this convention. It all began with The Grand Procession. Everyone got into their club uniforms (ours being stylish black shirts with pink sequins forming the New York skyline) and each club in orderly fashion descended the escalators, and filed into the ballroom to the tune of Pomp and Circumstance. The huge ballroom was decorated with all the club's banners hanging from the ceiling.

Once we were all there, the opening ceremony welcomed over 1600 dancers. As we assembled and the club names were called out, each group shouted their huzzahs, and I felt a huge swelling of pride that I was a part of this splendid gathering.

At my first Convention in Denver in our official Times Squares shirts

*The Grand Procession
(our club on the left escalator)*

Over 1600 dancers in one ballroom.

Sadly, I recently had to give up square dancing. I am developing neuropathy in my feet and legs, so it is difficult for me to keep my balance and it is getting harder and harder being sure on my feet. I fear I might just do-si-do right past my partner into the next square. But, I still go to some of the events to see the many friends and acquaintances I made at Times Squares and in other clubs.

Epilogue

Good Night, Sweet Prince

The winter I retired from Merck, a month after my 65th birthday, I was scheduled to direct a community college production of *Into the Woods*. Before I began rehearsals, the rights were pulled by the publishing company, so the production was cancelled. I now had the dreary winter months of January, February and March ahead of me with virtually nothing to do. I am not good at "idle" and I knew I had to find something to fill my time. I had always been pretty good at memorizing lines of a play (except lyrics, which oddly were always harder for me), so I thought, why not give myself a real challenge, just to keep the ol' brain cells active.

I landed upon the almost one-man play, *Barrymore*, which presented a day in the life of John Barrymore, shortly before he died. He is imagined by playwright, William Luce, to be rehearsing for a revival of *Richard III* in front of an audience. It won Christopher Plummer a Tony Award for Best Actor, many years before.

I thought I would give myself the project of memorizing all the lines, with no production in mind, just for the process and exercise of it. I turned our guest room, now with a pull out sofa instead of a bed, into my work room for all memorization and the process began. I tried to learn a new page every day, always reviewing what I'd learned before and adding the new page. This work was an exhilarating challenge and by March I had pretty much conquered the entire script.

Since there was a secondary character (the offstage "Prompter"), it was a help at this point to have someone read the other character's part and follow my script to catch errors. It was the first of the summers that the French boy, Thomas, was visiting us, and I got him to follow the script for me several times, helping me rehearse, as well as helping his English.

Just for fun I hooked several other people into doing this, including my cousin Marianne, whom I visited in Chicago. Now I wasn't trying to "act" the role really, but it was easy falling into the part when I had a

Prompter/audience, so John Barrymore got more and more established in my readings.

After hearing some excellent feedback, I came to the conclusion that, indeed, this could be an appropriate role for me to play in a theater. I had been directing some plays at the Bickford Theater, an Equity house in Morristown, and the producer was a man named Eric Hafen. I approached him with the idea of doing the play at the Bickford, with him as director. Thomas came with me and we did the script for Eric to get his opinion of my work. He seemed pleased and said he'd think about it and get back to me.

Within a week he called and told me that we should get to work on the play, because he was planning to schedule it for next season. Though, this was not what I started out to do, I was thrilled that it turned out this way.

Eric and I worked well together. Since I had done a lot of the work myself already, he guided me and made some excellent suggestions of how to make it play better in a large theater. We honed the play and I stretched the character, making him bigger than I would have thought – but on the other hand, keeping him as real as possible.

John Barrymore was a self-destructive drunk, and after years of abusing himself, his body and mind were seriously failing. Therefore, the concept of doing a revival of *Richard III*, which he had done so brilliantly many years before, was a failure before it started. Doing a live rehearsal for an audience was a major mistake, so they are allowed to see him slowly get drunker and watch his mind flounder, forgetting lines, quoting the wrong play and generally disintegrate before their eyes. Though the Prompter tries to keep him on track, it becomes virtually impossible.

Barrymore does, however, try to keep the audience entertained with jokes and anecdotes from his life, going on long ramblings of reminiscences about his past performances and his famous brother and sister, Lionel and Ethyl. These stories are funny, sad, revealing, and as the play goes on, tragic. In the second act he actually gets into a Richard III costume, hump and all, but is so drunk, he does Hamlet's "To be, or not to be" soliloquy instead. This is the one time he demonstrates what a great actor he was in his prime.

Since it was quite awhile until this was scheduled at the Bickford, I was chomping at the bit to play it to an audience. An old Roselle Park High student of mine, Gordon McConnell, who had gone on to make a profession of acting and directing, contacted me. When I told him that I was working on this play, he told me that he ran a small theater, TheaterWest, near West Palm Beach, Florida and asked if I could do a run of *Barrymore* at his theater. How exciting, an out-of-town try out, and in Florida in October.

I was thrilled and accepted the gig.

It was necessary for me to drive down to Florida, because of all the props and costumes needed for the play. My bulky, but beautifully handmade, costume for Richard III alone would have been difficult to pack for air travel. Any long automobile trips I had made previously were always with another driver (David Munro usually), so I was not looking forward to this long drive alone, but I set out excited about the prospect of doing the play in a real theater.

The day I left it was raining hard and it continued to rain hard all the way to the North Carolina boarder. Somewhere just past of Washington DC, I stopped at a turnpike gas station to fill up. I'm not used to pumping my own gas ("Jersey Girls Don't Pump Gas") but I got out of the car in the pouring rain and managed. When I went into the store for some coffee, I noted that the TV was talking about a sniper who had just killed someone who was pumping gas, on the turnpike – one rest stop after this one.

Everyone continued watching the TV while I, horrified, rushed back to my car, realizing that if I'd gone one more stop to get gas, I could have easily been that victim they spoke of on the TV inside.

I whizzed onto the turnpike just before the police cordoned it off, stopping traffic for hours to search for the killer. I sailed on south across the North Carolina border, into sunshine.

Before I arrived in West Palm Beach, I stopped off in Fort Lauderdale to visit an old friend, Debbie Cain. Debbie had a horrible traffic accident when she was in her 20s, when a drunk driver smashed into her car while she was on the way to a wedding, causing her to become quadriplegic. She was now residing in a nice home (thanks to a major insurance settlement) decked out for her electric wheelchair and was living as good a life as can be expected. Knowing that Debbie was a long-time theater lover, I wanted to give her a private reading of *Barrymore*.

With her living room as my stage, her grandmother and the caregiver sat as the audience, while Debbie read the role of the Prompter, and I did my best to give her a solid performance of the play. I've never had a more appreciative audience and it was well worth that side trip, especially to see Debbie who seemed to enjoy and appreciate it so much.

I finally arrived to the home of my friend, Gordon, in West Palm Beach, and settled into his attic apartment where I was to stay. His wife was perfectly pleasant and told me that she was a producer in an established mainstream theater in West Palm Beach. I hoped that this theater would be where I was to perform. I asked to see the space, but Gordon said we'd do it the next day.

The following morning, I urged Gordon to take me to the theater, and he seemed to be hedging, telling me we'd do it in the afternoon. At long last, we got into the car and set off for TheaterWest. En route, I realized why it was named "Theater<u>West</u>", because it was way-out West from West Palm Beach, nowhere near the center of the popular city.

As we drove past swamps with alligators and seedy strip malls, we came to an ugly industrial park, wound around cinderblock buildings and came to one that was a dance studio. That was where TheaterWest was housed.

The "theater" was one room, that was part of the dance studio, it had a one foot platform for a stage and flimsy plastic chairs for the audience. There wasn't even a sign out front with the name of the theater, let alone a marquee, and it was in the middle of this maze of buildings. *How would anyone find this theater, even if they wanted to?*

This was *not* what I was picturing back in New Jersey. It turned out that Gordon was not getting the acting work he'd hoped for, so his wife had rented this space for him to create a theater where he could direct his own shows. He was just getting started and I was an experimental beginning for his new theater.

I learned one valuable lesson about *Barrymore* when I had my first rehearsal in this tiny space. I had done all my rehearsals at the Bickford, which is a fairly large theater, that lacked quality acoustics. So my interpretation of Barrymore at the Bickford was necessarily even bigger than John Barrymore seemed in life. When I rehearsed it for Gordon the first time, I didn't change my performance much from what I'd rehearsed, and of course it landed far too huge for this venue. Gordon directed me to tone it way down for this space. So later when I did it in smaller venues, I found that "John" was able to adjust his performance to whatever size room or audience he was presented, and I used that lesson many times in the future.

Several of Gordon's friends came to my opening night, but other nights were pretty sparsely attended. The worst was one Sunday matinee. There were three reservations and we hoped for some "walk-ins" to make up some kind of audience. None appeared and the party of three weren't showing up either, so I was told that we were cancelling the show after I had prepared and was in costume. Then the three with reservations called on a cell phone and said that they were wandering around the industrial park looking for the theater. I got back in costume and they finally found the place. They were three ex-New York, theater-loving widows, who took the front row and turned out to be a gracious and responsive audience.

Since Barrymore talks directly to the audience, entertaining them with jokes and anecdotes, it was new to talk to just these three ladies, and getting their reactions only five feet away. At the end of the play, they gave me a standing ovation, and I said to them, "Aw, come on ladies, let's just do a group hug!". This turned out to be one of my favorite performances.

On the bare stage of TheaterWest

My out-of-town tryout wasn't what I'd hoped it would be, especially since I got paid a cut of the ticket sales, making it financially unprofitable, but I enjoyed myself and I was in Florida in October, so I wasn't complaining. David Munro flew down for my final weekend and then helped me with the drive back.

* * *

Back in New Jersey, I wanted to prepare for the opening at the Bickford. Being that it was an Equity theater and I wasn't a member of the actor's union, Eric had to hire a union actor to play the thankless, off-stage role of the Prompter that Barrymore rants and rails at. The character seems to have known Barrymore for many years, and I believe was secretly in love with him, so he stays with it as long as he can stand it and finally gives up.

Looking back, the actor wasn't ideal for the role (not gay enough, basically), but still the production was a success. It was amazing to have a real, beautifully designed set, especially after the tacky non-set I had in Florida. When the play opened, it was extremely well received and reviewed, which was a gratifying thrill for me, and a boon for Eric and the Bickford Theater.

On the full set at the Bickford

The journey wasn't over. There is an amateur theater in New Jersey called the Edison Valley Playhouse. It is housed in an old church, but has been a theater for decades, going back to the 1960s. Over the years I had acted and directed several times in that cozy theater and always loved the place.

Near the end of the 90s, it had fallen upon hard times and the building was in desperate need of repair and was subsequently closed by the fire department. Saddened, all of us that had worked in this charming space assumed it would be bull-dozed into oblivion. But Bill Sessellberg and another man, who had been on the board directors of the playhouse, got together and fought the destruction of the playhouse.

First they had it designated an historical landmark, so it couldn't be torn down. Then they raised funds to have the major constructive improvements made, like a new roof and back wall that was crumbling. Finally, they got helpers and cleaned it out, filling endless dumpsters, and began restoring it back into a living theater again.

Two years after I figured my John Barrymore was dead and buried, Bill asked me if I would recreate the role as the grand re-opening of Edison Valley Playhouse. I was quite honored, because I loved the playhouse and was delighted that it was re-opening. But, I was torn by this request because the idea of learning all those lines again was frightening and stressful. I had acted in three productions and directed three productions since I closed *Barrymore*, so that memory bank was thoroughly wiped out.

But I made the decision to restore John B. along with the restored theater, and my work began. Fortunately, I had a video copy of the Bickford production, so this helped in my re-memorization. It probably took a month to get the play back into my head, and I was ready to go for the re-opening.

I will always be extremely pleased that I did the play in this venue, because I gave a much deeper performance of the role in that theater than I had at the Bickford. The main reason was the intimacy of EVP compared to the Bickford.

At the larger theater, my audience was in the dark, beyond my vision most of the time, the first row being thirty feet away from the stage. I had to "project" my voice even broader than John Barrymore would have done, and I never felt that I was actually talking to anyone.

But at the 100-seat Edison Valley Playhouse, I could see all the audience clearly, all the time, and they, appropriately, played the third character in the play. When Barrymore told a joke, he saw how it landed and it helped him when it got a big laugh – as well as depressed him when the joke fell flat. When he completely fell apart at the end of the play, I feel the audience's disappointment and horror and it made it all the more tragic for John when leaving the stage in defeat.

For over the course of three years, my Barrymore got the chance to bow to a huge house on a beautiful set at a professional theater, to my friend in her living room, to three New York widows in the middle of the swamps of Florida, and finally in a local, intimate theatre that I knew well and loved. For the curtain call, the actor playing the Prompter, whom the audience never saw, only waved from off stage, a clever gimmick I suggested.

I stood onstage alone.

David Christopher's John Barrymore

Made in the USA
Columbia, SC
25 March 2020